Nietzsche as Phenomenologist

Nietzsche as Phenomenologist

Becoming What One Is

Christine Daigle

EDINBURGH
University Press

Edinburgh University Press is one of the leading university presses in the UK. We publish academic books and journals in our selected subject areas across the humanities and social sciences, combining cutting-edge scholarship with high editorial and production values to produce academic works of lasting importance. For more information visit our website: edinburghuniversitypress.com

© Christine Daigle, 2021, 2023

Edinburgh University Press Ltd
The Tun – Holyrood Road, 12(2f) Jackson's Entry, Edinburgh EH8 8PJ

First published in hardback by Edinburgh University Press 2021

Typeset in 11/13 Foundry Sans and Foundry Old Style
IDSUK (DataConnection) Ltd

A CIP record for this book is available from the British Library

ISBN 978 1 4744 8784 9 (hardback)
ISBN 978 1 4744 8785 6 (paperback)
ISBN 978 1 4744 8787 0 (webready PDF)
ISBN 978 1 4744 8786 3 (epub)

The right of Christine Daigle to be identified as the author of this work has been asserted in accordance with the Copyright, Designs and Patents Act 1988, and the Copyright and Related Rights Regulations 2003 (SI No. 2498).

Contents

Preface	vi
Acknowledgements	viii
List of Abbreviations	x
Introduction: Reading Nietzsche	1
1 Nietzsche's 'Wild' Phenomenology	14
2 Nietzsche's Phenomenological Notion of the Self	39
3 Multi-layered Embodied Consciousness	73
4 Being-in-the World—Being-with-Others	100
5 Fettered and Free Spirits	116
6 Becoming Overhuman	145
Conclusion: From the Ethical to the Political	165
Bibliography	180
Index	195

Preface

In his entry about *Human, All Too Human* in *Ecce Homo*, Nietzsche quipped that what allowed him to think and write was that he had to stop reading out of ill health.

> My eyes put an end to all bookwormishness . . . I was redeemed from the 'book', for years at a time I read nothing – the greatest favour I have ever done myself! – That deepest self, as it were buried and grown silent under a constant *compulsion to listen* to other selves (– and that is what reading means!) awoke slowly, timidly, doubtfully – but at length *it spoke again*. (EH 'Human, All Too Human' §4)

Nietzsche here speaks of his own move from philology to philosophy, namely from a scholarly to a creative activity. I would not claim that the present book represents such a move. This book is scholarly and presents an interpretation of Nietzsche's works and their meaning and it contains the usual scholarly apparatus of notes and references. However, I relate to this quote because in many ways, my decision to stop reading allowed me to write this book. The field of Nietzsche studies is quite vibrant, and the number of studies published every year in article or book format is quite large. The bulk of it is simply overwhelming and in many ways it is impossible to keep up with everything that is published about Nietzsche's philosophy. I have therefore stopped trying – I was failing anyway – and I decided to add to the overwhelming flow by writing this book on reading

Nietzsche as a phenomenologist. It is ironic that I should complain about the never-ending flow of publications – is it really a complaint? – and at the same time contribute to it. But this book had been in my system long enough, even before Élodie Boublil and I co-edited the book *Nietzsche and Phenomenology*, and I needed to put it out there. It is my hope that readers who have not stopped reading will see some value in it.

Acknowledgements

This book has been a long haul, and the many interactions and conversations I had with Nietzsche scholars and phenomenologists nourished it. I not only benefited from the support of many friends who believed in the project but also from the objections thrown at me along the way in both friendly and, less often, not so friendly manners. These expressions of scepticism pushed my thinking and forced me to dig further into the issues I wanted to address. Supportive friends were not always completely sold on the ideas either, and pushed me to articulate them in better form. This book is the outcome of my efforts to do so. I have also had the great fortune to teach Nietzsche's philosophy to both undergraduate and graduate students. I even taught a whole course on *Human, All Too Human* in which we examined the work in detail; not something one frequently has the luxury to do. Students' often candid puzzlements and questions were stimulating and, together, we worked out what Nietzsche might have been up to. These discussions and joint enquiries also contributed to the development of the ideas proposed in this book.

My thanks go to Keith Ansell-Pearson for hosting me during a short research visit at Warwick University where I had the occasion to discuss the first steps of my project with him and Peter Poellner. I also thank him for his ongoing support through the years. Sara Heinämaa and Marguerite La Caze each hosted me for a research visit at the Helsinki Collegium for Advanced Studies and Queensland University respectively.

At both locations, I had the fortune to present and discuss my work to groups of faculty members and graduate students, which further nourished my thinking. I also wish to thank Élodie Boublil whose collaboration for the edited volume *Nietzsche and Phenomenology: Power, Life, Subjectivity* helped shape and consolidate some of the ideas I was working through over the years.

Rebecca Bamford was an invaluable interlocutor and friend, and her work has inspired me greatly. I also deeply appreciate the support offered by Babette Babich, Vanessa Lemm and Daniel W. Conway. I am thankful for Horst Hutter's early encouragements for me to pursue a graduate education and what turned out to be a very long-term engagement with Nietzsche's philosophy. Friends from the Society for Existential Phenomenology and Culture (EPTC) have been precious interlocutors over the years. They have heard me present on various aspects of Nietzsche's thought and provided invaluable feedback. Thanks to David Koukal and Chris Nagel in particular. Antonio Calcagno has also been very supportive and offered provocative questions that helped my work. Everyone needs a friend like him. I am also deeply appreciative for Christinia Landry's friendship and support over the years, academic and personal.

I also wish to thank Carol Macdonald, editor, and all the staff who helped in the production of the book at Edinburgh University Press. Thanks are also due to the anonymous reviewers of the manuscript who offered constructive feedback that helped improve the book.

The Humanities Research Institute and internal programmes at Brock University have funded my work and allowed me to hire research assistants who have contributed to this project. Thanks go to Michael Braund, Christopher Wood, Megan Penney, Terrance McDonald and Brett Robinson. Thank you to Riina Koskela who assisted with the index.

Finally, I want to acknowledge that this book draws on research supported by the Social Sciences and Humanities Research Council of Canada.

List of Abbreviations

References to Nietzsche's texts will be made using the abbreviations below, followed by the aphorism number or section title as is standard in Nietzsche scholarship. The editions used for Nietzsche's works are listed in the bibliography.

A	*The Anti-Christ*
AOM	*Assorted Opinions and Maxims*
BGE	*Beyond Good and Evil*
BVN	Briefe von Nietzsche
D	*Daybreak*
EH	*Ecce Homo*
GM	*The Genealogy of Morals*
GS	*The Gay Science*
HH	*Human, All Too Human*
NF	Nachgelassene Fragmente
SE	*Schopenhauer as Educator*
TI	*Twilight of the Idols*
TL	'On Truth and Lies in a Nonmoral Sense'
TSZ	*Thus Spoke Zarathustra*
WP	*The Will to Power*
WS	*The Wanderer and His Shadow*

Introduction: Reading Nietzsche

> My patient friends, this book desires for itself only perfect readers and philologists: learn to read me well!
>
> ('Preface' §5, *Daybreak*)

Nietzsche's call to his readers to learn to read him well is oft repeated throughout the body of his work. A philologist by training, Nietzsche is aware of the power of words and discourse as a whole and thus he is always extremely careful in how he presents his views in his writings. Concerned as he is to communicate his ideas clearly to his readers, he still adopts a writing style that leaves his philosophy open to a multitude of interpretations. It may be the case that it is not just *Thus Spoke Zarathustra* that is 'for every one and no one', but rather this may hold true for his entire body of work. To some readers, Nietzsche's philosophy will appear to be merely a series of psychological observations in the vein of La Rochefoucauld and Fontenelle, French moralists whom Nietzsche admired. To others, Nietzsche's philosophy will appear to be very rich and offer multiple layers of meaning. There is indeed a great level of complexity to the Nietzschean corpus and the history of the reception of Nietzsche's philosophy is itself complex. Over the course of the twentieth and early twenty-first centuries, he has been understood to have held many different, and sometimes contradictory, viewpoints. He has been read as an existentialist, a naturalist, a nihilist, a moralist, a national-socialist, a psychologist, a postmodern *avant la lettre*, and so forth. And yet, among these varied interpretations, very little has been written about the possibility of interpreting his philosophy as a phenomenology.

Of the many phenomenologists who have taken an interest in Nietzsche's works, such as Martin Heidegger, Emmanuel Lévinas and Henri Birault, none has read his philosophy as being itself phenomenological. In the middle period works, *Human, All Too Human* (1878), *Daybreak* (1881) and *The Gay Science* (1882), as well as the posthumous notes of this period, Nietzsche's investigations reveal that he is realigning his thought, freeing himself from previous influences, such as that of Arthur Schopenhauer and Richard Wagner, and struggling to find his own path. It can be shown that his preferred methodology at the time, as well as in the mature works that follow, is a phenomenology *avant la lettre*, what I will refer to as a wild phenomenology. His phenomenological explorations and experimentations amount to an investigation of the way consciousness interacts with the world of objects and how the web of relationships between objects, humans and consciousness all affect the being of the human. This leads him to investigate embodiment and how an embodied subjectivity relates to itself and the world. In these works and beyond, Nietzsche makes use of the phenomenological concepts of intentionality and *epochè* (reduction) without naming them as such.

A close analysis of Nietzsche's position in the middle period works, one that unearths phenomenological concepts such as intentionality, being-in-the-world, and being-with-others of the human, reveals that he anticipates many Husserlian proposals and themes. Given that both Nietzsche and Husserl are considered to be harbingers of the twentieth-century's existentialist movement, each in their own way, it is fascinating to explore how they might share a similar phenomenological stance, especially since they come from very different philosophical traditions. It is all the more interesting if we consider that thinkers like Gilles Deleuze and Michel Foucault turned towards Nietzsche in an effort to distance themselves from phenomenology, a philosophical position they disliked.[1] Turning to Nietzsche allowed them to move away from a type of existential/phenomenological humanism. However, Nietzsche is closer to Husserl and the phenomenological movement than they, along with many others, realised. The notion that Husserl's and Nietzsche's critiques of the philosophical rationalistic tradition are of the same order has been recognised before.[2] Nonetheless, many interpreters have balked at interpreting Nietzsche as a phenomenologist, emphasising that while their critical stance is very close, their proposals are importantly different; at the very least, scholars contend, Nietzsche would reject Husserl's rationalistic position which makes for an unbridgeable difference in fundamental tenets between the two.[3] However, a more nuanced position can be adopted as evidenced by Peter Poellner, who also argues that Nietzsche can be seen as a precursor to the phenomenological movement. Without going as far as suggesting that Nietzsche was engaged in phenomenology, he recognises Nietzsche anticipated phenomenological modes of enquiry and claims 'it is in

---

[1] In particular, and as Dermot Moran explains, they both 'interpreted Merleau-Ponty, with his appeal to lost origins, as a foundationalist and defender of a humanism which structuralism was seeking to overcome' (*Introduction to Phenomenology*, p. 432).

[2] See, for example, Rudolf Boehm, 'Husserl and Nietzsche'.

[3] Boehm is also hesitant to think beyond this objection. Here is a selection of such objections: Jacob Golomb holds Nietzsche's ideal to be existential while Husserl's ideal is rational ('Nietzsche's Phenomenology of Power', p. 298); while digging under the surface of a seeming opposition between the two schools (Nietzsche's and Husserl's) and comparing their views on the living body, Alain Beaulieu still thinks that there is a radically different stance on consciousness in both thinkers, Nietzsche instrumentalises it while Husserl privileges it as a starting point ('L'Enchantement du corps chez Nietzsche et Husserl', p. 351); Andrea Rehberg points out that Nietzsche 'is struck by [consciousness's] capacity for falsification under the reign of herd values' and that phenomenology's focus on intentionality ends up in an anthropocentric position that Nietzsche would reject ('Introduction', p. 4ff.); and Jocelyn Benoist argues that Nietzsche's philosophy is about meaning and not about being, and that because phenomenology attempts to unveil true being, Nietzsche is not a phenomenologist ('Nietzsche est-il phénoménologue?', p. 322).

Nietzsche that we find the philosophical underpinnings of the phenomenological turn in philosophy'.[4] Therefore, Nietzsche elaborates positions and methods that open the way for the full-blown phenomenological enquiry as proposed by Husserl.[5] Ulrich Haase concurs and explains:

> to speak of Nietzsche and phenomenology does not only mean to identify certain points or methods in Nietzsche's text that can be counted as phenomenological, whereby we would first have to establish an essence of phenomenology in terms of its central claims and methods. Rather, the success of phenomenology in the sense that Heidegger understands it, is wholly dependent on this interpretation of Nietzsche.[6]

And yet, only a few studies consider the relationship between Nietzsche's philosophy and phenomenology.[7] Most commentators come to this topic obliquely while addressing some phenomenological concepts in the works of Nietzsche or others,

---

[4] Peter Poellner, 'Phenomenology and Science in Nietzsche', p. 303. This is a claim that John Sallis would agree with as he suggests that a similar aim is operative in both Nietzsche and phenomenology; namely, the inversion of Platonism that allows to go back to things themselves ('Shining in Perspective', p. 25). Sallis goes on to argue that while Nietzsche conducts his own inversion of Platonism, he shows that what we uncover is not things as they are but, rather, things as we colour them. He thus emphasises perspectivism in Nietzsche. He says: 'In Nietzsche's interpretation of the sensible as perspectival shining, as shining in perspective, the proximity of his later thought to phenomenology is evident' (p. 29).

[5] Perhaps it is the case, as has been suggested by Ammar Zeifa, that phenomenology needed Nietzsche's rejection of Schopenhauer in order to emerge. Zeifa also claims that Nietzsche did not have enough time to be a phenomenologist. See Ammar Zeifa, 'Nietzsche and the Future of Phenomenology'.

[6] Ulrich Haase, 'Dikè and Iustitia', p. 28. In this piece, Haase is specifically enquiring into Heidegger's relation and indebtedness to Nietzsche.

[7] The most recent one is the volume I co-edited with Élodie Boublil, *Nietzsche and Phenomenology. Power, Life, Subjectivity*. Aside from the already mentioned edited volume by Andrea Rehberg, there is also a special issue of *JBSP: Journal of the British Society for Phenomenology* on 'Nietzsche and Phenomenology' edited by Keith Crome. Some articles from this special issue will be referenced throughout the book.

such as embodiment. Kristen Brown and Rosalyn Diprose, among others, have offered important studies in which they position Nietzsche close to Merleau-Ponty.[8] They do so by way of discussing the body and the related notion of the self, concepts that will also be key to my analysis as core phenomenological concepts. Diprose positions Nietzsche in the phenomenological trend arguing that his view of the self is for the most part in agreement with Merleau-Ponty's views. Brown agrees and offers evidence for this connection by way of the 'dynamic non-dualism' she finds at work in both philosophers' thinking, namely a philosophical position that goes beyond any dichotomous approach to the human being.[9] While both position Nietzsche as close to Merleau-Ponty's phenomenology, neither offer a reading of Nietzsche as a phenomenologist. To be fair, their specific goal is not to demonstrate that Nietzsche was engaged in a phenomenological enquiry and yet the work they did, comparing his ideas to Merleau-Ponty's, certainly provides grounds to establish that Nietzsche's enquiry in matters related to the body-self is phenomenological.

Other studies, focusing on other aspects of his thinking as their main point of analysis have also investigated specific questions that pertain to the connection between Nietzsche and phenomenology. For instance, Nietzsche's musings on aesthetics and various art forms seem to have been of particular interest for some scholars; many have focused on Nietzsche's views of sensory and artistic experience, tragedy, music and other arts.[10] However, such specific investigations are not enough to establish, nor are they intended to establish, that Nietzsche's philosophy is

---

[8] See Kristen Brown, *Nietzsche and Embodiment*, and Rosalyn Diprose, *Corporeal Generosity*. I will come back to their respective analyses in later chapters.

[9] Brown brings Nietzsche into dialogue with Merleau-Ponty and claims that the latter's views of human experience as a dynamic whole can be compared to Nietzsche's since, 'It too suggests an experience of self and world as non-dual' (Brown, *Nietzsche and Embodiment*, p. 23).

[10] See for example Günther Figal, 'Aesthetically Limited Reason'; Michel Haar, 'Nietzsche and Van Gogh'; Jocelyne Lebrun, 'Pour une phénomenologie de l'imagination poétique'; Bernard Flynn, 'Merleau-Ponty and Nietzsche on the Visible and the Invisible'; Gary Shapiro, 'Übersehen'.

phenomenological.[11] They have, as per their intent, only shown that some aspects of Nietzsche's philosophising resemble some phenomenological endeavours. I believe that one of the reasons why the aforementioned attempts fail to establish Nietzsche as a phenomenologist, even in the rare cases where this is their end goal, is that they do not examine the Nietzschean texts on which I focus. Interestingly, most studies examine later texts such as *On The Genealogy of Morals*, *Beyond Good and Evil* and *Thus Spoke Zarathustra*. In addition, scholars often devote much attention to the early essay *The Birth of Tragedy*. This focus is misplaced. Only a very small number of works on Nietzsche take into account and focus on Nietzsche's middle period writings. By ignoring these works, commentators cut themselves off from an important source for understanding how Nietzsche's philosophy not only shares some concepts with phenomenology but is itself phenomenological, albeit in a non-orthodox and experimental way. In fact, paying little attention to or even ignoring these texts may be the reason why it did not even occur to many commentators to read Nietzsche as

[11] For example, Martine Prange's study of Nietzsche's aesthetics provides insightful analyses of the reasons why Goethe comes to replace Wagner in the middle period works. Prange claims that Goethe is the 'key-figure in Nietzsche's new aesthetics and "free spirit" philosophy' (*Nietzsche, Wagner, Europe*, p. 202). Nietzsche's appreciation for Goethe's understanding of measure and moderation, 'Greek' virtues that he is also attracted to, partly explains that. Goethe's interculturalism as well as his sensualist philosophy, the attention he pays to hearing and seeing, are also influences on Nietzsche and the latter would have paved the way for Nietzsche's turn from a musical to a pictorial aesthetics. Most importantly, as Prange points out, 'Not only did Goethe set out to harmonize art and knowledge, as is generally known, but also to integrate body and mind – and all senses for that matter' (p. 218). This is important in terms of the interpretation I will develop about embodied consciousness. Perhaps it is the case that Goethe's sensualist philosophy influenced the development of what I will call Nietzsche's wild phenomenology. See Prange's analyses in her *Nietzsche, Wagner, and Europe* for more details on the turn from Wagner to Goethe.

a phenomenologist. By focusing on these works my analysis aims to remedy this shortcoming.[12]

The enquiries I have mentioned investigate the question of the relation *between* Nietzsche and phenomenology by examining the linkage between his thought and that of various phenomenologists and/or various phenomenological concepts. The aim of this book is quite different. I will investigate Nietzsche *as* phenomenologist. My work will attempt to answer the question: What new insights can we gain from reading him as engaged in enquiries that are of a phenomenological nature?[13] Once it is established that Nietzsche's core concepts are phenomenological and that he offers a phenomenological understanding of the human being, how must we tackle the ethical ideals of the free spirit and the Overhuman? What kind of ethics is Nietzsche proposing on the phenomenological grounds he has established? Does understanding him as a phenomenologist perhaps provide us with a better understanding of his ethical and political proposals? While it may be the case that many phenomenologists wish to remain descriptive and pursue Husserl's call to

---

[12] While I will privilege the middle period works and remind the reader that doing so sheds a new light on Nietzsche's philosophy, I do not think it is possible to consider them separately from later works. Therefore, I will also take into consideration later iterations of the concepts I will examine and contrast some early and late formulations of the same concepts.

Another note about the material that will be used is in order. Throughout my analysis, I will not confine myself to invoking commentators from either the Anglo-American analytic tradition or the Continental tradition. Instead, I will put to work any helpful analysis and interpretation, regardless of its author's theoretical and interpretative background and commitments. I find that adopting one tradition or the other and ignoring what stems from the other is quite limiting, to put it mildly.

[13] In many ways, the current study is responding to the implicit call contained in the introduction I co-wrote with Élodie Boublil for *Nietzsche and Phenomenology*. We said: 'Our volume will inevitably leave some questions unanswered. In fact asking the question of "Nietzsche and phenomenology" is an opening of the inquiry. We hope to settle a number of issues and indeed demonstrate that this undertaking is valid and fruitful both historically and philosophically. Readers will be convinced, as we are, that our question(s), rather than being *Holzwege*, in fact open(s) up rich pathways that must be explored' ('Introduction', p. 5).

go 'back to the things themselves', many also wander in the realm of the normative and the prescriptive. This is certainly Nietzsche's case for whom, I will argue, the task is eminently ethical and therefore also pressingly political. His phenomenological explorations and the concepts he puts in place – perhaps insufficiently developed for the modern-day phenomenologist who is the heir of Husserl and others – offer tools that allow for a fruitful connection between the descriptive, the normative and the prescriptive. Understanding his take on the human as embodied consciousness that constitutes its world and exists in relation to it and to others leads to a different appreciation of his ethical proposals.

My analysis will proceed in as systematic a fashion as possible through these questions. Chapter 1 will offer an explanation of how Nietzsche embraces a phenomenological method of enquiry that amounts to a wild phenomenology, a phenomenology that is not conscious of itself as phenomenological. I will briefly discuss the concepts I understand to be fundamental to the phenomenological movement, those that are articulated in a variety of ways by thinkers from that movement. Intentionality and lived experience as an embodied consciousness in the world will thereby emerge as central core ideas. As we will see in later chapters, those are also Nietzsche's focus. Additionally, Chapter 1 will clarify the issue of influence of Nietzsche on phenomenology as well as methodological issues. I will present Nietzsche's philosophical position as a pursuit of truth conducted in the Enlightenment spirit. I will also discuss the particular method Nietzsche embraces, namely that of aphoristic writing and historical philosophising, explaining how these are atypical of phenomenological enquiries, but are possibly better tools to achieve phenomenological aims.

Chapter 2 will tackle Nietzsche's views on intentionality and selfhood. I will first explain how his position takes shape given his critical relation to Kant and the related critique of metaphysics. Indeed, it is upon his critique of the distinction between the real and appearances that Nietzsche operates a return to immanence and to our fundamental experience of constituting the world as intentional consciousness. I will explain how both postmodern and naturalist understandings of Nietzsche miss the mark by claiming that he rejects the self. Nietzsche offers a notion of the self that may significantly differ from the one inherited from centuries of rationalist and idealist philosophising, but that does not amount to a rejection. Instead, he proposes that the human self is the colourist of its world, what amounts to a phenomenological concept of intentional consciousness.

Chapter 3 will further unpack Nietzsche's phenomenological view of consciousness as multi-layered and embodied. I will delineate the topology of consciousness which I see emerging in key passages of *Thus Spoke Zarathustra*, such as 'On the Despisers of the Body', and wherein his view of the body as 'grand reason' emerges. It is important to understand how he repositions the ego, and thereby repositions agency and the traditional cogito as a tool for the conscious body. This understanding leads to an exploration of the key Nietzschean concept of perspectivism which I revisit as yet another feature of Nietzsche's phenomenological thinking. I also discuss the notion of the soul as subjective multiplicity as it is presented in the first book of *Beyond Good and Evil*. This text is importantly connected to the topology of consciousness presented in *Thus Spoke Zarathustra* and to the notion of perspectivism. The soul, as multiple, is a dynamic becoming within which drives and affects compete in their interaction with the world, leading to the adoption of multiple perspectives. I conclude this chapter by revisiting one of the most important passages in Nietzsche's work with regard to the notion of will to power, aphorism 36 of *Beyond Good and Evil*. I show that this section serves to summarise Nietzsche's views on intentional consciousness and its constitution of itself and the world.

Chapter 4 focuses on the being-in-the-world and being-with-others of the multi-layered embodied consciousness. I proceed to show that consciousness needs the world to exist; it cannot be conceived without it. In so doing, I appeal to Heidegger's notion of being-in-the-world and demonstrate that Nietzsche anticipated it. This also entails, as it does in Heidegger, that consciousness is ontologically dependent on others, that it is fundamentally a being-with-others. Intentional consciousness constitutes itself and its world, but it is also constituted by the world it is in and the others with whom it interacts. This leads to a discussion of a Nietzschean form of structuralism which I then relate to Foucault's later enquiries into the subject and power and the notion of relation to oneself (*rapport à soi*) and care of the self (*souci de soi*). I see Foucault's turn away from an early structuralism to an aesthetics of the self as being very similar to what Nietzsche offers in terms of how the free spirit and the Overhuman can relate to their self-constitution. The descriptive work of phenomenology, which unearths the workings of embodied and intentional consciousness, the self and world constitution, opens up interesting ethical and political pathways.

With the foundation of Nietzsche's wild phenomenology firmly in place, I turn to an examination of the free spirit, the ethical ideal grounded in this phenomenology. In Chapter 5, I explain that the free spirits are the sceptics that are searching for truth while freeing themselves from received knowledge and external authorities. Indeed, their search for truth and knowledge entails a constructive type of nihilism that negates in order to create. Their scepticism allows them to be authentic. Their longing for authenticity and self-scrutiny leads them to embrace themselves as the dynamic becoming that they are. My analysis of the first section of *Schopenhauer as Educator* allows for an understanding of the imperative to become what one is. The human being as *homo poeta* seeks to become oneself but this entails needing the other for one's own flourishing. Indeed, as required by the phenomenological conception of the self as a being-with-others, we need to pursue relationships with others that will foster our overcoming and our becoming what we are. Nietzsche offers that agonistic friendships among equals will open the path for this and will pave the way for the Overhuman.

Chapter 6 closely examines the ethical ideal that supersedes that of the free spirit: the Overhuman. I explain that the agonised subject, the one that embraces itself as dynamic becoming by itself and in its agonistic relations with others, is the Overhuman. When Nietzsche refers to the Overhuman as the meaning of the earth, he is pointing to the radical immanence of his ethical ideal.

The dynamic becoming is a this-worldly endeavour: it is as being-in-the-world and being-with-others in this world that one may become what one is. This amounts to an incorporation of truth which necessitates a transformation of oneself. I examine closely 'Of the Vision and the Riddle' and 'Of the Three Metamorphoses' from *Thus Spoke Zarathustra* along with aphorism 341 of *The Gay Science* to show what is involved in the ethical transformation Nietzsche is seeking. Affirmative ethical becoming, the overcoming of oneself and the affirmation of oneself as the being one is, is only possible if one rejects alienating moralities and asceticism. One may do so based on a phenomenological understanding of the human as proposed by Nietzsche. This phenomenological view offers the necessary ground for the ethical ideal of becoming oneself to emerge. I explain that Nietzsche's ethical perspective is that of a virtue ethics that shares with ancient virtue ethics a focus on the good life – an attention to small things and to one's flourishing in the immanent realm of being.

The final chapter offers considerations on the political ramifications of Nietzsche's phenomenological and ethical positions. Even if I conclude that Nietzsche is not a political thinker per se – that is, he is not offering an elaborate and sustained analysis of political systems and institutions nor does he offer us a clear proposal for what he considers to be the best organisation of the political – he still has some views on the political insofar as the political impacts our individual and collective flourishing and insofar as those are intertwined. Nietzsche's views are therefore useful for democratic thinking. He is interested in an anti-identitarian perfectionist democracy that forwards the conditions needed for individual and collective flourishing that may arise out of agonistic relations. Such a democracy would be radically different than any of the democratic systems we have experienced.

In summary, this book examines Nietzsche's phenomenological explorations with the intent to decipher his understanding of the human being as an intentional embodied consciousness, as a being-in-the-world and as a being-with-others. Establishing this phenomenological conception of the human will allow me to revisit the Nietzschean notions of free spirit and *Übermenschlichkeit* and how they express the ethical and cultural-political flourishing Nietzsche envisions. In his preface to *Human, All Too Human*, Nietzsche offers a retrospective interpretation of the work accomplished in his book. He says it marks his overcoming of romanticism and his creation of the concept of free spirits. The free spirit is the one who, freed from the alienating discourses of metaphysics, morality, art and religion, can look at things anew and be astonished by the things closest to them, rediscovering those closest things just as they are. The free spirit does so as an intentional consciousness that is conscious of itself as the creator of the world. We will also see that the Nietzschean individual is a dividuum, that is, a multi-layered self that is an intentional consciousness, that is unconscious and conscious, that is and can become, that is itself, and in-the-world and with-others. Enquiring in-depth the notion of 'Subjekts-Vielheit' that Nietzsche advances in *Beyond Good and Evil* §12 and the various earlier phenomenological positions that lead to this mature construct will allow me to show that there is a self that one is as a dynamic becoming and a self that one must become. This self that one must become is the key to authentic becoming which amounts to self-constitution, to individuality as 'a task to be accomplished'.[14] I will demonstrate that the reconceptualisation of the self that Nietzsche operates allows for his ethics and its ideals to unfold. My enquiry will illuminate the lesser-known and arguably better Nietzsche that Ruth Abbey and Paul Franco see at work in the middle period works.[15]

This better Nietzsche is engaged in philosophical experimentation, a methodology that amounts to the wild phenomenology we are about to discuss and that puts forward new conceptualisations of the human and its world. Very simply, the objective of this book is to answer the questions: What does it mean to think of Nietzsche as some kind of phenomenologist, perhaps a 'wild' one? What is this phenomenology about and what concepts does it bring forward? The first few chapters of the book focus on answering these questions. Having done

---

[14] This is how Nuno Nabais puts it in his 'The Individual and Individuality in Nietzsche' (pp. 81–2).
[15] I discuss Abbey's and Franco's readings in the following chapter.

that and explicated the various concepts we see emerging in the middle period works which then consolidate in later works, the last chapters consider how we can reread his ethical and political proposals once we see them as grounded in the fundamental view of humans as embodied intentional consciousnesses. Again, the Nietzsche that emerges through this rereading is arguably better than the one we are used to encountering in the various commentaries on his work. Focusing on the philosophical experimentation and creativity of that period of Nietzsche's thinking - the middle period - yields interesting and novel modes of understanding his works.

1
Nietzsche's 'Wild' Phenomenology

In the preface of his *Phenomenology of Perception*, Merleau-Ponty indicates that 'phenomenology can be practiced and identified as a manner or style of thinking', and 'it existed as a movement before arriving at complete awareness of itself as a philosophy. It has been long on the way, and its adherents have discovered it in every quarter, certainly in Hegel and Kierkegaard, but equally in Marx, Nietzsche and Freud.'[1] He goes on to explain that one can find the phenomenology in these writings not by compiling quotes but rather by approaching them from a phenomenological point of view. Whether one agrees with this or not, it is interesting to note the influences and thinkers that Merleau-Ponty sees as inspiring phenomenological thinking and, for my purposes, that Nietzsche would find room among them. What type of phenomenology could Nietzsche have been practising?

Phenomenology

While there was a phenomenological turn in the nineteenth century, which unfolded in a phenomenological movement

---

[1] Maurice Merleau-Ponty, *Phenomenology of Perception*, p. viii. Although, as Lars Peter Storm Torjussen points out, 'it is only with Husserl that this "manner of thinking" became explicitly aware of itself as a philosophical method' ('Is Nietzsche a Phenomenologist?', p. 179). Torjussen might therefore agree with my use of de Coorebyter's phrase 'wild phenomenology'. See note 29 below.

that developed through the twentieth century and beyond, it is difficult to arrive at one simple and straightforward definition of phenomenology. Husserl may be the 'father' of the movement but, as Paul Ricœur once suggested, phenomenology is the history of Husserlian heresies. Indeed, Ricœur argued that the structure of Husserl's philosophy was such that it implied that a Husserlian orthodoxy was impossible.[2] Indeed there is not one Husserl and, thus, there is no one Husserlian phenomenology. The early descriptive phenomenology, such as the one found in *Ideas*, gives way to a more existential phenomenology such as the one found in the *Crisis of the European Sciences and Transcendental Phenomenology*. In his study on Merleau-Ponty, Eric Matthews explains that it is thanks to Heidegger's understanding of Dasein as being-in-the-world that existential phenomenology is made possible. Matthews suggests that Heidegger's views may have brought Husserl to develop his later views on the Lebenswelt. This new view according to which the Lebenswelt is pre-given, which is to say we cannot 'bracket it', transforms the phenomenological reduction into a method to

> put into brackets ... the theoretical constructions of science and metaphysics ... The aim of phenomenology thus becomes not the achievement of rational insight into the 'essences' or necessary structures of experience, but a deeper understanding of the meaning of our theoretical activities through grasping their roots in ordinary lived experience.[3]

Therefore, a genuine radical 'reduction' will make us aware of the priority of our lived experience over scientific constructs. It is this kind of approach that Merleau-Ponty puts at work in his philosophy, according to Matthews. It is also the approach taken by existential phenomenologists such as Beauvoir, Sartre and

---

[2] Paul Ricœur, 'Sur la phénoménologie', p. 836. Quoted in Jean-Dominique Robert, 'Approche rétrospective de la phénoménologie husserlienne', p. 28.
[3] *The Philosophy of Merleau-Ponty*, p. 29.

Heidegger.[4] It is a phenomenology that also embraces a perspectivism akin to Nietzsche's. As I will argue, Nietzsche's critique of metaphysics, morality, art and religion, launched in *Human, All Too Human*, is an instance of this type of phenomenological reduction.

The types of phenomenology present in Husserl's writings give birth to a proliferation of phenomenological enterprises of one strand or another. Therefore, providing a definition of phenomenology that would match every instance may just be impossible. That said, it is possible to identify the methodological stance that a philosophy must embrace as well as a set of questions that it must address for it to qualify as a phenomenology.[5] In his authoritative work on phenomenology, Dermot Moran indicates that there is a great diversity of interests among philosophers who identify as phenomenologists. Further, there is also great diversity with regard to what they consider to be the key issues in phenomenology or how to apply the phenomenological method. But this diversity should not lure us away from attempting to define phenomenology which is, for Moran, a thoroughly modernist outlook.[6] Moran explains that

> Phenomenology is best understood as a radical, anti-traditional style of philosophizing, which emphasizes the attempt to get to the truth of matters, to describe *phenomena*, in the broadest sense as whatever appears in the manner in which it appears,

---

[4] Interestingly, their interest in the later Husserl goes hand in hand with an interest in the existential descriptions found in the writings of Kierkegaard and Nietzsche. With regard to Sartre and Heidegger, this is an argument that Jean-Dominique Robert makes with regard to Sartre and Heidegger which I find compelling and extend to Beauvoir. He claims that existential philosophy uses phenomenology as a method in an attempt to clarify questions pertaining to existence. He sees Heidegger, Sartre and Merleau-Ponty as engaged in this type of enquiry. See Ibid. pp. 32-7.

[5] As Andrea Rehberg puts it, 'There is no such easily delimitable phenomenon which could be called "phenomenology," but at most a "certain continuity of concerns" between different phenomenologists, although even these concerns may be conceived in very different ways, and according to very different styles of thinking, by different practitioners of the philosophical "genre" of phenomenology' ('Introduction', p. 1).

[6] See Dermot Moran, *Introduction to Phenomenology*, p. 3.

that is as it manifests itself to consciousness, to the experiencer. As such, phenomenology's first step is to seek to avoid all misconstructions and impositions placed on experience in advance ...[7]

In order to do so, the phenomenologist must focus on 'concrete lived human experience'[8] and suspend all other judgements. Announcing a new way of doing phenomenology in his *Logical Investigations*,[9] Husserl points to the need to suspend our natural attitude while investigating experience. Through the phenomenological reduction (*epochè*), phenomenology allows the experience to emerge and, in so doing, illuminates the involvement of consciousness in the world. Moran explains,

> the whole point of phenomenology is that we cannot split off the subjective domain from the domain of the natural world as scientific naturalism has done. Subjectivity must be understood as inextricably involved in the process of constituting objectivity ... There is only objectivity-for-subjectivity.[10]

Jean-François Lyotard's image for this is that consciousness is 'weaved with the world'.[11] Intentional consciousness is a key

---

[7] Ibid. p. 4.
[8] Ibid. p. 5.
[9] Quoted in Ibid. p. 1.
[10] Ibid. p. 15. Further in his introduction, Moran points out that 'Phenomenology will continue to have a central role in philosophy because of its profound critique of *naturalism* as a philosophical programme. From the beginning, Husserl's phenomenology initially set itself against psychologism and more generally against all forms of naturalism. Husserl and his followers see naturalism as self-defeating because it consciously excludes consciousness, the very source of all knowledge and value' (Ibid. p. 21). Interestingly, we can use this to defeat the naturalistic interpretation of Nietzsche which has been so prominent in Nietzsche studies in recent years. If indeed Nietzsche is a phenomenologist concerned with knowledge and value as it is constituted by a human consciousness, then a naturalistic reading of his philosophy is impossible. I will discuss this further in the context of his views on consciousness and the self in Chapter 2.
[11] Lyotard's phrase is 'tissée avec le monde' (Jean-François Lyotard, *La Phémoménologie*, p. 6).

concept for phenomenology, one that Husserl inherited from Franz Brentano. From him, he also inherited the desire to be rigorous and systematic in the search for truth.[12] Intentionality's concomitant concept, the pre-given life-world, is also essential for phenomenology. Consciousness is as conscious *of* something; the world and its objects constitute consciousness and consciousness constitutes the world and its objects as it is conscious of it. For Husserl, intentionality is a process of co-constitution. As Robert Sokolowski points out, what is novel in this view is the dynamism of perception.[13] While every phenomenologist subscribes to a notion of intentionality and a pre-given world, their understanding of these concepts varies. The most notable divergence in these views pertains to Husserl's notion of pure consciousness. Indeed, despite embracing the view that consciousness is intentional, Husserl holds to the view that there is a pure ego that we can arrive at by a process of bracketing.

This is a view that is criticised and rejected by existential phenomenologists such as Jean-Paul Sartre and Merleau-Ponty. In *Transcendence of the Ego* and *Being and Nothingness*, Sartre offers a strong critique of the notion of pure consciousness. His claim is simple and he summarises it in his *Notebooks for an*

---

[12] Noting that a rigorous and systematic search for truth is at the heart of the phenomenological enterprise, Moran speaks of Brentano as a major precursor to Husserl. He points out that 'Brentano's view of philosophy as a rigorous science puts him at a considerable intellectual distance from his contemporaries who were proponents of idealism, existentialism, and life philosophy. Indeed he especially disdained Nietzsche as a practitioner of bad philosophy' (*Introduction to Phenomenology*, p. 24). For Brentano's assessment of Nietzsche as a philosopher, see his entry on Nietzsche in *Geshichte der Philosophie der Neuzeit* (pp. 297-8). He says that 'Nietzsche is a failed philologist and a philosophical dilettante', and, further, 'Nietzsche is a degenerate philologist and attended a bad school from the beginning as a philosopher' (my translation of 'Nietzsche ist ein mißratener Philologe und ein philosophischer Dilettant' (p. 297) and 'Nietzsche ist ein entarteter Philologe und als Philosoph von Anfang an in eine schlechte Schule gegangen' (p. 298)). I will be arguing that this view of Nietzsche is unfounded.

[13] Robert Sokolowski, *Introduction to Phenomenology*, p. 18.

Ethics: 'if you were to take the world away from consciousness, it would no longer be consciousness of anything, therefore no longer consciousness at all'.[14] Therefore, the notion of a consciousness without a world, what Husserl's pure consciousness would amount to, is absurd. Similarly, Merleau-Ponty argues an 'I' or 'cogito' can only exist as situated, that is as in a relation involving things and others.[15] At the end of the section on temporality of the *Phenomenology of Perception*, for example, he claims that, he has 'more effectively analysed the notion of presence', and 'linked together presence to oneself and presence in the world, and identified the cogito with involvement in the world'.[16] Furthermore, the 'new cogito' offered by Merleau-Ponty is one for which 'there is consciousness of something, something shows itself, there is such a thing as a phenomenon'.[17] This cogito is the 'deep-seated momentum of transcendence which is my very being, the simultaneous contact with my own being and with the world's being'.[18]

Existential phenomenology focuses on the experience of human consciousness in the world. It seeks to go 'back to the things themselves' not as a transcendent reality but rather, as experienced by humans. The object of enquiry is thus intentional consciousness as embodied and weaved in a pre-given world as well as its objects. The encounter between subjectivity and world is creative as the perceiving consciousness constitutes the world it is already in. I am using 'creative' cautiously here as I do not mean to say that consciousness creates the world. In fact, Lyotard warns against such usage of 'creative', pointing out that the 'creation' of consciousness always occurs in the world. Consciousness is nothing by itself.[19] The phenomenological reduction is a tool

---

[14] Jean-Paul Sartre, *Notebooks for an Ethics*, p. 558.
[15] Eric Matthews, *The Philosophy of Merleau-Ponty*, p. 33.
[16] Maurice Merleau-Ponty, *Phenomenology of Perception*, p. 503.
[17] Ibid. p. 345.
[18] Ibid. pp. 438-9.
[19] See his *La Phénoménologie*, pp. 29-30. This takes us back to Jean-Paul Sartre's *Being and Nothingness*, in which nothingness is clearly consciousness that encounters being.

we can use to show the process of co-constitution: consciousness constitutes its experience and the object of the experience constitutes the consciousness that intends it. Existential phenomenology focuses its analyses on the experience of that consciousness engaged in the process of co-constitution. It seeks to understand how the human being exists as a being-in-the-world that is an intentional consciousness.

In *Being and Time*, Heidegger convincingly argued that '*Ontology is possible only as phenomenology*'.[20] He diagnoses metaphysics as the history of the forgetting of being because it did not choose a method that allowed for it to unveil being, or rather to let being appear. Metaphysics was a concealing rather than an unveiling. If one is to let appearances appear, to go back to things themselves as is the motto of phenomenology, one must engage in philosophy as a hermeneutic of Da-sein – the logos of a phenomemology of Da-sein – since Da-sein is the gateway to being. Indeed, 'Da-sein has ontological priority over all other beings' and the 'discovery of the meaning of being and of the basic structures of Da-sein in general exhibits the horizon for every further ontological research into beings unlike Da-sein'.[21] Phenomenology is thus the only philosophical method possible and it focuses on the experiences of Da-sein and its encounter with being as being-in-the-world as being-with and being a self.[22] Heidegger's point of view is grounded in Husserl's definition of phenomenology as a science but also as a method and an 'attitude of mind, the specifically *philosophical attitude* of mind, the specifically *philosophical method*'.[23] In the introduction to *Ideas I*, he explains that for the science of phenomena 'a new style of attitude is needed which is entirely altered in contrast to the natural attitude in experiencing and the natural attitude in thinking'. One must 'move freely in it without relapsing into

---

[20] Martin Heidegger, *Being and Time*, p. 31. Emphasis in the original.
[21] Ibid. p. 33.
[22] While Heidegger himself would resist the label existentialism because of how he associates it with a humanism he seeks to reject, it is this focus on Da-sein as fundamental to an understanding of being that leads many interpreters to align him with existentialists such as Beauvoir and Sartre.
[23] Edmund Husserl, *The Idea of Phenomenology*, pp. 18–19.

the old attitudes, to learn to see, distinguish, and describe what lies within view'.[24] This is rendered possible by making use of the method of phenomenological reduction. As we will see, Nietzsche too aims for us to learn to see things differently and, most importantly, to prevent our received judgements or even thinking processes from getting in the way of our experiencing and being-in-the-world. In the aphorism titled 'Do not want to see prematurely', for example, he says 'For as long as one is experiencing something one must give oneself up to the experience and close one's eyes: that is to say, not be an observer of it while still in the midst of it. For that would disturb the absorption of the experience: instead of a piece of wisdom one would acquire from it indigestion' (WS §297). The eyes he is referring to here are the inquisitive eyes of reason.[25] One must give oneself to the experience and learn directly from it.

Nietzsche as Phenomenologist

While there are many interesting parallels to be drawn between Husserl's views and Nietzsche's views – for example on the concept of intentionality as I will discuss in Chapter 2 – I will show that Nietzsche has a greater affinity with existential phenomenology. However, and as I have explained in the introduction, I will not proceed to a systematic comparison of Nietzsche's thought with that of Husserl, Heidegger, Sartre, Merleau-Ponty and other phenomenologists in an effort to establish to whom he stands closer. Instead, I will show that his philosophy is elaborated through a method that can be said to be phenomenological and that it presents concepts such as intentionality, being-in-the-world, being-with-others and embodiment although they are not named as such. Since these are key phenomenological concepts, I will explore how he deals with them. I will work to

---

[24] Edmund Husserl, *Ideas*, p. xix.
[25] Although, as we will see shortly, Nietzsche's position is not an outright rejection of reason but a reconceptualisation of reason as embodied. He does see himself as an Enlightenment thinker who continues to seek truth with the light of reason, an embodied one.

unearth these concepts as they occur in his writings which is to say without using this specific terminology. While conducting this enquiry, I will draw from the works of the aforementioned phenomenologists to illustrate both the similarities and differences between their views and those belonging to Nietzsche. Inevitably, this will lead to the question of influence. Nietzsche cannot be considered an influence on Husserl. In fact, Brentano was the major influence on Husserl, and given that Brentano displayed such a dislike for Nietzsche it is rather improbable that Husserl paid much attention to Nietzsche. Conversely, the question of influence of Nietzsche on Heidegger is not nearly as clear. Heidegger was an avid reader of Nietzsche and wrote an extensive two-volume study on his philosophy.[26] Although, it is hardly debatable that Nietzsche had an influence on Heidegger, I do not think he directly influenced Heidegger's phenomenology. Heidegger after all was a student of Husserl and it is clearly to Husserl's phenomenology that he responds in his own works, especially *Being and Time*. A similar relationship holds between Nietzsche and other figures like Sartre, Merleau-Ponty and Simone de Beauvoir who are responding primarily to Husserl and appropriating his propositions for their own uses. Therefore, Nietzsche's influence on their phenomenological thinking was indirect at best.[27]

The reason for this is that none of them read him as a phenomenologist, although as quoted earlier Merleau-Ponty does insightfully put Nietzsche among the ranks of those who were

---

[26] Martin Heidegger, *Nietzsche*.
[27] Sartre's and Beauvoir's relation to Nietzsche is very interesting. Both are very critical of Nietzsche, but their critique rests on a misunderstanding of Nietzsche's proposals. They both read him as a philosopher who champions the exercise of crude power and thus they misunderstand his ethical ideal of the *Übermensch*. If we move beyond this misreading, it can be shown that they both shared many ideas and methodologies with him. See note 64 below. With regard to the question of influence, I have conducted an extensive comparative study of Nietzsche and Sartre showing that their views on nihilism, question of meaning, and ethics are very similar. See my *Le Nihilisme est-il un humanisme?* I have also written on the connections between Nietzsche and Beauvoir, focusing on their views of the ethical imperative. See my 'A Nietzschean Beauvoir?'

engaged in phenomenological enquiries.[28] If indeed his philosophical method is a phenomenological one and if these thinkers were influenced by his methodological stance, albeit indirectly as I argue they were, then their own phenomenologies were devised under Nietzsche's influence. This will emerge as I proceed to analyse the phenomenological concepts at work in Nietzsche's thought although, again, I will not proceed to systematically compare views. For the moment, we may understand Nietzsche as a 'wild phenomenologist'. I take this characterisation from Vincent de Coorebyter who suggested that, prior to his encounter with Husserl's philosophy, Sartre was practising a wild phenomenology that was not quite self-conscious.[29] That is, Sartre was exploring human experience and consciousness and proposing to understand them through concepts and explanations that were akin to Husserl's properly articulated phenomenology. Sartre was already doing phenomenology but unknowingly and without using the vocabulary proper to this philosophical approach. The encounter with Husserl changed that. Had Nietzsche had such an encounter, his wild phenomenology might have consolidated in a phenomenology proper. There are indeed enough affinities for this possibility to be seriously contemplated. However, and to be very clear, it is a wild *existential* phenomenology I see at work in Nietzsche's thinking and not something like a descriptive or transcendental phenomenology. Indeed, there is no room in Nietzsche's thinking for such things as a transcendental ego or essences, be they of consciousness or of objects. But there is a concern with the being-in-the-world and being-with-others just

[28] Not only do they not read him as a phenomenologist, but they often conceive of themselves or are conceived of by commentators as engaged in a radically different project. Another example of this is Emmanuel Levinas. In the introduction to their edited volume, Bettina Bergo and Jill Stauffer explain that the two thinkers are often conceived as antithetical. And yet, there are a lot of similarities between their thoughts. Their volume seeks to unearth those, specifically with regard to their views on ethics and subjectivity (see *Nietzsche and Levinas*). While I will not engage with Levinas, I find it interesting that even a theistic phenomenologist would also have affinities with Nietzsche, as the contributors to the volume argue.
[29] See Vincent De Coorebyter, 'Introduction', p. 21. His phrase is 'phénoménologie sauvage et inconsciente de soi'.

as there is with embodied subjectivity. There is also a concern with adopting a critical and sceptical method which amounts to a constructive nihilism that dismisses discourses and theoretical constructs that have hidden the truth about the world and ourselves. This makes him a phenomenologist, albeit a 'wild one'.

Questions of Method

In order to conduct my analysis, I put the middle period writings, namely *Human, All Too Human* (1878), *Daybreak* (1881), *The Gay Science* (1882) and the notes from that period (1876 to 1881)[30] at the centre of my analysis. In the history of the reception of Nietzsche's philosophy, these works have been neglected, often because they are considered to be merely transitional. As Paul Franco indicates, when these works are studied it is mostly in relation to later works on which the emphasis is placed. However, Franco's study, along with work done on Nietzsche by Ruth Abbey, is an exception. These two recent studies have drawn attention to the middle period works and their importance.[31] In their respective works, Abbey and Franco show that reading these works allows for a different, and possibly better, Nietzsche

---

[30] Although, as will become evident, I will only rarely refer to the notes as I believe that the published writings contain whichever concepts, claims and ideas that Nietzsche considered to be, if not final, at least final enough to be ready for a readership to confront. What Nietzsche says about uncompleted thoughts, however, would seem to argue against me here. He says: 'Just as it is not only adulthood but youth and childhood too that possess value *in themselves* and not merely as bridges and thoroughfares, so incomplete thoughts also have their value. That is why one must not torment a poet with subtle exegesis but content oneself with the uncertainty of his horizon, as though the way to many thoughts still lay open. Let one stand on the threshold; let one wait as at the excavation of a treasure: it is as though a lucky find of profound import were about to be made' (HH I §207).

[31] In addition to Franco's and Abbey's works, the volume edited by Rebecca Bamford chooses to focus on the middle period works too and places them under the light of the concept of the free spirit (see her *Nietzsche's Free Spirit Philosophy*). There is also an interesting, edited volume in French dedicated to *Human, All Too Human*. See Paolo D'Iorio and Olivier Ponton (eds), *Nietzsche: Philosophie de l'esprit libre*. Most recently, Rebecca Bamford and Keith Ansell-Pearson have published *Nietzsche's Dawn: Philosophy as a Way of Living*, providing an analysis of this other neglected middle period work.

to emerge. Indeed, they unveil a Nietzsche that is less radical and vindictive than in the later writings. Abbey suggests that the middle period writings are 'superior to the subsequent works by some measures and some of these measures are Nietzsche's own'.[32] She points out that these works are more traditional, less radical and carry on the Enlightenment project.[33] Franco has a similar assessment and goes so far as to title his own investigation *Nietzsche's Enlightenment: The Free-Spirit Trilogy of the Middle-Period*.[34] Not only does Nietzsche free himself from previous influences, starting with *Human, All Too Human*, but he also adopts a new writing style and carves out his own philosophical path. This is the work in which Nietzsche begins to be Nietzsche according to Arthur C. Danto.[35] Nietzsche himself considered his middle period writings as pursuing a common set of aims. In a letter written on 3 July 1882, he tells Lou Salomé that he has finished *The Gay Science* and that this concludes his work of the last six years; he labels it his 'Freigeisterei', that is, his free-spiritedness or the free-spirit cycle.[36]

[32] Ruth Abbey, *Nietzsche's Middle Period*, p. xv.
[33] Ibid. p. xvi.
[34] Paul Franco, *Nietzsche's Enlightenment*. It ought to be noted that to refer to these texts as a 'trilogy' is in fact a misnomer since there were five separate texts: *Human, All Too Human* (1878, now referred to as HH I), 'Assorted Opinions and Maxims' (1879) and 'The Wanderer and his Shadow' (1880) which he republished with a preface as HH II in 1886 when he was also busy writing prefaces for his other works in an effort to republish them and reach a broader readership; *Daybreak* (1881); and *The Gay Science* (1882).
[35] See his essay 'Beginning to be Nietzsche'.
[36] 'Letter to Lou von Salomé' (BVN-1882, 256 – Brief an Lou von Salomé: 03/07/1882). In his mature works, Nietzsche's tone and approach is more critical. His critique rests upon the philosophy that was written in his earlier period. Abbey points out that 'he did not always present himself as a radical critic of the Western tradition whose own thought was unprecedented and whose development owed little to postclassical philosophers' (Ruth Abbey, *Nietzsche's Middle Period*, p. 149). The middle period Nietzsche thinks for himself, but he is still responding to the philosophical tradition. It is in his mature works that the critique radicalises itself. *Thus Spoke Zarathustra* is considered to open the mature period, along with *Beyond Good and Evil*. These two works consolidate Nietzsche's mature philosophy. Thus, *Zarathustra* is really a hinge between the middle period and the mature period. It is the result of the work undertaken in the middle period and serves as ground for what follows. Nevertheless, the works that follow are more radical in their critique.

That cycle opens up with what he considers to be 'the memorial of a crisis'. *Human, All Too Human* 'calls itself a book for *free* spirits: almost every sentence in it is the expression of a victory – with this book I liberated myself from that in my nature which *did not belong to me*' (EH 'Human, All Too Human' §1). His writings are the history of his own overcomings as he puts it in the Preface to volume II of *Human, All Too Human*: 'One should speak only when one may not stay silent; and then only that which one has *overcome*' (1). He explains that 'I realized it was high time for me to think for *myself*' (EH 'Human, All Too Human' §3) and this was made possible because of his ill health and how it prevented him from reading anything, allowing for his deeper self to speak again (EH 'Human, All Too Human' §4). What ensued was the first step towards the liberation of the spirit, namely the rejection of metaphysics and the critique of morality which is pursued in all three books of the *Freigeisterei*. *Daybreak* and *The Gay Science* pursue the same objectives as *Human, All Too Human* while adopting a positive tone. This is necessary because one rejects in order to build anew: 'We negate and must negate because something in us wants to live and affirm – something that we perhaps do not know or see as yet.' (GS §307) While *Daybreak* kickstarts his 'campaign against *morality*' (EH 'Daybreak' §1), it is also 'an affirmative book, profound but bright and benevolent. The same applies once again and in the highest degree to the *gaya scienza*' (EH 'The Gay Science'). After all, 'This whole book is nothing but a bit of merry-making after long privation and powerlessness, the rejoicing of strength that is returning' (GS 'Preface' 1). The writings from the middle period therefore all pursue the same goal: to free the spirit by rejecting certain views and opening up the ground for affirmation. This all starts with *Human, All Too Human* and its explicit embrace of the Enlightenment pursuit.

In *Ecce Homo*, Nietzsche remarks, 'The name of "Voltaire" on one of my writings – that was true progress – *towards myself*' (EH 'Human, All Too Human' §1). In reference to this observation, Dirk K. Johnson points out, 'Nietzsche later claimed that his public embrace of the Enlightenment tradition as well as its most famous exponent allowed him to recognize and articulate his own philosophical perspectives'.³⁷ Johnson further suggests that there is an alliance between Nietzsche and rationalism. Although I think that Johnson may be right, I think it is necessary to elucidate the nature of this alliance. Examining Nietzsche's path in *Human, All Too Human* and beyond allows us to understand this more clearly.

Human, All Too Human is one of Nietzsche's most neglected writings. It is often considered to be a positivistic interlude, one that would not offer the foundation for Nietzsche's philosophy as found in subsequent texts. However, I consider this reading to be erroneous. I agree with Danto that one's perspective on the work will be very different whether one reads it retrospectively to illuminate the later works or whether one reads it prospectively, from the point of view of its author.³⁸ I also agree with Abbey and Franco: if one reads the work very closely, one discovers a Nietzsche that is quite different, a new Nietzsche. This Nietzsche is engaged in an important dialogue with the philosophical tradition that he is critically re-evaluating, and, that, in the true Enlightenment spirit. Despite Nietzsche's description of the book as a monological book in its epigraph, it is in fact a genuine dialogue. The epigraph reads:

> This monological book, which came into being during a winter residence in Sorrento (1876 to 1877), would not have been given to the public at this time if the proximity of the 30th of May 1878 had not aroused all too intensely the wish to offer a timely personal tribute to the greatest liberator of the human spirit.

This great liberator of the spirit is none other than Voltaire. This dedication is a clear indication that Nietzsche embraces the Enlightenment spirit.³⁹ It is interesting that this epigraph

---

³⁷ Dirk K. Johnson, *Nietzsche's Anti-Darwinism*, p. 30.
³⁸ Arthur Danto, 'Beginning to be Nietzsche', p. ix.
³⁹ It should also be noted that Nietzsche refers to himself and the free thinkers – *Human, All Too Human* is a book for free spirits – as 'children of the Enlightenment' (HH I §55).

and the quote from Descartes used in his preface in the 1878 edition of *Human, All Too Human*, are not always included in English editions of the work. The Cambridge edition from 1996 does not include them while the Stanford edition from 1995 does.[40]

The quote that Nietzsche chooses from Descartes as his preface to the 1878 first edition of *Human, All Too Human* is also illuminating. It shows a Nietzsche concerned with the search for truth and embracing a sceptical stance. It is worth reproducing the quote from part three of *The Discourse on Method*:

> Finally, to conclude this moral code, I decided to review the various occupations which men have in this life, in order to try to choose the best. Without wishing to say anything about the occupations of others, I thought I could do no better than to continue with the very one I was engaged in, and devote my whole life to cultivating my reason and advancing as far as I could in the knowledge of the truth, following the method that I had prescribed by myself. Since beginning to use this method I had felt such great satisfaction that I thought one could not have any sweeter or purer enjoyment in this life. Every day I discovered by its means truths which, it seemed to me, were quite important and were generally unknown by other men; and the satisfaction they gave me so filled my mind that nothing else mattered to me.[41]

In his 1886 Preface, Nietzsche elaborates in his own words. He indicates that his writings 'have been called a schooling in suspicion, even more in contempt, but fortunately also in courage, indeed in audacity. And in fact I myself do not believe that anyone has ever before looked into the world with an equally profound degree of suspicion' (HH I Preface §1) What he is indicating here is that his scepticism and critical stance is magnified in comparison to that of Descartes and Voltaire, and also

---

[40] The latter is part of the series 'The Complete Works of Friedrich Nietzsche' that is based on the Colli-Montinari authoritative edition of the complete works in German.
[41] René Descartes, *Selected Philosophical Writings*, p. 33.

to that of Kant. Nevertheless, it is still in all of its profundity informed by Descartes's and Kant's critique.[42] The fact that Nietzsche would opt to quote from *The Discourse on Method* as his preface to the first edition should be an indication that, even if he does not embrace the philosophical positions of rationalism, he is at the least interested in its method of enquiry.[43] The search is for truth and the means to attain it is to use one's reason and not to trust any received authority.[44]

[42] In his study, *Nietzsche and the French*, W. D. Williams points out that 'both the dedication to Voltaire and this passage were cut out of later editions, as if Nietzsche were aware that neither of these two was fundamentally akin to himself' (p. 42). Williams understands Nietzsche as slowly drifting away from Voltaire over the course of his writing of the middle period texts. After quoting from *The Gay Science*, Williams says 'Here Nietzsche is emancipated from Voltaire; he has progressed from the Socratic temper of *Menschliches* [*Human, All Too Human*] to the attitude that knowledge is not the final goal in life, which will bear its full fruit only later' (Ibid. p. 90). However, Voltaire is again present at the very end of *Ecce Homo*. The very last words of the book are: 'Have I been understood? *Dionysus versus the Crucified* –' (EH 'Destiny' §9). But the preceding section, which opens with the same question, 'Have I been understood?', proceeds to explain that the overcoming of Christian morality is essential. It ends by quoting Voltaire's call against the Church: '*Écrasez l'infâme!*' (crush the infamous, the vile).

[43] Indeed, he rejects vehemently key Cartesian tenets such as the cogito. In *Beyond Good and Evil* Part Two, 'On the Prejudices of Philosophers', for example, he summarises his critique towards this concept: 'When I analyze the process that is expressed in the sentence, "I think," I find a whole series of daring assertions that would be difficult, perhaps impossible, to prove ... it has, at any rate, no immediate certainty for me' (BGE §16) and again 'it is a falsification of the facts of the case to say that the subject "I" is the condition of the predicate "think." *It* thinks; but that this "it" is precisely the famous old "ego" is, to put it mildly, only a supposition, an assertion, and assuredly not an "immediate certainty"' (BGE §17). I will come back to these passages when discussing consciousness in Chapter 3.

[44] He could also have quoted the following from the *Meditations on First Philosophy* since *Human, All Too Human* can be read as an exercise in such methodical enquiry: 'I realized that it was necessary, once in the course of my life, to demolish everything completely and start again right from the foundations if I wanted to establish anything at all in the sciences that was stable and likely to last ... I will devote myself sincerely and without reservation to the general demolition of my opinions ... for the purpose of rejecting all my opinions, it will be enough if I find in each of them at least some reason for doubt' (Descartes, *Selected Philosophical Writings*, p. 76). Interestingly, Husserl quotes this passage in his *Cartesian Meditations*.

The rejection of rationalism is not a rejection of reason. Rather, it consists in re-evaluating the role of reason and in grounding it in the body, as we will see in the next chapters. Very systematically Nietzsche's work proceeds to critically examine and reject received philosophical opinions on metaphysics, morality, religion, art, and so forth, leaving him free to form his own opinions on all such matters. This critique is liberating for Nietzsche – allowing him to 'progress toward himself' – and it is also liberating for his readers.[45] His intended readers are the free spirits, those who have been freed from all alienating metaphysical illusions. However, simply being a liberating book and one for the free spirit (or one for the spirit to be freed) does not make *Human, All Too Human* a rejection of the quest for truth. Quite the contrary: the task for Nietzsche is to reject everything that has passed as truth in order to uncover the true nature of the human, its place in the world, and the relation between the human being and the world. Thus, Nietzsche puts Kant's call to work: 'Sapere Aude!' – dare to know. This is the Enlightenment call for the human being to stop relying on authority and to seek knowledge for oneself by using the power of one's spirit.

In the introduction to his essay 'An Answer to the Question: What Is Enlightenment?', Kant explains:

> Enlightenment is mankind's exit from its self-incurred immaturity. *Immaturity* is the inability to make use of one's own understanding without the guidance of another. *Self-incurred* is this inability if its cause lies not in the lack of understanding but rather in the lack of the resolution and the courage to use it without the guidance of another. Sapere

---

[45] This progress towards himself is what he claims to have accomplished in *Human, All Too Human* (see EH 'Human, All Too Human' §1 and the discussion of the dedication to Voltaire above). In the last section of *Ecce Homo*, 'Why I am a Destiny', he also speaks of this progress, this time about smelling the lie of morality: '*Revaluation of all values*: this is my formula for an act of supreme coming-to-oneself on the part of mankind which in me has become flesh and genius' (§1). I will return to this in my discussion of the free spirit in Chapter 5.

Aude! Have the courage to use your own understanding! is thus the motto of the enlightenment.[46]

In his translator's note to this passage, Schmidt explains that the Latin phrase, Sapere Aude!, is taken from Horace's *Epistles*. Furthermore, in 1736 this phrase was struck on a medal for the Société des Alétophiles of Berlin (a society of friends and lovers of truth – aletheia – 'dedicated to the spreading of truth in general and the Leibniz-Wolff philosophy in particular'). As Schmidt indicates, the phrase was widely used in the eighteenth century.[47] The Enlightenment's appetite for knowledge and truth, paired with the courage that is necessary for it, implies a critique and a questioning of the philosophical tradition. It informs Descartes's queries, the French and Scottish Enlightenment's pursuits, Kant's endeavours and Nietzsche's work. Following Nietzsche's own assessment, I take *Human, All Too Human* as a starting point for his Enlightenment-type of enquiry, and I see it as continuing to unfold in the following two works of the middle period and beyond. As he puts it in *Daybreak*, 'This Enlightenment we must now carry further forward' (D §197). In fact, he poses as an Enlightenment thinker who is a better Enlightenment figure than even Kant.[48] By rejecting the German attitude towards morality which is one of obedience, and which finds its heightened form in Kant's categorical imperative (D §207), and seeking to become the master of himself (D §206), and by grounding reason in the body, understanding consciousness as intentional, Nietzsche takes the Enlightenment further forward and, he would argue, puts it on firmer ground.

It should be noted that the problem of truth and method is one that Nietzsche begins to tackle rather early. The essay 'On Truth and Lies in a Nonmoral Sense' from 1873 already

---

[46] In James Schmidt (ed.) *What Is Enlightenment?*, p. 58.
[47] See the translator's note (ibid. p., 64).
[48] I am thankful for Bamford's and Ansell-Pearson's analyses of Book III of *Daybreak* which drew my attention to this claim.

puts the problem forth: In what consists truth and does it rely on a transcendent realm of the in-itself? He posits the latter as out of our reach and thereby inconsequential and not worth striving for. Nietzsche suggests that the critical enquiry of the philosopher can demonstrate that 'truth' is a

> movable host of metaphors, metonymies, and anthropomorphisms: in short, a sum of human relations which have been poetically and rhetorically intensified, transferred, and embellished, and which, after long usage, seem to a people to be fixed, canonical, and binding. Truths are illusions which we have forgotten are illusions . . . (TL 117)

In this early essay then, Nietzsche already sows the seeds of his future thinking on metaphysics and on the problem of truth. *Human, All Too Human* and later works revisit this in greater depth as we will see.[49]

Nietzsche's Phenomenological Method: Aphoristic Writing and Historical Philosophising

Human, All Too Human marks the beginning of a new philosophical approach for Nietzsche; it also marks the beginning of a new methodological stance. Two features of his philosophical style appear in *Human, All Too Human* for the first time: aphoristic writing and historical philosophising. Thereafter, and with the exception of the *Genealogy of Morals* and *Thus Spoke Zarathustra*, aphoristic writing is Nietzsche's preferred writing style.[50] Against Safranski, who thinks that this type of writing

---

[49] This serves to show that Nietzsche's philosophical preoccupations remained consistent throughout the different periods in which we can organise the corpus.

[50] I say 'preferred' because he also uses other writing techniques and methods throughout his writings. One interesting feature of his books, for example, is the writing in songs and poems. For complete sections of such, see: '"Joke, Cunning, and Revenge": Prelude in German Rhymes' and the appendix 'Songs of Prince Vogelfrei' to *The Gay Science*. See also 'From High Mountains. Aftersong' in *Beyond Good and Evil*.

lacks coherence and systematicity,[51] I argue that aphoristic writing is the only methodologically appropriate tool for Nietzsche's philosophy and that it does display coherence or systematicity, albeit one that requires unearthing through the more involved efforts of a reader. Such a reader would be 'a reader such as I deserve, who reads me as good old philologists read their Horace' (EH 'Books' §5) and further: 'When I picture a perfect reader, I always picture a monster of courage and curiosity, also something supple, cunning, cautious, a born adventurer and discoverer' (EH 'Books' §3). Now, it is true, as Safranski claims, that Nietzsche's stance towards philosophical systems such as Hegel's became more critical in his mature philosophy. But to go so far as to say that he was aiming for such system-building and that the aphoristic style marks a failure seems exaggerated to me. I think it is helpful to approach aphorisms as Nietzsche would want every reader to, namely, as parts of *Gedanken-kette*, chains of thoughts that are connected to one another.[52] The context of every aphorism, its location in a book, its neighbouring aphorisms, and the chapters in which it is presented, all contribute to the implicit argumentative and systematic philosophising that Nietzsche offers in his writings. Certainly, this offers a great deal of coherence and systematicity.

It has also been claimed that it was in fact Nietzsche's health that commanded the use of aphoristic writing. That Nietzsche was suffering at the time with disabling health problems that 'rendered him incapable of writing or even thinking for extended periods of time'[53] leads Richard Schacht to claim that aphoristic writing may not have been a methodological choice but rather the only option if Nietzsche was to write anything. However, he does not deny coherence and systematicity to Nietzsche for

---

[51] For Safranski's arguments, see his *Nietzsche: A Philosophical Biography*, pp. 158-61. He argues that aphoristic writing is not a methodological objective for Nietzsche and that he had conceived of *Human, All Too Human* as a series of essays.

[52] This is a proposal that Paul Franco offers in his preface to his *Nietzsche's Enlightenment*. I find this concept apt and very helpful in uncovering the inner coherence of Nietzsche's arguments.

[53] Richard Schacht, 'Introduction', p. xi.

that matter, saying that it would be unwarranted 'to assume that Nietzsche's recourse to it is indicative of the absence of any underlying unity and coherence of thought and intention here and subsequently'.[54] He calls on Nietzsche's own warning for support: '*Against the shortsighted.* – Do you think this work must be fragmentary because I give it to you (and have to give it to you) in fragments?' (HH II §128)

Indeed, I argue that because Nietzsche wants to tackle the lived experience of the individual as an embodied being, one that is a subjective multiplicity,[55] his philosophy has to be expressed in this type of narrative which, on the surface, appears to be non-systematic and non-linear. However, the fact that each piece appears to be isolated is not indicative of a lack of coherence or even the lack of a Nietzschean 'system'. This aphoristic style may not be typical of most phenomenological enquiries (to say the least), but it could be a closer rendition of human experience than any theoretical treatise could ever hope to be.[56] Nietzsche offers that writing is about communicating 'a state, an inner tension of pathos through signs' and that 'Every style is good which actually communicates an inner state' (EH 'Books' §4). It seems that the aphoristic style is particularly advantageous for his endeavours but the fact that he also uses other styles, such as poetry, essay writing and even gospel-like writing in *Thus Spoke Zarathustra*, indicates the need for a style that is multiple in order to describe life, as argued by Eric Blondel.[57] According to him, Nietzsche adopts aphoristic writing in order to go back to concrete reality. This entails that genealogy – which will be

---

[54] Ibid.
[55] We will see in the next two chapters how this understanding of human subjectivity shapes up.
[56] Nietzsche shares the existentialist attempt to render the human experience through various types of writing. Existentialists are famous for their use of literature as a tool for exploring human experience. In addition, Nietzsche also leaves systematic theoretical enquiries aside. This is not to say that there is not a deeper systematicity at work in his thinking/writing. Any careful reader – the only type of reader Nietzsche is interested in – will recognise his body of work as a cohesive systemic whole.
[57] Eric Blondel, *Nietzsche: The Body and Culture*, pp. 22–3.

discussed shortly – is essayistic, an aphoristic and fragmentary play that renders a reality that is itself a dynamic play of forces.[58] Reality, as experienced by a consciousness, is always fragmentary and aphoristic writing allows for the encapsulation of such fragments and presents them for what they are. Pieced together in *Gedanken-kette*, they can then offer us better insights into what reality is than a systematic theoretical treatise can.

The Nietzschean method allows us to 'go back to things themselves', as they appear in their non-systematic and non-linear way, and it does so by offering multiple perspectives on things. The aphoristic style Nietzsche adopts is indicative of how he conceives of human experience: not as a rationalistic, systematically organised, continuous, linear narrative, but rather as a collection of perspectives gained through a plentitude of experiences. Further, aphoristic writing is a methodologically sound choice for Nietzsche's perspectivism. The aphorism does not aim to unveil the truth about a specific reality or experience; instead it aims at unveiling a possible truth, one truth among many others.[59] While Nietzschean aphorisms address a theme or

---

[58] Ibid. p. 83ff. He says, 'He committed himself to the path of *Versuch*: a metaphorical plurality in which language, he thinks, instead of simplifying, can try to regain a multiplicity of perspectives on life' (p. 203). This reinforces the idea that Nietzsche is an experimenter.

[59] Jacob Golomb explains that Nietzsche offers phenomenological descriptions and that he 'performs all this with an avoidance from providing us with an empirical-causal explanation and an ontological hard-core context for the explicated phenomena. This, of course, reminds us of the Husserlian *epochè*, that function as the necessary condition of any phenomenological investigation' (Golomb, 'Nietzsche's Phenomenology of Power', p. 295). In an essay on *Human, All Too Human* and the critique of ideals, Mathieu Kessler suggests that the essayistic nature of Nietzsche's philosophy and his embrace of the aphoristic style and perspectivism protects him from the dogmatism inherent to materialism, i.e., it would posit a given and measurable reality. In fact, one could use Kessler's claim to argue against the naturalist reading of Nietzsche (see 'La critique des idéaux dans *Choses humaines, trop humaines*', p. 150). Luca Lupo, for his part, considers that aphorisms are the expression of an interior monologue experienced in solitude. He considers the passage from the Platonic dialogues to the Nietzschean monologues as indicative of the passage from an absolute notion of truth in Plato to a perspectival notion in Nietzsche (see his 'Ombres: Notes pour une interprétation', p. 109).

a particular topic, they are not definitions in the strict sense.[60] They open up to a multiplicity of interpretations, but, and as Franco also claims, it would be a mistake to take this multiplicity as indicative of a kind of 'interpretive nihilism'.[61]

Jill Marsden's take on the aphoristic style is convincing to me. She says, '[aphorisms are] only fragmentary to the extent that [they fragment] expectations. By failing to supply the "connective tissue" that would impose a semblance of unity on the text, Nietzsche compels his readers to be active in their reception of his ideas.'[62] In other words, aphorisms present the spontaneity of thought and trigger a reflective response in the reader. The careful reader Nietzsche wants, as described above, will navigate the fragmentary by reconstituting that 'connective tissue'. Discussing the methodological shift we see at work in *Human, All Too Human*, Franco refers to aphorism 178, concurs with Marsden, and says '[Nietzsche] also recognized that [the aphorism's] fragmentary nature could be very effective in conveying philosophical ideas. The incompleteness of an aphorism forces the reader to fill in what is left unsaid and thereby to think along with the philosophical writer.'[63] In that aphorism, titled 'The effectiveness of the incomplete', Nietzsche explains:

---

[60] In our introduction to *Nietzsche and Phenomenology*, Élodie Boublil and I clarified that 'the Greek *aphorismos* means determination and is derived from the verb *aphorizo* which means to mark off with boundaries' (p. 8 n6).

[61] Franco is worried that interpreters like Kofman, Deleuze, Derrida and Blondel present exaggerated claims with regard to the inherent meaninglessness of aphorisms. He is dissatisfied with their emphasis on what they perceive to be an endless play of perspectives (see Franco, *Nietzsche's Enlightenment*, pp. xiii–xiv). I share Franco's worry and disagreement with this type of reading of Nietzsche's style. Nonetheless, an interpreter like Blondel has very interesting things to say about the aphoristic style; for example, he suggests that aphoristic discourse is 'subversive' (see *Nietzsche: The Body and Culture*, pp. 22–41). As he points out, it is the right method for a philosophy that aims to go beyond the metaphysical while simultaneously critiquing language. Giorgio Colli also suggested that the aphoristic style is revealing of Nietzsche's distrust of logical proofs and argumentative series (see 'Nachwort', pp. 708–9).

[62] Jill Marsden, 'Nietzsche and the Art of the Aphorism', p. 30.

[63] Franco, *Nietzsche's Enlightenment*, p. 14.

Just as figures in relief produce so strong an impression on the imagination because they are as it were on the point of stepping out of the wall but have suddenly been brought to a halt, so the relief-like, incomplete presentation of an idea, of a whole philosophy, is sometimes more effective than its exhaustive realization: more is left for the beholder to do, he is impelled to continue working on that which appears before him so strongly etched in light and shadow, to think it through to the end, and to overcome even that constraint which has hitherto prevented it from stepping forth fully formed. (HH I §178)[64]

There are also interesting parallels to be drawn between Nietzsche's notion of historical philosophising – what will later become genealogical thinking – as delineated and proposed in *Human, All Too Human* and the phenomenological notion of reduction. In his second *Unfashionable Observation* on history, Nietzsche discussed the various ways one may approach historical practice, namely the monumental, the antiquarian and the critical. However, it is in *Human, All too Human* that he offers historical philosophising as a method to counter metaphysics and he does so in the very first aphorism. There he confronts metaphysical philosophy with historical philosophy which 'can not be separated from natural science, the youngest of all philosophical methods' (HH I §1). Metaphysics posits absolute truths but, as he puts it in the next aphorism: 'Lack of historical sense is the family failing of all philosophers' (HH I §2). Metaphysicians who lack this historical sense take as their starting point the human being and the world as they are now, and by so doing they fail to appreciate their historical becoming. Because 'everything has become', as he puts it, 'there are *no eternal*

---

[64] This is reminiscent of Sartre's and Beauvoir's views on literature. For them, writing is a communicative act in which a writer appeals to a reader's freedom via the written piece. The reader responds to the writing and may act upon the world or oneself as a result. See my '*The Second Sex* as Appeal' for a discussion of how this view of literature is applicable to philosophical writing. Nietzsche's description of the effectiveness of the incomplete is in the same vein and entails a similar appeal to the reader.

facts, just as there are no absolute truths. Consequently what is needed from now on is *historical philosophizing*, and with it the virtue of modesty' (HH I §2). Philosophising historically means to trace the history of concepts and our understanding of things, and ultimately to uncover their origin. This uncovering will allow for things to emerge as they are while we divest them of our human interpretation and meaning. Our world and the objects therein have acquired meaning through our religious and metaphysical interpretation of them. Therefore, philosophising historically will allow us to divest things of the beliefs we have superimposed on them. We will indeed go 'back to the things themselves'. This does not mean going back to the realm of the in-itself – a notion Nietzsche rejects as we will come to see – but rather it means to go back to the things as they are before our human interpretation comes into play. Nietzsche embraces this method in *Human, All Too Human* and beyond. His work is replete with genealogical accounts of concepts and values. These are exercises in phenomenological reduction that help Nietzsche make his case against metaphysics, morality, art and religion. When these discourses are shown to be merely human, the individual may rediscover oneself as what one is and seek out one's own flourishing.

There are possibly as many phenomenologies as there are phenomenologists. But certain themes and concepts as well as theoretical presuppositions and methods are common to all. If phenomenology is a style of philosophising as I have described it, then Nietzsche certainly embraces this style. If his is a 'wild' phenomenology it is because, in addition to not being fully conscious of itself as a phenomenology, it also predates its official birth. The similarities in methodological aims, if not expressions, are too many to ignore. The chapters that follow will unearth phenomenological concepts as they are elaborated in Nietzsche's philosophy, further supporting reading Nietzsche as a phenomenologist.

2
Nietzsche's Phenomenological Notion of the Self

> It seems to him as if his eyes are only now open to what is *close at hand*. He is astonished and sits silent: where *had* he been? These close and closest things: how changed they seem! what bloom and magic they have acquired! ... Only now does he see himself--and what surprises he experiences as he does so! What unprecedented shudders!
>
> (*Human, All Too Human* 'Preface' §5)

While Nietzsche does not provide his readers with the equivalent of Locke's *Essay Concerning Human Understanding* or Kant's *Critique of Pure Reason*, his works are replete with statements about the nature of the human being, and these allow us to draw a portrait of consciousness as Nietzsche conceived it. By examining closely how he tackles the problem of knowledge and truth, which is arguably the most pressing problem in the middle period works and especially in *Human, All Too Human*,[1] we can unearth his understanding of consciousness as intentional. In this chapter, I will proceed by first examining his critique of metaphysics, including his relation to Kant, and

---

[1] As mentioned earlier, *Human, All Too Human* is not the first work in which Nietzsche tackles the notion of truth. See the discussion on 'On Truth and Lies in a Nonmoral Sense' in the previous chapter and note 26.

then turn to his view of the self. We will see that understanding Nietzsche's philosophy as rejecting the self altogether is mistaken. Indeed, he holds on to a notion of selfhood whereby we are the colourists of the world, engaged in processes of constitution as the intentional consciousness that we are.

Critique of Metaphysics

As I have explained in the preceding chapter, Nietzsche conceives of himself as embracing the spirit of the Enlightenment and seeks to establish knowledge for himself, without recourse to tradition or received opinions. His dedication to Voltaire as well as the quote from Descartes in lieu of a preface are tips to the reader that this is the programme that will pan out in the book. The first chapter of *Human, All Too Human*, titled 'Of First and Last Things', seeks to establish the foundation for what will follow. The point of departure is a critique of metaphysics that misconceives of the world, superimposing a realm of things in themselves and appearances over it and thus preventing the human being from attaining knowledge about the world and about him- or herself. A genealogical enquiry into metaphysics, putting Nietzsche's wild phenomenological method of historical philosophising to work, shows that it was human beings who came up with these fictions in the first place.

The critique of metaphysics sets out with a critique of Kant. Nietzsche's relation to Kant is very complex and not mediated through Schopenhauer, as has often been suggested.[2] Nietzsche was particularly interested in Kant's critical philosophy. This

---

[2] In his book, R. Kevin Hill has shown that Nietzsche was a very attentive reader of Kant and that his knowledge and understanding of Kant did not rely either on Schopenhauer's treatment of him or on other secondary sources on Kant. Hill shows that Nietzsche read Kant directly and that he read the *Critique of Judgment* first, before the *Critique of Pure Reason* (see Hill, *Nietzsche's Critiques*). Hill's study is an excellent analysis of the relation between the two philosophers and of Nietzsche's reception of Kant. For another, less exhaustive but equally interesting study, see Olivier Reboul's *Nietzsche Critique de Kant*. With regard to the mediating role Schopenhauer may have played, João Constâncio's analysis sheds a new

is easily understood given that Nietzsche's aim in *Human, All Too Human* is similar to that of Kant's; namely, to determine the possibility and limits of knowledge.[3] For Kant, an enquiry in the nature of reason is the key to providing an answer to these questions. Similarly, Nietzsche's search for knowledge and truth entails an understanding of the subject of knowledge, i.e., human consciousness. Like Kant, Nietzsche seeks to provide an answer to the question of how truths are erected and upon what.

However, Kant's answer to the problem turns out to be too rationalistic for Nietzsche's taste. In the Kantian epistemic process, a rational consciousness perceives an object. Perception is made possible and is conditioned by the categories of understanding of reason. These categories allow for perception to happen but also shape the perception itself. The thing in-itself is limiting and allows for the epistemic relation between subject and object to take place. According to some interpretations – which Nietzsche appears to follow at times – Kant's proposal rests upon the view that the object of perception is causally supported by the thing in-itself. The object is a phenomenon for the subject and, as such, it is not the genuine object which remains hidden, so to speak, behind the epistemic relation. In some way, the object in-itself would ground the object as phenomenon for the subject. It is tempting for Nietzsche to posit a

light on this. He argues that it is not so much to Kant as to Schopenhauer that Nietzsche's concept of consciousness responds. Because he conceives of subjectivity as that of a body or organism, he rejects Descartes's and Kant's views and takes an interest in Schopenhauer's views. When he does so, he develops them in radical new ways. This means that there are a lot of agreements between Nietzsche and Schopenhauer. I read Constâncio's analyses as indicative that it is not so much Schopenhauer's take on Kant that interests Nietzsche, rather, it is the tools he finds in Schopenhauer to defeat any overestimation of consciousness. His analysis of drives and what they mean for Nietzsche is particularly interesting and I will come back to it in a later section (see Constâncio, 'On Consciousness: Nietzsche's Departure from Schopenhauer').

[3] In his *Critique of Pure Reason*, Kant indicates that philosophy must answer the following three questions: 'What can I know? What should I do? What may I hope?' (*Critique of Pure Reason*, A805/B833, p. 677).

noumenal world to explain the phenomenal world, which is the only world to which we can ever have access, but this is not the path he takes.[4] As Hill points out, while Nietzsche is interested in Kant's critical endeavour, his 'references to Kant's metaphysics and epistemology stress the skeptical motif at the expense of any positive claims about the thing-in-itself'.[5]

Indeed, Nietzsche's stance is utterly sceptical in the classical sense of the word. Jessica Berry has argued, quite convincingly, that his interest in Montaigne in the period preceding the writing of *Human, All Too Human* combined with his extensive reading and appreciation of the Greeks, and his desire to overcome Schopenhauer's metaphysics led Nietzsche to embrace a Pyrrhonian type of scepticism.[6] The overcoming of Schopenhauer goes hand in hand with the critique of Kant. As Berry further indicates, Nietzsche's scepticism takes the form of an anti-transcendentalism, 'treating human beings as continuous with the rest of the natural world'.[7] This position also entails a rejection of transcendent realms of any type that takes the following form: we cannot assert whether it is the case or

---

[4] Hill suggests that *The Birth of Tragedy* contains an aesthetical metaphysics which is the outcome of this temptation. He thinks that Nietzsche had given in to the temptation and explored its possibility in this early work (Hill, *Nietzsche's Critiques*, pp. 74–5 and 104).

[5] This is an important point that Hill makes in his analysis of the references to Kant in the middle period works (Ibid. p. 21).

[6] Berry believes that reading Nietzsche as a sceptic gives us the key to coherence and continuity in his works (see *Nietzsche and the Ancient Skeptical Tradition*, p. 6). She points out that 'many of Nietzsche's remarks about "free" and "fettered" spirits in *Human, All Too Human* are echoes or even paraphrases of Montaigne's various condemnations of the uncritical acceptance of tradition–especially religious tradition' (Ibid. p. 81). I will discuss the free spirit in Chapter 5.

[7] Ibid. p. 9. As we will see later, Nietzsche's 'naturalism' entails a sceptical outlook that necessitates the rejection of any transcendent foundation. Anthony Jensen argues that what we find at work in Nietzsche is rather a Langean type of scepticism that makes him more of a naturalist than Descartes, Kant and Schopenhauer, with whom he shares a degree of scepticism but who would reject the naturalism he develops on the basis of their thought as well as that of Spinoza and Leibniz. For details of this argument, see his 'Helmholtz, Lange, and Unconscious Symbols of the Self'.

not that there is a realm of the in-itself. However, R. Lanier Anderson takes this too far when he claims that 'precisely because there are no things in themselves, Nietzsche concludes that the *only* kinds of reality are phenomenal'.[8] Yet, Nietzsche does not assert the inexistence of things in themselves. His argument in *Human, All Too Human* is the following:

> It is true, there could be a metaphysical world; the absolute possibility of it is hardly to be disputed. We behold all things through the human head and cannot cut off this head; while the question nonetheless remains what of the world would still be there if one had cut it off. This is a purely scientific problem and one not very well calculated to bother people overmuch ... For one could assert nothing at all of the metaphysical world except that it was a being-other, an inaccessible, incomprehensible being-other; it would be a thing with negative qualities. – Even if the existence of such a world were never so well demonstrated, it is certain that knowledge of it would be the most useless of all knowledge: more useless even than knowledge of the chemical composition of water must be to the sailor in danger of shipwreck. (HH I §9)

In a sense, one might say that Kant too leaves the problem aside in order to focus on the operations of reason and how it acquires knowledge. However, Kant might not go as far as to say, with Nietzsche, that 'the thing in itself is worthy of Homeric laughter ... it appeared to be so much, indeed everything, and is actually empty, that is to say empty of significance' (HH I §16). Given the task that he has set himself in *Human, All Too Human*, it is important for Nietzsche to insist on the

---

[8] R. Lanier Anderson, 'Nietzsche on Truth, Illusion, and Redemption', p. 190. Even if he gets this point wrong, Anderson does proceed to an interesting discussion of how this leads Nietzsche to talk of the constitution of the phenomenal world. He points to a distinction in Nietzsche between types of representation: the way things appear in consciousness and the underlying content of unconscious sense impressions which he thinks are derived from Leibniz's 'petites perceptions'. See especially pp. 190–1.

liberatory aspect of this discovery: we cannot know whether the realm of the in-itself exists, nor does it matter. He argues that the metaphysical discourse that has put in place a realm of things in themselves opposed to a realm of appearances has perverted the human being's take on the world. He says: 'What is "appearance" for me now? Certainly not the opposite of some essence: what could I say about any essence except to name the attributes of its appearance! . . . Appearance is for me that which lives and is effective' (GS §54). The knower only ever has access to appearances. He further explains that appearance is 'thrown over things like a dress and [is] altogether foreign to their nature and even to their skin' (GS §58). We are in fact the creators of such appearances and names of things that veil the thing itself and 'What at first was appearance becomes in the end, almost invariably, the essence and is effective as such' (GS §58).[9] This is how a 'real world' is established. But, he asks: 'What is "real" in that? Subtract the phantasm and every human *contribution* from it, my sober friends! If you can! . . . There is no "reality" for us – not for you either, my sober friends' (GS §57).

However, this means that the human being has erred for centuries, seeking a truth which does not exist, misconstruing truth as what it is not. Historical philosophising, or genealogy, is Nietzsche's tool for demonstrating this. It allows for bracketing off all the false judgements that have built the world, that have veiled the raw experience of the world, thereby creating an illusory world. It provides access to that raw experience, to things themselves, as is the goal of the phenomenological method. 'How the "Real World" at last became a Myth. History of an Error', from *Twilight of the Idols* summarises this very well. There, Nietzsche recounts the whole history of the real world, the realm of the thing in-itself, and how it gained the

---

[9] In what follows in the aphorism, he takes this line of argument in the direction of what I have labelled his constructive nihilism (see my *Le Nihilisme est-il un humanisme?*). He points out that 'We can destroy only as creators' (GS §58). By this he means that we need to create new names and new values for new things to emerge and therefore for reality to change. This is similar to what he claims later in GS §307 and which I have quoted in the previous chapter.

prominence and value it did for human beings. He concludes by saying: 'We have abolished the real world: what world is left? the apparent world perhaps? . . . But no, with the real world we have also abolished the apparent world!' (TI) It is crucial to note that Nietzsche is not rejecting the phenomenal world of experiences with this. He explains that the construct 'real world' came along with the construct 'apparent world', the needed opposite to the real world. The point is that both *together* were veiling the phenomenal reality of human experience in the world. This phenomenal reality is the raw experience of the world. It is impossible to experience if one has not shown the illusions of the 'real world' and 'apparent world' to be what they are through historical philosophising.[10] Uncovering the insignificance of the in-itself is instrumental in focusing on human experience which is a phenomenal one. As he puts it in 'The Wanderer and his Shadow', 'We must again become *good neighbours to the closest things* and cease from gazing so contemptuously past them at clouds and monsters of the night' (WS §16). That is to say, we must do away with metaphysics and its 'deep explanations' as the title of the next aphorism has it (WS §17).[11] The exercise of focusing on the human relation to the closest things leads to the fundamental relation between consciousness and the world. It allows a focus on the fundamental phenomenon which is that of consciousness as 'weaved with the world'.

---

[10] What is interesting to note here is that this later text from 1889 reproduces the views expressed in Nietzsche's first full-blown attack on the metaphysical concept of the in-itself. This example supports my view that the foundation for Nietzsche's philosophy is built in the middle period texts.

[11] As Nietzsche puts it, 'being unknowledgeable in the smallest and most everyday things and failing to keep an eye on them – this it is that transforms the earth for so many into a "vale of tears". Let it not be said that, here as everywhere, it is a question of human *lack of understanding*: on the contrary – there exists enough, and more than enough understanding, only it is *employed in the wrong direction* and *artificially* diverted away from these smallest and closest things' (WS §6). This is the work of metaphysics and the reason why it must be rejected. The wanderer is motivated by a search for truth, what he describes as a 'penchant and passion for what is true, real, non-apparent, certain' (GS §309).

This was also Kant's worry, but it can be argued that Nietzsche radicalises Kant. Ibáñez-Noé's claims are interesting in that regard, even if I have my reservations about them. He points out that both Kant and Nietzsche agree that categories are grounded in the subject. He understands Nietzsche's critique of the subject as aimed towards a substantial notion of the subject à la Descartes.[12] However, Kant's subject is different: 'this transcendental ground which is precisely the *subject*, in Kant's sense, is not a thing but rather the non-thingly ground of the being or intelligibility of all things'.[13] He further claims that not only does Nietzsche agree with Kant's notion that the subject is foundational of knowledge but he takes this a step further by adopting an 'absolutely subjectivist position, for which the precedent would be found in Berkeley and, more consistently, in Fichte'.[14] While I agree with Ibáñez-Noé that there are strong affinities between Kant and Nietzsche in their claim that the subject shapes its own perceptions and thus stands at the foundation of knowledge, I resist referring to Nietzsche's subject in terms of categories of understanding. As we will see below, we can conceive of subjectivity in better and more fruitful terms. Also, to say that Nietzsche adopts an absolutely subjectivist position is to deny the nature of this subjectivity as embodied and worldly, which is what I see

---

[12] While the rejection of Descartes is usually understood as wholesale in Nietzsche, there are reasons to think that there are some affinities. Beyond the sceptic line I have identified in the first chapter as evidenced by his use of Descartes as epigraph to *Human, All Too Human*, there is still room for the cogito in Nietzsche, albeit a much reduced and somewhat insubstantial one. As we will see, the prevalence of the ego as cogito is reduced to the little reason as a tool of the body. Isabelle Wiemand has interestingly argued that there are affinities between Descartes's naturalism as expressed in his theory of the animal as machine and Nietzche's naturalistic views that emphasise drives and instincts as well as affinities along the line of adopting the first-person perspective to engage in one's philosophising. See her 'Writing from a First-Person Perspective'.

[13] Javier Ibáñez-Noé, 'Nietzsche and Kant's Copernican Revolution', p. 139.

[14] Ibid. p. 144.

Nietzsche as offering.¹⁵ However, I do not wish to go as far as Barbara Stiegler, who argues that the Nietzschean subject is a biologised Kantian subject. She explains that the Nietzschean subject is both an empirical and a transcendental subject and that it is, at all times, in flux and a unificatory act.¹⁶ The latter part of her description seems to me precisely to distinguish Nietzsche's notion from Kant's. Hill's description seems more apt as he claims that we find in Nietzsche a 'Kantian constructivist account of how the mind produces phenomena'.¹⁷ This production of phenomena, which amounts to the constitution of the world, is achieved by a consciousness that is embodied and not by a solely rational subject, a pure reason and its categories of understanding.

I find myself closer to Tsarina Doyle's reading, which suggests that Nietzsche uses Kant for his own purposes in his search for truth.¹⁸ She rightly indicates that while Nietzsche is committed to truth, he does object to the a priori as well as the fixed status of categories. I think this is right and to attribute these views to Nietzsche would be mistaken. However, when Doyle further argues that Nietzsche's anthropomorphism is milder than Kant's, I disagree. Her point is that Kant's anthropomorphism is of the first degree, i.e., that we constitute the world,

---

¹⁵ In her 'Die große Vernunft des Leibes: Nietzsches Dekonstruktion des Subjekts', Annemarie Pieper argues that Nietzsche follows Kant epistemologically in embracing the distinction between the thing in-itself and appearance. She says: 'Our knowledge is "anthropomorphic through and through," all things are rendered human by means of language, even objectivity, and consequently remain "highly subjective products" – precisely appearances, according to the Kantian terminology.' (My translation of 'Unsere Erkenntnis ist "durch und durch anthropomorphisch", alle Gegenstände sind mittels der Sprache "menschenartig" zugerichtet, und selbst die Objektivität und bleiben daher "höchst subjective Gebilde" – Erscheinungen eben, gemäß der Kantischen Terminologie' (pp. 59-60).) She sees them parting ways on the notion of the subject that is engaged in that epistemic relation with objects.
¹⁶ See Barbara Stiegler, *Nietzsche et la biologie*, pp. 20-1.
¹⁷ R. Kevin Hill, *Nietzsche's Critiques*, p. 103.
¹⁸ Tsarina Doyle, 'Nietzsche's Appropriation of Kant', p. 184.

but that Nietzsche's is of a second degree, namely that 'we explain phenomena in anthropomorphic terms'.[19] What Doyle seems to forget with this claim is that, according to Nietzsche, it is precisely the human subjectivity which is the creator of these interpretations and explanations. As Richard S. G. Brown rightly suggests, 'The subject therefore does not actively materialize the object or create it ex nihilo but, in a literal sense, it is said to construct it by making the manifold permanent, united, and causally related.'[20] The subject encounters the world and constitutes it for itself. To Nietzsche, interpretation and world constitution amount to the same and it is not because he rejects fixed categories of understanding that a constitution process cannot take place, as we will see. In that sense, I don't conceive of Nietzsche's position as milder than Kant's but, to the contrary, as more radical.

This brings us to the view that we falsify and veil objects when we encounter the world. A very important point needs to be made before we delve into this view, a point made very clearly by Eric Blondel. He suggests that, just like Kantian phenomena, the phenomena and sensory impressions experienced by the Nietzschean subject are representations, but they are not illusions: they are realities, they are *the* reality.[21] The only real world is the world that is constituted by subjectivity's creative and interpretive activity as it encounters being. As Houlgate indicates, the view according to which we falsify and veil objects is something that Nietzsche takes from Kant who says, for example, that 'the things which we intuit are not in

---

[19] Ibid. p. 201.
[20] This is a point that he makes in the context of his analysis of Nietzsche's relation to Kant with regard to knowledge and the notion of permanence. As he indicates, it seems that Nietzsche takes this view from Kant (see Brown, 'Nietzsche and Kant on Permanence', p. 40). Likewise, Paul Swift argues that Nietzsche presents the understanding as creative of the world as early as in his 'Teleologie seit Kant', an essay written in 1869 and related to Nietzsche's doctoral project (see 'Nietzsche on Teleology and the Concept of the Organic', p. 32).
[21] Eric Blondel, 'Critique et généalogie chez Nietzsche, ou *Grund, Untergrund, Abgrund*', p. 203. Blondel believes that Nietzsche takes this idea from Kant.

themselves what we intuit them as being'.[22] We will examine later how Nietzsche's self proceeds to construct its world as the embodied intentional consciousness that it is, a self that is significantly different from the traditional rationalistic subject that is still operating in Kant.

View of the Self: Between Postmodernism and Naturalism

As my forthcoming analyses will show, Nietzsche's phenomenological views lead him to undertake an important deconstruction of the classical rationalist notion of subject. However, this deconstructive act does not lead to a complete dismissal of the subject which is needed precisely for the phenomenal experiences to occur. I wish to argue against two strands of Nietzschean interpretation that offer that conclusion, albeit each in a different way. The naturalist interpretation of Nietzsche has emphasised the organic origin of consciousness and thereby wanted to dismiss completely the notion of a subject to whom agency or responsibility could be ascribed. The popular postmodern reading of Nietzsche has also taken the stance according to which his philosophy amounts to a complete dissolution of the self.[23] However, as I will show here and through an examination of both positions, Nietzsche does not reject the self. Rather, his critique of the notion of self is oriented towards a specific one; namely, the traditional understanding of the self

---

[22] This is a quote from the *Critique of Pure Reason*, quoted in Stephen Houlgate, 'Kant, Nietzsche and the "Thing in Itself"', p. 118. Houlgate claims that Nietzsche is not careful in his critique and does not distinguish Kant from Plato, Schopenhauer and others (see Ibid. pp. 128-9). It could be that Nietzsche does not in fact conceive of 'appearance' and 'in-itself' in a Kantian way (Ibid. pp. 138-41). This would be why he makes extensive use of quotation marks when referring to those. He says 'Nietzsche's apparent Kantianism is merely a mask barely concealing his profoundly deconstructive aim' (Ibid. p. 143). And he further concludes that Nietzsche uses Kant's language but eventually 'twists free of' Kant (Ibid. pp. 155-7).

[23] This line of interpretation is taken by scholars whom David B. Allison takes to offer a 'new Nietzsche', such as Maurice Blanchot, Gilles Deleuze and Pierre Klossowski.

as something fixed and to be nurtured. Conversely, as we will see and as I have already hinted at, the Nietzschean self is a dynamic one, the image that best represents it is that of the polyp, as discussed in *Daybreak* §119.[24]

Many postmodern, or more aptly labelled poststructuralist, thinkers have claimed to have been inspired by Nietzsche's philosophy and to be walking the path he had opened for them.[25] I do not want to engage here in an extended analysis of the different ways in which poststructuralist thinkers have received Nietzsche's thought as it would take us too far afield.[26] I only

---

[24] In their study of *Daybreak*, Rebecca Bamford and Keith Ansell-Pearson indicate that it was Julien Offray de La Mettrie who first discussed the polyp philosophically in his essay *L'homme machine* from 1748. They refer to Aram Vartanian's article which traces the philosophical uses to which Abraham Trembley's 1740 discovery of the polyp as animal with surprising capacities was put. Vartanian notes that 'the polyp became involved in speculations on matters ranging from the nature of the soul to the teleology of organic forms' ('Trembley's Polyp, La Mettrie, and Eighteenth-Century French Materialism', p. 260). The polyp was most prominently used by materialist thinkers such as La Mettrie and Diderot in his *Rêve de d'Alembert*. In light of the Nietzsche-Spinoza connection I bring up later, it is interesting to note that La Mettrie's reflections on the polyp led him to reinterpret Spinoza's determinism favourably (see Vartanian, p. 277).

[25] If there is any substance to the suggestion I will offer in what follows that there is a significant structuralist trend in Nietzsche's view of the being-in-the-world and the being-with-others (see Chapter 4), we may be faced with a situation where Nietzsche is both a structuralist and a poststructuralist. The openness of his corpus and the apparent unsystematicity with which he presents his ideas may allow for such a contradictory reception of his work. However, as I will argue here, I think that although poststructuralist thinkers were clearly influenced by him, he himself would not have embraced the radical claims they offer and see him as forwarding, namely that of the death of the subject.

[26] James Winchester has pointed out how thinkers who belong to this group have a very different understanding and use of Nietzsche. In particular, and discussing the notion of truth, he explains that while Deleuze's attempt at systematising Nietzsche on truth goes too far, Derrida's approach remains too unsystematic (*Nietzsche's Aesthetic Turn*, p. 6). He insists that while postmodernists are interested in his rejection of truth, Nietzsche remains convinced of the necessity of creating truths for ourselves. Interpretations, or what Winchester refers to as 'necessary fictions', are key to our existence, as is language that allows for such to be erected.

wish to point to the main elements of interest to them as a means to unearth the Nietzschean view of the self. In particular, they accept and embrace Nietzsche's critique of metaphysics, his critique of truth and the possibility of knowledge, his critique of language and, importantly for me here, his critique of the notion of subject. These readers of Nietzsche place a great deal of emphasis on his view according to which logic, grammar and language have obfuscated the fact that there is no ego nor world in which it would be located. For Allison and the thinkers he gathers in his volume, it is clear that there is no such thing as a subject in Nietzsche, nor is there such a thing as a will, an author for a deed. Emphasising passages on the parallels between grammar and thoughts, in aphorism 20 of *Beyond Good and Evil*, for example, Allison says:

> The grammatical functions determine the terms of thought as well as the rules of thought: thus, subject, predicate, affirmation, and negation will permit the development of a double axiomatic set (identity and causality) and favor only certain operations to be performed upon this set (e.g. binary opposition).[27]

Given that 'Man and world, world and thing, both belong to the order of the signifier, the *only* order of things . . .',[28] this means that there is no grounds to establish a subject or a consciousness in Nietzsche. All these would amount to would be linguistic constructs to which we mistakenly ascribe substance and existence.

The influence of Nietzsche on poststructuralist thought has been very important. It has, in fact, led to the elaboration of extremely creative philosophies and lineages of thinking.[29] However, it seems to me, and other commentators agree, that

---

[27] David B. Allison, 'Introduction', p. xxii.
[28] Ibid. p. xix.
[29] One such lineage that is of great interest to me is that leading from Spinoza to Nietzsche, from Nietzsche to Deleuze and from Deleuze to posthumanism. Terrance McDonald and I have explained such lineage in the introduction we co-wrote for *From Deleuze and Guattari to Posthumanism*.

their understanding of Nietzsche's position on the subject is a misinterpretation because they take too literally statements such as 'The "subject" is merely a fiction; there is no ego whatsoever about which one speaks, if one criticizes egoism.'[30] Or this other statement: 'all these people, unknown to themselves, believe in the bloodless abstraction "man," that is to say, in a fiction;' (D §105), and again when he refers to 'the so-called "ego"' (D §115). What they fail to take into account, however, is that Nietzsche's critique and rejection of the ego is aimed at one specific concept. What is identified here as a fiction is the ego as conceived in transcendental philosophies and Christian beliefs. That that ego is a fiction does not entail that an ego is impossible or that the idea of it ought to be dismissed. One must ask 'to what extent it is life-promoting, life-preserving, species-preserving, perhaps even species-cultivating' (BGE 4). As David E. Cooper argues:

> It is wrong therefore to read Nietzsche as a nihilist. To do so is to ignore the scare-quotes in which, almost always, he places words like 'truth' and 'knowledge' in his apparent onslaughts on these notions. They are, in fact, onslaughts on *misconceived* accounts of truth etc.[31]

This is also true of the critique of the notion of ego.

Kathleen Higgins also makes a very important point in suggesting that Nietzsche is not to be aligned with postmodernism. As wary as he is of the totalising and unifying view of the subject offered by modern philosophies, Nietzsche is equally

---

[30] My translation of 'Das "Subjekt" ist ja nur eine Fiktion; es giebt das Ego gar nicht, von dem geredet wird, wenn man den Egoism tadelt' (NF-1887 p. 9[108]).

[31] David E. Cooper, 'The "New" Nietzsche', p. 860. Cooper's article points out that the fascination for perspectivism and metaphors on the part of proponents of a 'new Nietzsche', namely the postmodern reception of his work, tends to overemphasise these concepts. For Cooper, it is evident that 'the "new Nietzscheans" are frequently guilty of superficial, or downright wrong interpretations of important passages in Nietzsche' (p. 858).

wary of a view that would revel in sheer fragmentation. Higgins explains:

> Although both Nietzsche and the postmodernists advocate a fragmented, perspectivist orientation toward our experience, Nietzsche's purpose distinguishes him from his alleged intellectual heirs. Nietzsche's primary concern is the possibility of rich and meaningful subjective experience. His 'postmodernist' critique of the dangers of 'modern' pretentions serves this aim.[32]

Higgins interprets Nietzsche's philosophy as revolving around the central concern for the ethical development of individuals. The postmodernists who deny that there is such a thing as an 'individual' would fall under Nietzsche's critique according to her. Ken Gemes agrees with this and also understands Nietzsche's rejection of the rationalist subject as part of Nietzsche's ethical project of the construction of a unified self.[33] He also agrees that the postmodernists' dogmatic rejection of the self is nihilistic in Nietzsche's own terms. Like me, Higgins takes seriously Nietzsche's numerous admonitions to his readers throughout his writings and the call for 'existential, subjective self-transformation'[34] that they convey. Such a call can only be directed to a self, albeit a minimal one in Nietzsche's case. But even such a minimalist self is at odds with the postmodernist view according to which a coherent self is meaningless.[35]

As with the postmodern/poststructuralist reading of Nietzsche, I only want to broach briefly the naturalist reading

---

[32] Kathleen Higgins, 'Nietzsche and Postmodern Subjectivity', pp. 191–2.
[33] Ken Gemes, 'Postmodernism's Use and Abuse of Nietzsche', p. 339. Gemes points out that even Derrida recognised 'the possibility of the construction of a new unified subjectivity' (p. 339 n3).
[34] Kathleen Higgins, 'Nietzsche and Postmodern Subjectivity', p. 198. As we will see in a later section, Gemes also argues in this vein.
[35] Ibid. The whole volume edited by Koelb explores the question of Nietzsche's relation to postmodernism from various other angles.

and its main points in relation to my analysis in order to better illustrate what view of the self Nietzsche holds. I do so by appealing to Christa Davis Acampora's potent critique of a naturalism found in Nietzsche that is understood in terms of a strict scientism.[36] Indeed, Acampora wants to resist what she refers to as a narrow conception of naturalism and instead offers that Nietzsche's is an artful naturalism.[37] For the narrow naturalist,[38] Nietzsche embraces the scientific method and its aims wholeheartedly while rejecting the existence of supernatural entities and emphasising natural processes in the individual, privileging physiology and relegating consciousness to the status of a physiologically generated epiphenomenon that amounts to no more than an illusion. Examining the notion of consciousness as epiphenomenal in Nietzsche, Sebastian Gardner points out that epiphenomena are not the same as fictions. This means that his view goes against anti-realism about the self.[39] He sees a contradiction building in Nietzsche between his theoretical view of the self and the view of the self he needs for his ethics. He says, 'Nietzsche claims that his deconstruction of the self undermines the metaphysics of egoism, but it equally threatens to undermine his view of valuation as reflexive affirmation.'[40] According to him, there is no account of how the self experiences itself as self in Nietzsche and there is a need for 'a conception which holds together in a coherent manner *both* the unitary I of self-consciousness *and* the psychological manifold'.[41]

[36] Christa Davis Acampora, 'Naturalism and Nietzsche's Moral Psychology'.
[37] Ibid. p. 315.
[38] Examples of such interpretations are to be found in Gregory Moore, *Nietzsche, Biology, and Metaphor*; Robin Small, *Nietzsche in Context*; Gregory Moore and Thomas H. Brobjer (eds), *Nietzsche and Science*. Acampora sees Christoph Cox's *Nietzsche: Naturalism and Interpretation* as an example of a counter to narrow naturalism, what she calls 'artful naturalism', which is one that weaves together 'the centrality of art [in Nietzsche] in his critique and appropriation of science' ('Naturalism and Nietzsche's Moral Psychology', p. 317).
[39] See Sebastian Gardner, 'Nietzsche, the Self, and the Disunity of Philosophical Reason', pp. 3-4.
[40] Ibid. p. 10.
[41] Ibid. p. 13.

However, Gardner thinks that while it is possible to provide such a unified theory, Nietzsche did not. It is up to commentators to work this out.[42] But the naturalistic model held by some fails since 'though it coheres with Nietzsche's denial of the reality of the I, [it] conflicts with his practical presupposition of the self, and more generally frustrates the ambitions of Nietzsche's practical thought'.[43] Indeed, if there is an ethical project at work in Nietzsche, it requires some sort of ego that can engage in it.

Furthermore, and to conclude this brief discussion of the naturalist reading, I agree with Acampora: there is no doubt that Nietzsche denies the existence of supranatural entities, that he favours a philosophical approach that refrains from speculating beyond experience, and that he views science as a powerful tool. Likewise, he places an unprecedented importance on the body in his dealings with the human subject. However, Nietzsche is not a naive champion of science and its methods. He is critical of science as well as of any other type of human thinking that seeks to provide explanations and wants science to be mindful of its own explanatory and creative power. In addition, his attention to physiological processes is a matter of emphasis and not of dismissal of the conscious self. The naturalised subject that we find in Nietzsche is the figure that emerges out of his artful embrace of science, that is, an appropriation of science that also implicates art. Acampora says, 'What we call the individual, or "subject," is at best, for Nietzsche, a composite.'[44] She quotes aphorism 12 of *Beyond Good and Evil* where Nietzsche defines the subject as a subjective multiplicity as evidence for this. She posits that 'Nietzsche's naturalism leads him to consider

---

[42] As with many other things, Nietzsche's manner of arguing in favour of something is via a sustained critique of the notions that he sees as flawed or detrimental to the human. His 'arguing for' most often than not takes the form of an 'arguing against'. But there are also moments in his writings where he gives clear indications of what he favours and what we ought to aim for. These make it possible for us to extract the unified theory Gardner is referring to.
[43] Ibid. p. 21.
[44] Christa Davis Acampora, 'Naturalism and Nietzsche's Moral Psychology', p. 320.

replacing belief in the existence of individuals with a conception of the human being as a complex of forces.'[45] This amounts to a reconceptualisation of the subject that has ethical implications in terms of what each individual *qua* subjective multiplicity is to aim for to achieve the best life.[46]

While scholars have been attracted to the passages in Part One of *Beyond Good and Evil* in order to circumscribe Nietzsche's view of the subject as a multiplicity, especially as stated in aphorism 12, there are a few passages that are equally compelling in earlier writings. As he is preparing *Daybreak*, for example, Nietzsche writes:

> The self is not the position of one single being to many (desires, thoughts, etc.). Rather the ego is a multiplicity of person-like forces, of which sometimes this one, sometimes that one foregrounds itself as the ego and looks over to the others, much as a subject looks to an environment that influences and determines it.[47]

Nietzsche is already working with the idea of the inner multiplicity in each individual in the middle period works. This passage makes it clear that we are dealing with a multiplicity of drives and thoughts, presumably both conscious and unconscious elements, and the being that is this multiplicity constructs for itself an ego according to the various strengths of these drives and thoughts and according to how it finds itself in the world and impacted by it. Nietzsche's reflections in *Daybreak* revolve around his critique of morality and, as part of that critique, the

---

[45] Ibid. p. 321.
[46] See Ibid. p. 326. I will return to this question, as well as to an analysis of BGE §12, in what follows. Acampora proposes that the agonistic subject faces the task of keeping the tension that it embodies.
[47] My translation of 'das Ich ist nicht die Stellung Eines Wesens zu mehreren (Trieben, Gedanken usw.) sondern das ego ist eine Mehrheit von personenartigen Kräften, von denen bald diese, bald jene im Vordergrund steht als ego und nach den anderen, wie ein Subjekt nach einer einflußreichen und bestimmenden Außenwelt, hinsieht' (NF-1880 p. 6[70]).

enquiry into the notion of moral agent. The discussion of moral evaluations brings forth an investigation of what it is to be an agent and what the notion of agent entails in terms of an ontological ground for a self or subject.[48]

The Constitutive Work of Consciousness

What the examination of the postmodern and naturalist readings of Nietzsche's view shows is that there is indeed a notion of the self in Nietzsche. We must now examine how this self is constituted and what its inner operations are. Nietzsche explains the encounter between consciousness and being and the emergence of the world[49] in the following, previously

---

[48] It has often been argued that Nietzsche's main preoccupation is with morality and ethics. This, however, makes the question of the self as agent and an articulation of that self's relation to others and the world central to his thought. In the introduction to their edited volume, *Nietzsche and the Problem of Subjectivity*, João Constâncio, Maria João Mayer Branco and Bartholomew Ryan say: 'In Nietzsche's writings, the question of consciousness is closely linked with the question of agency' ('Introduction', p. 3). This is, among other things, what motivates them to publish their collection of essays since they also see him as being preoccupied with ethical questions. They further add: 'However, in the books that he actually published, including those he left prepared for publication before his mental collapse, he presents his theoretical positions on the problem of subjectivity in an extremely fragmented and condensed fashion – sometimes even *en passant* – and, most importantly, he often seems to take great care to embed them in a practical context, indeed in a context which may be called "existential", or perhaps "practical-existential"' (p. 6). One of my tasks here is to demonstrate that Nietzsche's positions on subjectivity can be pieced together if we read him attentively, as I will do in what follows.

[49] One of the problems faced by phenomenologists and, I will argue, by Nietzsche, is that they sometimes equivocate on terms. Here, I will be very careful in my use of 'being' as opposed to 'world'. Oftentimes, 'world' is used both for the constituted realm of phenomena emerging from the encounter between consciousness and being and for the realm of being itself. I wish to stir away from designating it as the realm of the in-itself because of the discussion above. I will refer to it as 'being'.

quoted, sentence: 'We behold all things through the human head and cannot cut off this head' (HH I §9). It is the human being that makes its world. As Merleau-Ponty puts it, 'the world is vision of the world and could not be anything else'.[50] This world is, as Nietzsche puts it, 'so marvelously variegated, frightful, meaningful, soulful, it has acquired colour – but we have been the colourists: it is the human intellect that has made appearance appear and transported its erroneous basic conceptions into things' (HH I §16). In aphorism 34 of *Beyond Good and Evil*, Nietzsche refers again to this 'colouring' activity. He says:

> Indeed, what forces us at all to suppose that there is an essential opposition of 'true' and 'false'? Is it not sufficient to assume degrees of apparentness and, as it were, lighter and darker shadows and shades of appearance – different 'values,' to use the language of painters? (BGE §34)[51]

This points out again the constitutive activity of human subjectivity. It is also related to the notion of the world as fiction that I talked about earlier. Indeed, the aphorism continues:

> Why couldn't the world that *concerns us* – be a fiction? And if somebody asked, 'but to a fiction there surely belongs an author?' – couldn't one answer simply: *why?* Doesn't this 'belongs' perhaps belong to the fiction, too? Is it not permitted to be a bit ironical about the subject no less than the predicate and object? (BGE §34)

---

[50] Maurice Merleau-Ponty, *The Visible and the Invisible*, p. 75. As Stanley Rosen puts it, 'In Nietzsche, *die dichtende Vernunft* [the poetic reason] schematizes chaos' (*The Ancients and the Moderns*, p. 214). He also says that 'The comprehensive process of world production is thus a process of the production of local perspectives' (ibid.).

[51] Again in *The Gay Science*, Nietzsche uses the colouring metaphor in the context of the death of God: 'We have given things a new color; we go on painting them continually' (GS §152).

The world that concerns us, the phenomenal world, is constituted by the subject.[52] Nietzsche says:

> Whatever has *value* in our world now does not have value in itself, according to its nature – nature is always value-less, but has been *given* value at some time, as a present – and it was *we* who gave and bestowed it. Only we have created the world *that concerns man*! (GS §301)[53]

But we have to be mindful of the fact that this creative subject is a subjective manifold as we will see. This is why Nietzsche mentions that we need to be ironical about the subject and reject a traditional notion of it as unified and self-enclosed.

It is possible to read the passages above as indicative of Nietzsche's proposal according to which human beings have created truths for themselves, 'truths which are illusions which we have forgotten are illusions' (TL 117). But HH I §16 is also pointing to the intentional nature of consciousness, the 'human head' Nietzsche refers to in HH I §9. He says: 'it is the human intellect that has made appearance appear'. Thus, it is our human head that makes the phenomenon exist as it encounters being, allowing for the world to emerge.[54] It encounters something, an *etwas*, and the human head colours it, interprets it, constitutes it as a phenomenon. In the aphorism titled 'Man

---

[52] Didier Franck speaks of a process of anthropomorphisation of the world ('humanisation du monde') in Nietzsche and refers to the following fragment from 1881 where Nietzsche says that we are like an arable land for things: 'We are an arable soil for things. Images of existence should grow out of us' (my translation of 'wir sind *Ackerland* für die Dinge. Es sollen *Bilder des Daseins* aus uns wachsen' (NF-1881 p. 11[21]). For Franck's discussion, see his *Nietzsche et l'ombre de Dieu*, p. 254ff.

[53] Later in *Twilight of the Idols*, he repeats this idea saying 'Man believes that the world itself is filled with beauty – he *forgets* that it is he who has created it ... Man has *humanized* the world: that is all' (TI 'Expeditions' §19).

[54] This is similar to – although different from – the encounter between the Kantian rational subject who imposes the categories of its understanding on its perception, as we saw previously.

and things' he says 'Why does man not see things? He is himself standing in the way: he conceals things' (D §438).[55] And in *The Gay Science* again, 'the human intellect cannot avoid seeing itself in its own perspectives, and *only* in these. We cannot look around our own corner' (GS §374). The reason for this is that the encounter with things is a constitutive one. We interpret and construct, we falsify the world by introducing our numbers, grammar and logic (see BGE §4, for example). Not only is this something that we do, but he goes further and claims that without such, we could not live for 'renouncing false judgments would mean renouncing life and a denial of life' (BGE §4). This is the notion of necessary fiction already referred to above. Speaking of morality later in *Beyond Good and Evil*, he says:

> just as little do we see a tree exactly and completely with reference to leaves, twigs, color, and form; it is so very much easier for us simply to improvise some approximation of a tree. Even in the midst of the strangest experiences we still do the same: we make up the major part of the experience and can scarcely be forced *not* to contemplate some event as its 'inventors.' All this means: basically and from time immemorial we are – *accustomed to lying*. (BGE §192)

We are creators, inventors, liars in that we falsify the beings we encounter via the process of constitution. He describes the activity of thinkers in the following way:

> Every thinker paints his world in fewer colours than *are actually there*, and is blind to certain individual colours ... By virtue of this approximation and simplification he introduces harmonies of colours *into the things themselves*, and these harmonies possess great charm and can constitute an enrichment of nature. (D §426)

This is true of thinkers but also true of every human being encountering being. In fact, it would be true of all beings since

---

[55] This of course is anticipatory of the Heideggerian proposals according to which being has been concealed.

he also says that all existence is 'actively engaged in interpretation' (GS §374).[56] However, and importantly for Nietzsche, this constitutive process is not unidirectional. Again, in *Daybreak*, Nietzsche says:

> Every moment of our lives sees some of the polyp-arms of our being grow and others of them wither, all according to the nutriment which the moment does or does not bear with it. Our experiences are, as already said, all in this sense means of nourishment ... (D §119)[57]

This is indicative that our interaction with the world is constitutive of our being. We constitute our experiences, and these experiences nourish the polyp that we are. The drives are what guide this activity since, 'This nutriment is ... a work of chance: our daily experiences throw some prey in the way of now this, now that drive, and the drive seizes it eagerly' (D §119). There are 'nutritional requirements of the totality of the drives' (D §119) and, as Constâncio rightly notes, 'Nietzsche sees the activity of the drives and instincts not as simply "blind", but as "intelligent", "smart" (*klug*)'.[58] I take this to mean that there are different levels or degrees of consciousness in Nietzsche. The level of consciousness of the intelligent drives is not where

[56] The German is 'ob ... nicht alles Dasein essentiell ein auslegendes Dasein ist'. Kaufmann notes: 'It is only in Heidegger that *Dasein* refers only to human existence. In Nietzsche and in ordinary German it refers to existence in general' (GS 336 n138). I see possible connections here with Spinoza's monism since, in Nietzsche, all life is will to power and the interpretive drive of all existence would be an expression of the will to power's self-overcoming, the striving for more power. The link to Spinoza is discussed further below (see notes 66 and 67).

[57] This passage has often been used in the literature to demonstrate Nietzsche's naturalism and rejection of consciousness. What allows commentators to do this is the emphasis on drives in the aphorism. What is missed by these analyses, however, is what Nietzsche says about his own talk of drives, gratification, strength, etc., 'these are all metaphors' (D §119). As discussed above, such a reading is problematic and misses the ethical aim of Nietzsche's philosophy. Consciousness is more than an epiphenomenon.

[58] João Constâncio, 'On Consciousness', p. 19.

thinking happens, rather this is where desiring and willing happens, which are conscious activities albeit pre-reflective and pre-linguistic conscious activities.[59] The drives are oriented towards their gratification. They can be such because there is something to which they relate. They are a 'relating to'. Constâncio continues and explains that:

> drives are not brute impulses, but rather *perceptions* – elementary perspectives that build interpretations in accordance with the goals they affectively pursue ... Accordingly, as elementary perspectives or perceptions, the drives *are* relations – namely, perceptual relations to the external world, but also *to each other*.[60]

The last sentence here captures in a nutshell the notion of co-constitution that is at work in Nietzsche. One is in the world as this bundle of drives that perceive being and constitute the world each from their own perspective. These perceptions are interpretive since the human head 'colours' what it encounters. Constâncio rightly points out that conscious mental states are not epiphenomenal. They are an 'active and interpretative force' as per GM III 12 and, 'Due to its active nature, consciousness adds something new to what is created by the instincts – it develops our relation to the external world (Nachlass 1887/88, 11[145], KSA 13.67f.) by transforming it into "a surface-and-sign-world" where social life becomes possible (GS 354, KSA 3.593).'[61] It is not merely a case of the organism adapting to its environment but really of actively affecting it. As Linda L. Williams puts it, 'Will to power allows the organism to initiate at least some action rather than be solely a consequence of determined causes.'[62]

---

[59] This relates to the topology of consciousness that can be devised from the important section of *Thus Spoke Zarathustra*, 'On the Despisers of the Body'. I provide this analysis below.
[60] João Constâncio, 'On Consciousness', p. 19.
[61] Ibid. p. 39.
[62] Linda L. Williams, *Nietzsche's Mirror*, p. 42.

Aphorism 119 of *Daybreak* is titled 'Experience and invention'. In it, Nietzsche starts off by saying that it is impossible for any individual engaged in self-examination to form a complete image of the 'totality of drives which constitute his being' (D §119). The section goes on to explain what these drives are and specifies that we are dealing with both physiological and moral drives. It is in this context that Nietzsche uses the image of the 'polyp-arms of our being'. Nietzsche posits that 'there is no *essential* difference between waking and dreaming' in that drives respond to stimuli in an interpretive manner in every circumstance. In the aphorism 'The logic of the dream', for example, he explains how a dreamer forms thoughts and representations as a result of 'a multiplicity of inner events', such as bowel movements and sensations had while lying in bed as well as external events that imprint themselves on the body of the sleeper, such as a sound or strapping the feet (HH I §13). He says: 'the dream is the seeking and positing of the causes of this excitement of the sensibilities, that is to say the supposed causes' (HH I §13). Pointing out that in dreams we are quick at incorporating events (internal or external) and to posit a cause explaining them (the straps on the feet becoming serpents coiled around them for example), we come to believe in the explanation that our mind has put in place:

> (For in dreams we believe in the dream as though it were reality, that is to say we regard our hypothesis as completely proved.) – In my opinion, the conclusions man still draws in dreams to the present day for many millennia mankind also drew *when awake*: the first *causa* that entered the mind as an explanation of anything that required explaining satisfied it and was accounted truth. (HH I §13)

And after explaining that in wakefulness we have similar experiences when we close our eyes and the imagination engages in interpretation in trying to identify a cause to the effects it perceives, namely the shapes and colours that one sees with closed eyes, he says:

> The imagination is continually providing the mind with images borrowed from the sight-impressions of the day, and

this is precisely the way in which it fashions the dream-fantasy: – that is to say, the supposed cause is inferred from the effect and introduced *after* the effect: and all with extraordinary rapidity, so that, as with a conjurer, a confusion of judgement can here arise and successive events appear as simultaneous events or even with the order of their occurrence reversed. (HH I §13)[63]

The whole analysis of the logic of the dream serves to illustrate the close relationship between consciousness and affects and the co-constitutive work they accomplish. Consciousness is creative in interpreting the sense impressions received.

We are interpreting animals, valuing and measuring creatures – 'the word "*Mensch*", indeed, means the measurer' (WS §21)[64] – and as such we constitute our world and ourselves as we have our experiences. This is not only true of the world we constitute for ourselves but also of the inner world. He says, 'all our so-called consciousness is a more or less fantastic commentary on an unknown, perhaps unknowable, but felt text'

---

[63] Nietzsche is not explicitly using this as a means to reject free will and the possibility for an agent to direct its action whichever way they want. Rather, he wants to demonstrate how the illusions that have become the core of metaphysical theories came to be put in place thanks to the workings of imagination that put in place imaginary causes to real effects. Interestingly, in his *Ethics* Spinoza uses a similar example but his aim is quite clearly to dismantle causality and freedom of the will. He says, for example, that while we dream we do not think we can suspend our judgement and 'when we dream that we are speaking, we think that we do so from free mental decision; yet we are not speaking, or if we are, it is the result of spontaneous movement of the body' (Part III, P2 schol). From which he concludes that 'those who believe that they speak, or keep silent, or do anything from free mental decision are dreaming with their eyes open' (ibid.). I briefly discuss Nietzsche's relation to Spinoza further below.

[64] In the *Genealogy of Morals*, Nietzsche designates this as the valuing and measuring activity of humans. He says: 'man designated himself as the being who measures values, who values and measures, as the "calculating animal as such!"' (GM II §8).

(D §119).⁶⁵ It is the commentary on the activity of the drives as they respond to nervous stimuli brought by experience, constructing for itself an agent, a unifying grounds for that multiplicity of experiences. But, he concludes, 'What then are our experiences? Much more that which we put into them than that which they already contain! Or must we go so far as to say: in themselves they contain nothing? To experience is to invent? –' (D §119). The invention that comes into play here is the world constitution and related self-constitution that is the result of the activity of consciousness encountering being. However, as Keith Ansell-Pearson rightly says, 'for Nietzsche it is never a question of unveiling Being in its truth or of rendering existence naked and bare, simply because we can never remove ourselves from a horizon of interpretation and evaluation'.⁶⁶ We are the colourists; we see things through the human head.

Richard A. Cohen has noted that there are many affinities between Nietzsche and Spinoza specifically with regard to the body and their understanding of the drives, as expressed above in D §119 for example. He says:

> Starting with the body, Nietzsche uncovers a philosophy of fragmentation, of various forces each pulling in its own direction to establish provisional moments of stasis, reflected as symptoms – ideas, images, or desires – in consciousness ... The

---

⁶⁵ This theme of the impossibility of fully knowing ourself is a recurring one in Nietzsche. An interesting passage to that effect and in the context of his discussion of art is in HH I §160, titled 'Created people'. There he says that artists fool themselves when they think they are doing something special by creating characters. He explains 'we understand very little of an actual living person and generalize very superficially when we attribute to him this or that character: well, the poet adopts the same *very imperfect* posture towards man as we do, in that his sketches of men are just as *superficial* as is our knowledge of men'. In HH II §223, he points to the fact that self-knowledge also entails a knowledge of history since 'for us to know ourselves, we require history, for the past continues to flow within us in a hundred waves; we ourselves are, indeed, nothing but that which at every moment we experience of this continued flowing'.

⁶⁶ Keith Ansell-Pearson, 'The Incorporation of Truth', p. 240.

Nietzschean self is thus constantly reinventing itself, releasing new energy configurations. Its 'overcoming' is a constant shattering of the 'idols' of pretended unity.[67]

The self that emerges from a section like D §119 certainly matches this description. It is no surprise that Nietzsche should have communicated his enthusiasm about Spinoza's philosophy in the following manner to his friend Franz Overbeck in a postcard dated 30 July 1881; namely, a few months after having completed *Daybreak*:[68]

> I am really amazed, really delighted! I have a precursor, and *what* a precursor! I hardly knew Spinoza: what brought me to him now was the guidance of instinct. Not only is his whole tendency like my own – to make knowledge the most powerful *passion* – but also in five main points of his doctrine

---

[67] Richard A. Cohen, 'Levinas, Spinozism, Nietzsche, and the Body', p. 179. The objective of Cohen's essay is to analyse Nietzsche's relation to Levinas via an enquiry into Spinoza. Cohen argues that Nietzsche's agreement with Spinoza rests upon a rejection of any metaphysical grounding to morality and this leads him to discuss the ethical position of Levinas in relation to that of Nietzsche.

[68] The relation between Nietzsche and Spinoza is more complicated than his enthusiastic postcard to Overbeck may suggest. Thomas Brobjer points out that the peak of Nietzsche's interest and enthusiasm for Spinoza is the summer of 1881, the time at which he writes this postcard to Overbeck. This is a time of intense philosophical creativity for Nietzsche as he 'discovers' the eternal return, is conceptualising the Übermensch, and is refining his views on the will to power. Brobjer indicates, 'The possibility that Spinoza's philosophy worked as a stimulus or influence on these Nietzschean concepts [will to power, amor fati, eternal recurrence] cannot be ruled out' (*Nietzsche's Philosophical Context*, p. 77). However, as he points out, Nietzsche did not read Spinoza. The work to which he would seem to be the closest, *The Ethics*, was sent to him by a publisher in the summer of 1875 but he decided against buying it and returned it. Most of his knowledge of Spinoza was mediated via his reading of historians of philosophy, commentators or other philosophers referring to Spinoza. It ought to be noted also that the peak of enthusiasm experienced in 1881 wanes into a much more critical stance towards Spinoza. Christian Emden points out that already as early as 1873–4, Nietzsche's reading of Roger Boscovich's work on atoms and

I find myself; ... he denies free will, purposes, the moral world order, the nonegoistical, evil ...[69]

Nietzsche sees himself as of the same mind as Spinoza who conceives of reality and human beings as part of that monistic realm as a dynamic realm of becoming. He says: 'We speak of nature and forget to include ourselves: we ourselves are nature, *quand même* -. It follows that nature is something quite different from what we think of when we speak its name' (WS §327). Whichever ego arises for this natural being is always and ever in flux and is 'unegoistische', that is, it bears very little relation to the ego offered by rationalist dualistic philosophies that oppose mind and body.

fields generated the distance that would remain between him and Spinoza. Christian J. Emden explains: 'While Spinoza's focus on God as the only existing substance delivered a unifying theory of nature, Boscovich argued that nature had to be structured by force fields so that matter, bodies, could only be understood as the centers of forces. This was still a unifying theory of nature, but its principles were more diffuse and dynamic than what Spinoza offered' (*Nietzsche's Naturalism*, pp. 105-6). Emden believes that Nietzsche's naturalism - which he sees him as offering - is grounded in such a view, rather than Spinoza's philosophy. Wollenberg, for his part, argues that there are many more affinities between Spinoza and Nietzsche than the latter ended up acknowledging. He puts this on the count of Nietzsche's misreading and mis-remembering of Kuno Fischer's *Geschichte der neuern Philosophie: Baruch Spinoza* which he had read in 1881 and which triggered his enthusiasm at the time. To him it is clear that the notion of an inner struggle of affects which Fischer sees at work in Spinoza is one that is in line with Nietzsche's own views and concept of will to power. For their full discussion of the relation between Nietzsche and Spinoza see Thomas H. Brobjer's *Nietzsche's Philosophical Context*, pp. 78-82; Christian J. Emden, *Nietzsche's Naturalism*, pp. 104-7; and David Wollenberg, 'Power, Affect, Knowledge'.

[69] 'To Franz Overbeck [Postmarked Sils Engd., July 30, 1881]', *Selected Letters of Friedrich Nietzsche*, p. 177. eKGWB/BVN-1881, 135. Note that Nietzsche says that Spinoza makes knowledge the most powerful 'Affekt', which has a different connotation than 'Leidenschaft', which, it seems to me, is the type of passion that carries Romantic connotations that Nietzsche would reject as problematic. In that same postcard to Overbeck, he also says: 'of course the differences are enormous, but they are differences more of period, culture, field of knowledge' (ibid.).

Aphorism 119 of *Daybreak* is part of an interesting *Gedanken-kette* which illustrates well Nietzsche's method of argumentation. Just prior to §119, in §118, Nietzsche talks about how we are changed by our neighbour, that they are a satellite of our own system. He identifies the relation to the other as constitutive of our being.[70] In §120, he speaks of how we are always acted upon and, in §121, he refers to the intellect as a mirror. The discussion of the inner multiplicity of the self proposed in §119 relates to these other discussions and is part of the argument Nietzsche proposes about the human being as a fluid and dynamic creature that is constantly making itself, at the same time that it is being constituted by its relations. The whole process is described in terms of the activity and responsiveness of drives that invent for themselves a doer, a self and a world. The fact that this consciousness is a 'fantastic commentary' does not dismiss the experience of being conscious and does not constitute a full-scale rejection of consciousness and its ego. Furthermore, the commentary is the expression of the constitutive work of consciousness.

In his 'Disarticulation of the Self in Nietzsche', J. Hillis Miller argues that the self becomes disarticulated as a result of the 'activity of the mind [which] is an activity of interpretation'.[71] As he points out, 'The inner world, the world of subjectivity, the ego, the self, has the same structure and nature as the external world man has constructed for himself in the primeval joy of his artistic shaping.'[72] While he does not refer to it as phenomenological, this artistic shaping is none other than the phenomenological intentional act of constituting the world and oneself. To offer his argument, he analyses the fragment from spring 1888 titled 'The phenomenalism of the "inner world"'. In it, Nietzsche offers some thoughts on the relation of cause and effect and how we typically conceive of inner experience as being caused by external events. He explains:

---

[70] I will discuss the notion of being-with-others as it emerges in Nietzsche in greater detail below.
[71] J. Hillis Miller, 'The Disarticulation of the Self in Nietzsche', p. 249.
[72] Ibid. p. 250.

we have learnt that the sense impression naively posited as conditioned by the outer world is actually conditioned by the inner world: that every real action of the outer world always takes its course unconsciously ... The bit of outer world we become conscious of is born only after the effect exerted on us from outside, and is retrospectively projected as its 'cause' ...

In the phenomenalism of the 'inner world' we invert the chronology of cause and effect.

The fundamental fact of 'inner experience' is that the cause is imagined after the effect has taken place ...

The 'inner experience' only enters our consciousness after it's found a language that the individual *understands* ... i.e., a translation of a state into states more familiar to the individual— (NF-1888 p. 15[90])

What Nietzsche is pointing to here is a multi-layered inner world, what I refer to as the pre-reflective consciousness that precedes the formation of the ego which is then in a position to interpret and name the experience. As we will shortly see, the topology of consciousness established in *Thus Spoke Zarathustra* allows for that. As Miller puts it, 'There is no solid object to cause subject but only one single "phenomenal" realm within which all these fictitious entities and the lines between them are constructed.'[73] These are fictitious entities insofar as they are created in order to make sense of a dynamic realm of experiencing. As Nietzsche put it earlier in *Human, All Too Human*: 'Our thinking and judgment are, it seems, to be made the cause of our nature [Wesens]: but in fact it is *our* nature [Wesen] that is the cause of our thinking and judging thus and thus' (HH I §608).[74]

Consciousness constitutes the world for itself, and the experiences that are had constitute it in return. This is akin

---

[73] Ibid. p. 252.
[74] In the original, Nietzsche uses 'Wesen' and not 'Natur' which leads me to think that he is referring here to our being as we experience it. Elsewhere, as in HH I §31, he refers to 'die Natur des Menschen'. As we will see shortly, the being he is discussing in HH I §608 is a dynamic multiplicity.

to the bidirectional process of intentionality as put forward by Husserl. Intentionality requires that an 'I' be in relation to being, that there be things and other people for consciousness to be conscious of something. This is precisely what is at work in Nietzsche, who sometimes refers to consciousness as 'Bewusstheit' rather than 'Bewusstsein', a potentiality for being conscious rather than a being conscious. Thus, in aphorism 11 of *The Gay Science*, titled 'Consciousness [Bewusstsein]', Nietzsche says 'Consciousness [die Bewusstheit] is the last and latest development of the organic and hence also what is most unfinished and unstrong' (GS §11). And later in the same aphorism,

> One thinks that it constitutes the kernel of man; what is abiding, eternal, ultimate, and most original in him. One takes consciousness [die Bewusstheit] for a determinate magnitude. One denies its growth and its intermittences. One takes it for the 'unity of the organism.' This [is a] ridiculous overestimation and misunderstanding of consciousness [des Bewusstseins] ... (GS §11)[75]

What are we to make of this distinction between the two terms? Are we dealing with something like Husserl's pure ego? In his *Cartesian Meditations*, Husserl argues that there is a pure ego that is the ground of possibility for conscious life. He says:

> I put myself above all this life and refrain from doing any believing that takes 'the' world straightforwardly as existing – if

---

[75] Rebecca Bamford touches on this aphorism in her essay '*Ecce Homo*: Philosophical Autobiography in the Flesh'. She points out that for Nietzsche, the fact that we take such pride in our consciousness is a welcome impediment to the further development of it, and therefore the enhancement of our alienation via the life-denying error of giving priority to consciousness. She explains: 'Knowledge, Nietzsche suggests in GS 11, needs to be reconceived by the free-spirited philosopher *as instinctual*: a more satisfactory understanding of knowledge, he suggests in this section, would be one in which knowledge is literally in-corporated, or returned, to the body' ('*Ecce Homo*: Philosophical Autobiography in the Flesh', pp. 9-10).

I direct my regard exclusively to this life itself, as consciousness *of* 'the' world – I thereby acquire myself as the pure ego, with the pure stream of my *cogitationes*. Thus the being of the pure ego and his *cogitationes*, as a being that is prior in itself, as antecedent to the natural being of the world – the world of which I always speak, the one of which I *can* speak. Natural being is a realm whose existential status [*Seinsgeltung*] is secondary; it continually presupposes the realm of transcendental being.[76]

This pure ego is of a transcendental nature and is the condition of possibility for intentional consciousness to exist as such since it orientates and directs intentionality. It seems contradictory, however, to posit a pure ego when one has defined consciousness in terms of intentionality as Husserl does in other sections of the same book. It is especially puzzling since he insists that it is not simply a structure that makes consciousness possible, although it is that too. Husserl seems to say that the pure ego is in possession of a pure flow of *cogitationes*. This would entail that this pure ego is something substantial. But in fact Husserl, distinguishing between the transcendental and the psychological ego, says that 'Just as the reduced Ego [the ego arrived at through the phenomenological reduction] is not a piece of the world, so, conversely, neither the world nor any worldly Object is a piece of my ego.'[77] The transcendental ego is a necessary premise for the world.[78] In the natural attitude, I do not realise that I am at every moment also a transcendental ego. Later phenomenologists, like Sartre and Merleau-Ponty, criticised this view, as we have seen. Nietzsche would reject it for the same reasons they did: there is no such entity separate from the world. Consciousness only exists because there is a world that it experiences. How is one to understand the notion of *Bewusstheit* then, if it is not such an entity? The next chapter undertakes this analysis.

---

[76] Edmund Husserl, *Cartesian Meditations*, p. 21.
[77] Ibid. p. 26.
[78] Husserl refers to it as an 'apodiktisch evidente Prämisse' (*Cartesianische Meditationen*, p. 66).

Nietzsche's critique of metaphysics is famous. Revisiting it with an eye to uncovering what it tells us about his take on the distinction between the real and appearances, truth, the self and its constitutive activity allows for an understanding of Nietzsche as engaged in phenomenological enquiry. He goes 'back to the things themselves', demonstrating that we are interpretive animals who constantly shape the world via our conscious activity. This consciousness is a multi-layered one and Nietzsche further explores the inner workings of it by offering a topology of conscious and unconscious states, embodied consciousness and the ego as a tool for it. What emerges is a complex view of a multi-layered embodied consciousness which bears little resemblance, if any, to the traditional subject of rationalist, idealist philosophies of which Nietzsche is so critical.

3
Multi-layered Embodied Consciousness

Nietzsche's view of the self and of consciousness is complex, to say the least. As discussed in the previous chapter, he makes a number of distinctions when talking about our being conscious. A difficult one to handle and track in his writings is the one we closed the previous chapter with, namely that between *Bewusstheit*, a potentiality for being conscious, and *Bewusstsein*, being conscious. To clarify this and other aspects of consciousness as manifold, I will delineate a topology of consciousness and explain the notion of subjective multiplicity he advances in *Beyond Good and Evil*. This will lead to a renewed discussion of perspectivism as the intentional constitutive process of a consciousness that is a manifold and a new assessment of Nietzsche's famous claim that the world is will to power and nothing else. While a number of concepts will be dealt with here, their analysis is necessary to clearly establish Nietzsche's phenomenological understanding of embodied intentional consciousness and its workings. This, as mentioned earlier, then forms the firm ground upon which to think the ethical and political thriving of humans.

A Topology of Consciousness

Analysing the section 'Of the Despisers of the Body' in *Thus Spoke Zarathustra* will yield an interesting view of the conscious self. It is worth quoting at some length:

> ... the enlightened man says: I am body entirely and nothing beside; and soul [*Seele*] is only a word for something in the

body. The body is a great intelligence [*eine grosse Vernunft*], a multiplicity with one sense, a war and a peace, a herd and a herdsman. Your little intelligence [*deine kleine Vernunft*], my brother, which you call 'spirit' [*Geist*], is also an instrument of your body, a little instrument and toy of your great intelligence [*deiner grossen Vernunft*]. You say 'I' and you are proud of this word. But greater than this ... is your body and its great intelligence [*seine grosse Vernunft*], which does not say 'I' [*ich*] but performs 'I' ... It [the Self] rules and is also the Ego's ruler. Behind your thoughts and feelings [*Gedanken und Gefühlen*], my brother, stands a mighty commander, an unknown sage – he is called Self [*Selbst*]. He lives in your body, he is your body. There is more reason [*Vernunft*] in your body than in your best wisdom [*Weisheit*] ... The creative body created spirit [*den Geist*] for itself, as a hand of its will. (TSZ 'Of the Despisers of the Body')

This passage eliminates the classical mind/body dualism in a clear fashion, making use of different terms to refer to the different parts of the human being that it identifies. As Douglas Burnham remarks, 'N[ietzsche] employs an array of terms to discuss what we might otherwise call "the self". Although there are differences among them, they do not form a clear taxonomy.'[1] Further, Kristen Brown notes that 'Nietzsche's mix

[1] Douglas Burnham, *The Nietzsche Dictionary*, p. 294. In the entry 'self', Burnham distinguishes between Ich, Herz, Seele, spirit, ego and Selbst. In his entry on 'consciousness', Burnham claims simultaneously that 'For the most part, N[ietzsche] is simply not interested in consciousness' and 'there is in N[ietzsche] something that looks like a traditional view of consciousness as the becoming aware and taking charge of something' (Ibid. pp. 76–7). Burnham is here one step away from identifying that the critique of the traditional notion of consciousness, for which Nietzsche indeed has no interest, serves to clear the ground for a more accurate notion of consciousness.
  Burnham's book provides valuable tools for tracking the use of different concepts in Nietzsche's body of work, including the concepts of 'consciousness', 'conscience' and 'self', concepts for which he does not always use the same term, as Burnham notes and as I have noted about the world and being in note 49, Chapter 2, above. A similar, more exhaustive, tool is the *Nietzsche-Wörterbuch*, published by the Nietzsche Research Group (Nijmegen) under

tries to interconnect, but not reduce, body to mind or mind to body.'² She thinks that, in this way, his view avoids both material and spiritual monism as well as Cartesian dualism. In 'Of the Despisers of the Body' we can note that there are many different terms being used to refer to the 'spiritual' part of the human being which relate to the self which is in fact the body: *Seele, Vernunft, Geist, Selbst, ich, Weisheit*. These are far from equivalent and, in fact, refer to various modes of consciousness that all relate to the body. Nietzsche may not be offering a clear taxonomy in this passage, or any other for that matter, but there is definitely a topology of consciousness that is taking shape here.

The mind/body dualism is eliminated in that Nietzsche does not contrast the body to the spiritual parts of the human being since he says that the body is a *grosse Vernunft*, a grand reason which is itself a multiplicity. The term 'Vernunft' has been translated as intelligence. However, I think that translating it this way erases what I see as an implicit critique of Kant and I prefer to translate it as 'reason'. By positing a little reason, *kleine Vernunft*, and a grand reason, *große Vernunft*, Nietzsche is moving away from the Kantian pure reason, *reine Vernunft*. In fact, the latter can be equated with the *kleine Vernunft* in Nietzsche's topology.³ Nietzsche says that the grand reason, the body, is both war and peace. I take this to mean that there is both an inner struggle between the drives and a peace among them as the body *qua* grand reason commands them towards one goal. The translation has 'one sense' but the German is *Einem*

---

the direction of Paul van Tongeren, Gerd Schank and Herman Siemens. The first volume, Band 1: Abbreviatur – Einfach, presents sixty-seven out of the 300 terms the *Wörterbuch* aims to track, among which 'Bewusstsein' has its entry.

² Kristen Brown, *Nietzsche and Embodiment*, p. 17. She sees Nietzsche as offering a 'dynamic non-dualism'. She argues that he stands close to Merleau-Ponty who also views human experience as a dynamic whole. The experience of the self and world in both is non-dual (Ibid. p. 23).

³ This does constitute a rejection of rationalism but only in the sense that it resituates reason and minimises its importance. It does not make of Nietzsche an irrationalist thinker as has been sometimes claimed.

Sinne. Interestingly, the indefinite article is capitalised, which marks emphasis since only nouns are capitalised within German sentences. *Sinn* refers to both meaning and direction or goal. Thus, the body is this multiplicity that orientates itself. As both shepherd and herd, it goes about the world experiencing it and itself as a manifold. It is a mighty commander; it is the self as multiple. Annemarie Pieper refers to the grand reason as a relation that relates to itself ('als Verhältnis, das sich zu sich selbst verhält'[4]), a net of relations between different elements within the human being.

What this passage presents us with is a multi-layered embodied consciousness. The body encounters the world and has experiences through its senses. In order to process these, the body creates a tool for itself: the little reason which human beings refer to as spirit.[5] In a notebook entry from 1885 titled 'Morality and physiology' Nietzsche reinforces this point:

> In fact, what is more astonishing is the *body*: there is no end to one's admiration for how the human *body* has become possible; how such a prodigious alliance of living beings, each dependent and subservient and yet in a certain sense also commanding and acting out of its own will, can live, grow,

---

[4] Annemarie Pieper, 'Die große Vernunft des Leibes', p. 71. She explains that the body constitutes itself, the grand reason makes itself body, by building a net of relations between the forces and affects of the head, the heart, the belly and the hand. She states: 'In this way the grand reason embodies itself so to speak, insofar as the head, heart, belly, and hand are interconnected and this network of relations in its turn relates back to itself: as a relation that relates to itself.' (My translation of 'Auf diese Weise verleiblicht sich die große Vernunft gewissermaßen, insofern sie Kopf, Herz, Bauch und Hand miteinander vernetzt und dieses Beziehungsnetz wiederum auf sich selbst zurück bezieht: als Verhältnis, das sich zu sich selbst verhält' (ibid.).)

[5] For a different and in-depth enquiry of the concept of reason in Nietzsche and how it relates to the body as the interpretive agent, see Günter Abel, 'Interpretatorische Vernunft und menschlicher Leib'. While some of the points that Abel makes are similar to mine, his analysis takes a different approach to Nietzsche's views insofar as he focuses on a typology of rationality. As Didier Franck notes, in making the body the 'essence' of the human being, Nietzsche is in fact making the hierarchy of drives the foundation of knowledge (see *Nietzsche et l'ombre de Dieu*, p. 251).

and for a while prevail, as a whole – and we can see this does *not* occur due to consciousness! For this 'miracle of miracles', consciousness is just a 'tool' and nothing more – a tool in the same sense that the stomach is a tool ... this whole phenomenon 'body' is as superior to our consciousness, our 'mind', our conscious thinking, feeling, willing, as algebra is superior to the time tables. (NF-1885 p. 37[4])[6]

The body as embodied consciousness, the grand reason that Zarathustra identifies, is considered to be creative in that it provides itself with the necessary tool to understand the world it constitutes.[7] This tool is also a 'hand of its will'. It is the doer, the tool with which the body performs 'I'. In *Daybreak*, he refers to this tool as a 'fellow worker':

We are none of us that which we appear to be in accordance with the states for which alone we have consciousness and

---

[6] I am thankful for Alain Beaulieu's dealings with this fragment in his essay 'L'Enchantement du corps chez Nietzsche et Husserl' which drew my attention to it. Beaulieu argues that Husserl and Nietzsche share an emphasis on the lived body that serves their common rejection of metaphysical transcendence (Ibid. p. 339). With regard to this specific fragment, Beaulieu claims that Husserl uses the same phrase 'Wunder der Wunder' to refer to the body. However, the passage he quotes from *Ideas III* does not tie the phrase to the experience of the living body but rather to that of the pure ego (Ibid. p. 340). That said, he sees Husserl as articulating an alliance between the lived body and the pure ego, which is the wonder that Husserl is referring to. For Husserl, according to Beaulieu, the living body is the starting point and centre of orientation (Ibid. p. 349). While this may also be true of Nietzsche, Beaulieu sees an important distinction in that Husserl privileges consciousness after all while Nietzsche instrumentalises it (Ibid. p. 351).

The rest of the notebook entry further discusses the body in terms of an apparatus, a multiplicity and an 'interplay of many intelligences' (NF-1885 p. 37[4]). Given the time at which this entry was written, June–July 1885, namely the period during which Nietzsche was working on *Beyond Good and Evil*, I think it is safe to identify it as a draft for BGE §12 which I will discuss below.

[7] As mentioned above in note 50, Chapter 2, Stanley Rosen speaks of a poetic reason in Nietzsche, a *dichtende Vernunft*. This reason 'schematizes chaos' (*The Ancients and the Moderns*, p. 212).

words, and consequently praise and blame; those cruder outbursts of which alone we are aware make us *misunderstand* ourselves, we draw a conclusion on the basis of data in which the exceptions outweigh the rule, we misread ourselves in this apparently most intelligible of handwriting on the nature of our self. *Our opinion of ourself*, however, which we have arrived at by this erroneous path, the so-called 'ego', is thenceforth a fellow worker in the construction of our character and our destiny. (D §115)

We experience ourselves as having thoughts and feelings but, Nietzsche warns us, this is only a small part of our being and our experiencing since there is the great reason that stands *behind* these thoughts and feelings and, as he put it in *Thus Spoke Zarathustra*, there is more reason there than in the little reason. This entails that the activity of thinking, feeling and perceiving also happens at that level even if it does not make its way into the thinking of the little reason. We have to move away from the misguided notions of ourselves and understand that there is more to us than the ego. As Nietzsche puts it,

To this day the task of incorporating knowledge and making it instinctive is only beginning to dawn on the human eye and is not yet clearly discernible; it is a task that is seen only by those who have comprehended that so far we have incorporated only our errors and that all our consciousness relates to errors. (GS §11)

As we will see below, GS §354 clarifies this even further.

Of further interest, in 'Of the Despisers of the Body' from *Thus Spoke Zarathustra*, is the way Nietzsche resituates the ego. Traditionally conceived as the agent and even the whole self that uses its body to accomplish the deeds it wills, the ego is now conceived of as a creation of the body. It is the body that performs the ego through its interactions with the world. This is very much akin to the views presented in *Transcendence of the Ego* by Sartre. In this essay, Sartre posits that the ego is a contingent being of the world, that it is transcendent to consciousness.

Rejecting Descartes's notion of the cogito, Sartre explains that the fundamental irreducible fact is 'there is consciousness' and not an 'I think'. Sartre offers that 'there is consciousness, therefore I am' is a more correct way to describe conscious and thinking processes. In the essay, Sartre proposes to conceive of consciousness as being concomitantly pre-reflective, reflective and self-reflective. It is because there is a pre-reflective consciousness that is further ramified into a reflective and self-reflective consciousness that one can be as an 'I'.[8] In Sartre as well as in Nietzsche, Husserl and other phenomenologists, consciousness is intentional. It finds itself engaged in a world of which it is conscious. The co-constitution of consciousness and world is a process out of which the ego emerges.[9] The way Nietzsche describes the body as grand reason in Zarathustra makes it akin to Sartre's pre-reflective consciousness, which is anything but a transcendental ego.

I would like to conclude my analysis of 'Of the Despisers of the Body' with some considerations on the beginning of the section that I have left out when I quoted it previously. Nietzsche says '"I am body and soul" – so speaks the child. And why should one not speak like children?'[10] (TSZ 'Of the Despisers of

[8] One could say that while the 'therefore' is superfluous in Descartes's formula, 'cogito ergo sum' in *The Discourse on Method* – he does not use it in the *Meditations* and says instead 'I am, I exist' and defines the 'I am' as a thinking substance – it is completely meaningful and necessary in Sartre's revision of it. Indeed, it is precisely because there is consciousness that the 'I' can exist as one of its extensions, a contingent one that emerges out of the encounter between consciousness and being.

[9] Husserl would disagree with this as he sees the ego as the condition for this co-constitutive process to happen.

[10] *Thus Spoke Zarathustra* is replete with metaphors and characters, some of which recur in various sections and sometimes in other works. The figure of the child is certainly a very important one. In the section 'Of the Three Metamorphoses', Nietzsche discusses the process through which the spirit must evolve in order to approach *Übermenschlichkeit*. There are three stages: the camel, the lion and the child. There, the child spirit is presented positively as the type of spirit that has overcome many of the burdens under which the other types of spirit suffer. This child spirit is the closest to the *Übermensch*. It is the spirit that is free because it is 'innocence and forgetfulness' (TSZ 'Of the Three Metamorphoses'). It is also creative of values. While the camel spirit lets itself be burdened by transcendent values and

the Body'). While Volker Gerhardt reads this as indicating that the child is naive and possesses an unenlightened understanding of itself,[11] one that embraces dualism, I read this instead as indicative of the child's belief that we are body-subjects. It appears that Gerhardt understands the 'and' as exclusive while I read it as inclusive. I take the phrase to mean that the child is a body and a soul, that it is concomitantly a body and a soul, i.e., a body/soul. 'Why should one not speak like children?' Nietzsche asks. Because: 'the enlightened man [der Erwachte, der Wissende] says: I am body entirely and nothing beside; and soul [*Seele*] is only a word for something in the body.' I believe that one must read this in the following manner: the child, in 'innocence and forgetting', exists as a body/soul. According to the topology of embodied consciousness that I have been elaborating, the child is thus a self, a reason and an I which it performs as body/soul. What does the enlightened man stand for then?

While the child is in the natural attitude, the enlightened man is a phenomenologist who sees through our use of language.

> while the lion spirit is content with rejecting these, the child spirit initiates a process of creation of values and, by the same token, of creation of oneself. The child spirit engages in a playful creation. It is a sacred Yes, sacred because it is the sole originator of that Yes. As Annemarie Pieper explains, the child is the embodiment of the aesthetic reason that can take us towards the *Übermensch*. She says that it is the first step for the human being to become fully human and thereby be on its way to *Übermenschlichkeit* (see Annemarie Pieper, 'Die große Vernunft des Leibes', p. 68; the *aesthetische Vernunft* she refers to is akin to what Stanley Rosen identifies as the *dichtende Vernunft*, see note 50, Chapter 2, and 7 in this chapter). As I mentioned before, Nietzsche is a careful writer. The fact that it is the child that utters the statement 'I am body and soul' ought to be indicative that to conceive of oneself as such is a positive thing, one way of moving towards the *Übermensch*. Indeed, 'why should one not speak like children?' In later chapters, we will see that to view and embrace oneself as a multi-layered embodied consciousness is an essential part of the ethical life Nietzsche associates with the free spirit and the Übermensch.

[11] Gerhardt reads this as meaning that the child presents a naive dualist view of the self as composed of a body and a soul which are two separate entities, two types of substances. Thus he says: 'The child interprets an *attribute* of the body as an independent *substance*' ('The Body, the Self, and the Ego', p. 283).

'I am body and soul', says the child and we should speak like children. However, it is crucial to remain aware that 'soul' is a word we use to refer to something in our body, something bodily and not something that has a life of its own. Historical philosophising allows us to see that we use 'soul' for convenience's sake but the phenomenological enquiry shows that in fact it encompasses a multiplicity of processes. It is noteworthy that, in this section, 'soul' is only used in these two instances and that the term is discarded to offer a non-metaphysical mapping of the human being as body-subject. What emerges is a body-subject that is a multi-faceted conscious being that is a worldly situated embodied consciousness. The analysis of this section unearths a Nietzschean conception of the body-subject that I find to be akin to that of Merleau-Ponty.[12] While I will explore this at greater length in the next chapter, I want to emphasise one point here. As Merleau-Ponty says in *Phenomenology of Perception*, 'My body is the fabric into which all objects are woven, and it is, at least in relation to the perceived world, the general instrument of my "comprehension".'[13] Orientating oneself in the world, intending the world, constituting it and oneself is all done as an embodied being. This body that I am is my point of view on the world, the place of my emergence as conscious being. Merleau-Ponty further says the body is that 'through which we can consequently "be at home in" that world, "understand" it and find significance in it'.[14] It does that as our point of insertion in the world. This ties in nicely with an important feature in Nietzsche's philosophy, namely perspectivism. There is a beautiful passage in *Daybreak*

---

[12] Lars Peter Storm Torjussen sees Nietzsche's proposals as far more radical than Merleau-Ponty's. He says: 'Nietzsche's reflections are more radical than Merleau-Ponty's, but perhaps too radical. The human body is not a unity but an incoherent mosaic' ('Is Nietzsche a Phenomenologist?', p. 187). While it is the case that the body for Nietzsche can be conceived as a mosaic, I would disagree that it is an incoherent one. The mighty commander that the self is provides coherence and unifies the mosaic with its life affirming will. We will see how this can take the form of striving to become an *Übermensch* in later chapters.

[13] Maurice Merleau-Ponty, *Phenomenology of Perception*, p. 273.

[14] Ibid. p. 275.

that gives us insight into the connection between Nietzsche's perspectivism and his understanding of consciousness as intentional. Again, this is a passage that is worth quoting at some length:

> *In prison.* – My eyes, however strong or weak they may be, can see only a certain distance, and it is within the space encompassed by this distance that I live and move, the line of this horizon constitutes my immediate fate, in great things and small, from which I cannot escape. Around every being there is described a similar concentric circle, which has a mid-point and is peculiar to him . . . Now it is by these horizons, within which each of us encloses his senses as if behind prison walls, that we *measure* the world . . . The habits of our senses have woven us into lies and deception of sensations: these again are the basis of all our judgments and 'knowledge' – there is absolutely no escape, no backway or bypath into the *real world!* We sit within our net, we spiders, and whatever we may catch in it, we can catch nothing at all except that which allows itself to be caught in precisely *our* net. (D §117)[15]

---

[15] This brings to mind Pieper's characterisation of the self as a 'Beziehungsnetz'. Our spider-being is itself and its net, a web of relations between all its different parts. See note 23 in this chapter. In the aphorism immediately before this one and which is part of the *Gedanken-kette* formed of D §§115-21, Nietzsche also says 'We have expended so much labour to learning that external things are not as they appear to us to be – very well! the case is the same with the inner world! Moral actions are in reality "something other than that" – more we cannot say: and all actions are essentially unknown' (D §116). It ought to be noted also that the image of the spider's net in relation to knowledge and interpreting the world is already present in the early essay 'Truth and Lies in an Extra Moral Sense'. Speaking of the anthropomorphisation of the world, he says: 'Here one may certainly admire man as a mighty genius of construction, who succeeds in piling an infinitely complicated dome of concepts upon an unstable foundation, and, as it were, on running water. Of course, in order to be supported by such a foundation, his construction must be like one constructed of spiders' webs: delicate enough to be carried along by the waves, strong enough not to be blown apart by every wind.' And later in the same section: 'All that we actually know about these laws of nature is what we ourselves bring to them – time and

This passage is important because it expresses a few key things. First, Nietzsche points out that our embodied presence constitutes the point from which we perceive, and the horizon of our perception constitutes our fate, our existence. Second, he points out that this is the case for every being, pointing to an array of intentional consciousnesses constituting their world and themselves.[16] Third, the judgements we pass on the world we experience are deceptions since they do not refer to the 'real world', to being in-itself. They are interpretations we make of being, constituting a world for ourselves. Again, Nietzsche expresses this view in *The Gay Science* as he says 'How should explanations be at all possible when we first turn everything into an image, our image! It will do to consider science as an attempt to humanize things as faithfully as possible; as we describe things and their one-after-another, we learn how to describe ourselves more and more precisely' (GS §112). This is the case because the things that are part of our world are constitutive of our selves, and vice versa.

Aphorism 354 of *The Gay Science*, titled 'On the "genius of the species"', provides more information on the inner multiplicity of consciousness in addition to giving an account of

---

space, and therefore relationships of succession and number. But everything marvelous about the laws of nature, everything that quite astonishes us therein and seems to demand explanation, everything that might lead us to distrust idealism: all this is completely and solely contained within the mathematical strictness and inviolability of our representations of time and space. But we produce these representations in and from ourselves with the same necessity with which the spider spins' (TL §1).

[16] In *Being and Nothingness*, Sartre talks about the co-presence of being for-others in similar terms. When one encounters another being for-others, one's world is 'stolen' by the other as the objects that were part of my world are taken in the other's gaze and world constituting. He explains: 'Thus suddenly an object has appeared which has stolen the world from me. Everything is in place; everything still exists for me; but everything is traversed by an invisible flight and fixed in the direction of a new object. The appearance of the Other in the world corresponds therefore to a fixed sliding of the whole universe, to a decentralization of the world which undermines the centralization which I am simultaneously effecting' (*Being and Nothingness*, p. 279).

the origin of consciousness.[17] In this aphorism, Nietzsche questions our worry with consciousness, the fact that we see becoming conscious as a problem, since he thinks we could dispense with it. It appears to me that he equivocates here on the notion of consciousness and that, in light of what was said above, it is important to distinguish what he means by 'consciousness' when he says we could dispense with it. He thus claims: 'we could think, feel, will, and remember, and we could also "act" in every sense of that word, and yet none of all this would have to "enter our consciousness" [*in's Bewusstsein zu treten*] (as one says metaphorically)' (GS §354).[18] Further in the aphorism he explains:

---

[17] This aphorism is part of Book V of *The Gay Science* and thus qualifies as a later piece of writing. It was in fact written after *Thus Spoke Zarathustra* and *Beyond Good and Evil*, in 1887. Chronologically, then, it does not belong to the middle period. However, I believe a case can be made that Book V qualifies, to a certain degree, as middle period-like, in spirit and content. As an author who was always so careful in the preparation of his books, selecting and organising aphorisms and other parts meticulously, Nietzsche had to have a good reason for choosing to append the series of aphorisms that constitute Book V to *The Gay Science* rather than to append them to another work or even to have them stand alone as a book. He must have seen a continuity of thought and themes from the first four books to this one even if the emphasis of the book is more physiological and concerned with the future of Europe, like *Beyond Good and Evil*, for example. In fact, at one point he wanted to add Book V to this latter work but due to a type-font issue opted to append it to *The Gay Science* instead. If one considers that *The Gay Science* I to IV was originally planned as the second part of *Daybreak* and *Beyond Good and Evil* was planned as a reworking of *Human, All Too Human* (there are many parallels between the two beyond the number and themes of chapters), one is entitled to consider them, Book V and *Beyond Good and Evil* as part of the free-spirit period. This goes to show that characterising Nietzsche's corpus as organised in three neatly separated periods is to misconstrue the expression and evolution of his thought.

[18] A notebook entry provides another formulation of this idea while claiming that we need to prioritise the body: 'Everything which enters consciousness as "unity" is already tremendously complicated: we only ever have a *semblance of unity*. The phenomenon of the *body* is the richer, more distinct, more comprehensible phenomenon: to be given methodological priority, without determining anything about its ultimate significance' (NF-1886–1887 p. 5[56]). I want to thank Dan Ahern for drawing my attention to this note.

Man, like every living being, thinks continually without knowing it; the thinking that rises to consciousness is only the smallest part of all this – the most superficial and worst part – for only this conscious thinking takes the form of words, which is to say signs of communication, and this fact uncovers the origin of consciousness. (GS §354)

Analysing this, Paul Katsafanas argues that there is a clear distinction between conscious and unconscious mental states in Nietzsche and that consciousness is presented as the sum total of conscious mental states.[19] Rather than refer to it as an unconscious, however, I prefer to refer to it as the pre-reflective/ prelinguistic consciousness that we are as the body that thinks, the grand reason discussed above. In a fragment from 1887, Nietzsche re-affirms his views:

> I maintain that the *inner* world is phenomenal as well: everything *we become conscious of* has first been thoroughly trimmed, simplified, schematized, interpreted – the *real* process of inner 'perception', the *causal association* between thoughts, feelings, desires is absolutely hidden from us, like that between subject and object – and may be just a figment of our imagination. This 'apparent *inner* world' is managed with quite the same forms and procedures as the 'outer' world ... *Between* two thoughts there are, in addition, *all sorts of affects* at play: but they move so fast that we *mistake* them, we *deny* them ... (NF-1887 p. 11[113])[20]

---

[19] He explains that part of 'what Nietzsche means when he says that consciousness is a multiplicity is that there is no faculty named Consciousness, which stands apart from our conscious mental states; rather, there is only a host of conscious mental states' (Katsafanas, 'Nietzsche's Theory of Mind', pp. 12–13).

[20] This is to be related to the discussion above on the inner world as Nietzsche brings it up in NF-1888 p. 15[90]. I am thankful for J. Hillis Miller's article, 'The Disarticulation of the Self in Nietzsche', for drawing my attention to these two fragments as he juxtaposed them with BGE §12 which I shall analyse shortly.

This thinking is done by the body, the being that is affected.[21] Rehberg explains that there is an 'always already open channel between a body and its thought' and physiological thinking 'reinstates and embodies the smooth transitions between phenomena that we habitually attribute to consciousness and those that we tend to attribute to our bodily being'.[22] We have seen that there is a rationality of the body as the grand reason, indeed as Nietzsche puts it 'There is more reason in your body than in your best wisdom' (TSZ 'Of the Despisers of the Body'). In aphorism 333 of *The Gay Science*, Nietzsche points to the origin of consciousness as raising to the surface of a swarm of non-conscious activity:

> Since only the last scenes of reconciliation and the final accounting at the end of this long process rise to our consciousness, we suppose that *intelligere* must be something conciliatory, just, and good – something that stands essentially opposed to the instincts, while it is actually nothing but *a certain behavior of the instincts toward one another*. For the longest time, conscious thought was considered thought itself. Only now does the truth dawn on us that by far the greatest part of our spirit's activity remains unconscious and unfelt . . . Conscious thinking, especially that of the philosopher, is the least vigorous and therefore also the relatively mildest and calmest form of thinking; and thus precisely philosophers are most apt to be led astray about the nature of knowledge. (GS §333)

Here again, the 'conscious thinking' he is referring to is that of the little reason. The grand reason of the body is operative at the unconscious level and constitutes a stronger form of thinking that then constitutes for itself the ego as a tool, the little

---

[21] Barbara Stiegler who sees Nietzsche engaged in the biologisation of the Kantian subject (see the discussion on the naturalist reading of Nietzsche in Chapter 2) sees Nietzsche's strategy as one that emphasises that any living subject is first and foremost an affected subject (see Barbara Stiegler, *Nietzsche et la biologie*, p. 35).

[22] Andrea Rehberg, 'Nietzsche and Merleau-Ponty', p. 152.

reason that allows for communication and relating with other human beings.

Nietzsche explains that '*consciousness has developed only under the pressure of the need for communication*; ... Consciousness is really only a net of communication between human beings' (GS §354).[23] The 'consciousness' he is referring to here is none other than the little reason, the tool of the body. According to him then, the little reason emerges with the development of language and language develops because we interact with other human beings. The desire to communicate generates that layer of consciousness. Nietzsche says that 'consciousness does not really belong to man's individual existence but rather to his social or herd nature' (GS §354). Again, this is not to say that if we were removed from a social setting we would not be conscious beings. However, there would be no need for the development of the little reason. The intersubjective realm of language and communication further shapes the consciousness of every individual. In proposing this view of the origin of that part of consciousness, the little reason, Nietzsche is making the human subject ontologically dependent on the other: the being of others is part of our own being as we will see in what follows.

Nietzsche also notes that 'Fundamentally, all our actions are altogether incomparably personal, unique, and infinitely individual; there is no doubt of that. But as soon as we translate them into consciousness *they no longer seem to be*' (GS §354). This is because we put them into words and signs for the purpose of communicating. But, also, it is because 'all becoming conscious involves a great and thorough corruption, falsification, reduction to superficialities, and generalization' (GS §354). This is a claim he also made in the fragment I quoted above and in aphorisms 11 and 333 of *The Gay Science*. Further, he explains that, 'The human being inventing signs is at the same time the human being who becomes ever more keenly conscious of himself. It was only as a social animal that man

---

[23] Note here again the use of the image of a net. This recurring image in relation to consciousness and its operations supports the view according to which subjectivity is a dynamic multiplicity of relations.

acquired self-consciousness – which he is still in the process of doing more and more' (GS §354). With this, he has identified three different ways of being conscious in the aphorism: (1) the 'unconscious' thinking and feeling, (2) the conscious rendering of these 'unconscious' thoughts and feelings through language and signs, and (3) the consciousness of oneself. There is therefore an inner multiplicity and various degrees of consciousness. Identifying these three different modes of consciousness may give a false sense of a neatly structured inner life. As he puts it in *Daybreak*, however, 'If we desired and dared an architecture corresponding to the nature of our soul (we are too cowardly for it!) – our model would have to be the labyrinth!' (D §169). Indeed, the inner activity of the drives and instincts in their relating to one another, to the world and to conscious thinking results in a field of tensions that gives the appearance of the incoherent mosaic Torjussen sees emerging in Nietzsche.[24] That the self is a multiplicity is clear, but I would reject that it is incoherent. An analysis of an important *Gedanken-kette* from Part One of *Beyond Good and Evil*, 'On the Prejudices of Philosophers', is in order to help explain this.

Aphorism 12 of *Beyond Good and Evil* is among the most cited of Nietzsche's. As per usual in his works, one must pay attention to the context in which an aphorism appears. The theme of the overall book, the subsection in which it is inserted – in the current case Part One, 'On the Prejudices of Philosophers' – and the theme of the neighbouring aphorisms are all clues about what is being said here. First, it is interesting to note that the first three parts of the book mirror the first three of *Human, All Too Human* with regard to themes and that many of the themes explored in Book I of *Human, All Too Human* are revisited in other parts. Part One is a renewed discussion of many questions brought forth in the first chapter of *Human, All Too Human*, 'Of First and Last Things'. Therein, Nietzsche explores the possibility that untruth or uncertainty might be better than truth, which is what philosophers have traditionally longed for. It is in this context that the notions of the self and consciousness emerge again.

---

[24] See note 12 above.

In aphorism 3, he explains that:

> by far the greater part of conscious thinking must still be included among instinctive activities ... 'being conscious' is not in any decisive sense the opposite of what is instinctive: most of the conscious thinking of a philosopher is secretly guided and forced into certain channels by his instincts. (BGE §3)

Although the discussion here pertains directly to philosophers and how they form their ideas, this is also true of any human being as we have seen above. In aphorism 2 just before, he rejects the idea that there are any opposites saying, 'For one may doubt, first, whether there are any opposites at all' (BGE §2).[25] In aphorism 12, against the Christian soul atomism which conceives of human beings in dualistic (opposite) terms and as having a soul that is immortal, indivisible and monistic, he posits that we need to open ourselves to new interpretations of the soul. The idea is not so much to dismiss the soul.[26] Rather:

> the way is open for new versions and refinements of the soul-hypothesis; and such conceptions as 'mortal soul,' and 'soul as subjective multiplicity,' and 'soul as social structure of drives and affects,' want henceforth to have citizen's rights in science. (BGE §12)

As J. Hillis Miller puts it, 'The endpoint of Nietzsche's dismantling of the notion of the substantial self is the idea that a

---

[25] This is reminiscent of what he says, for example, in 'The Wanderer and his Shadow': 'Habit of seeing opposites – The general imprecise way of observing sees everywhere in nature opposites (as, e.g., "warm and cold") where there are, not opposites, but differences of degree. This bad habit has led us into wanting to comprehend and analyse the inner world, too, the spiritual-moral world, in terms of such opposites. An unspeakable amount of painfulness, arrogance, harshness, estrangement, frigidity has entered into human feelings because we think we see opposites instead of transitions' (WS §67).

[26] The argument here is similar to the one brought forth about truth and ethical values. Nietzsche's nihilism is not one that squashes and dismisses but one that aims to uncover the roots of these notions and reconceptualise them.

single body may be inhabited by multiple selves.'[27] In an entry to his notebooks from the autumn of 1885, as he is refining the manuscript of *Beyond Good and Evil*, which he completed in June of the same year, Nietzsche remarks: 'Man as a multiplicity of "wills to power": each one with a multiplicity of means of expression and forms' (NF-1885-1886 p. 1[58]). This is the multiplicity of drives, of affects, he has been uncovering and which generates the multi-layered consciousness that I have been discussing. He further notes: 'Thoughts are signs of a play and struggle of the affects: they are always connected to their hidden roots' (NF-1885-1886 p. 1[75]), which is reminiscent of this earlier claim: 'Thoughts are the shadows of our feelings – always darker, emptier, and simpler' (GS §179). And furthermore he explains that:

> Everything which enters consciousness is the last link in a chain, a closure ... Every *thought*, every feeling, every will is *not* born of one particular drive but is a *total state*, a whole surface of the whole consciousness, and results from how the power of *all* the drives that constitute us is fixed at that moment – thus, the power of the drive that dominates just now as well as of the drives obeying or resisting it. (NF-1885-1886 p. 1[61])

The Nietzschean self is this complex structure and using any one word or concept to refer to it is merely a means to simplify what is in fact manifold. While this may be a strategy to think about such things, one needs to remain mindful that it is a distortion of what is actually happening within this subjective multiplicity.

Aphorisms 16 and 17 complement this by revisiting and rejecting the cogito. In aphorism 16, Nietzsche rejects the idea according to which there are any immediate certainties and

---

[27] J. Hillis Miller, 'The Disarticulation of the Self in Nietzsche', p. 259. In a similar vein, Philip J. Kain claims that for Nietzsche, and in opposition to Kant, the subject is 'a simplified and falsified flux of chaotic becoming' ('Nietzsche, the Kantian Self, and Eternal Recurrence', p. 231).

thereby rejects that of the 'I think'. He attributes our mistake about the cogito to the seduction of words, that is the way in which grammar establishes a subject for every verb. Grammar leads us to think that if we have 'thinking', there must be something that does the thinking. But he challenges that and says that we operate with a number of daring assumptions such as 'that there is an "ego," and, finally, that it is already determined what is to be designated by thinking – that I *know* what thinking is'. (BGE §16) The following aphorism continues this reconceptualisation by offering that:

> it is a falsification of the facts of the case to say that the subject 'I' is the condition of the predicate 'think.' *It* thinks; but that this 'it' is precisely the famous old 'ego' is, to put it mildly, only a supposition, an assertion, and assuredly not an 'immediate certainty.' After all, one has even gone too far with this 'it thinks' – even the 'it' contains an interpretation of the process, and does not belong to the process itself. (BGE §17)

In the fragment I have already quoted from 1887, he revisits this thought, this time explicitly connecting the ego to action and rejecting both. He says:

> The 'mind', *something that thinks:* maybe even 'the mind absolute, pure, unmixed' – this conception is a derivative, second consequence of the false self-observation that believes in 'thinking': here *first* an act is imagined that doesn't occur, 'thinking', and *secondly* a subject-substratum is imagined in which every act of this thinking, and nothing else, originates; i.e., *both doing and doer are fictions.* (NF-1887 p. 11[113])

It is tempting to read these passages as a reformulation of David Hume's view on the subject. In his *Treatise on Human Nature*, Hume famously uses the image of the theatre to explain his view on personal identity. He states:

> The mind is a kind of theatre, where several perceptions successively make their appearance; pass, re-pass, glide away, and

mingle in an infinite variety of postures and situations . . . The comparison of the theatre must not mislead us. They are the successive perceptions only, that constitute the mind.[28]

Indeed there is no stage as such, no substratum for the perceptions to occur and be inscribed on. Nietzsche offers something similar when he speaks of 'our world of desires and passions . . . the reality of our drives – for thinking is merely a relation of these drives to each other' (BGE §36). As David E. Cooper explains, 'his rejection of the *ego* or *cogito* as a fiction is a rehearsal of Hume's point that nothing in our experience warrants the postulation of such substantive entities'.[29] Ken Gemes indicates that Nietzsche and Hume share a rejection of any transcendental grounding to the I, but, and I agree with his assessment here, 'the claim that there is no doer behind the deed need not be taken as a blanket rejection of the notion of a doer . . . For Nietzsche, the doer is literally in the deeds.'[30]

This doer is the 'mighty commander' as offered in 'Of the Despisers of the Body', the 'soul as multiplicity' from BGE §12. In aphorism 19, he analyses the will and how it relates to sensations and argues that 'the will is not only a complex of sensation and thinking, but it is above all an affect, and specifically the affect of the command' (BGE §19).[31] There is no will in-itself

[28] David Hume, *A Treatise of Human Nature*, p. 301.
[29] David E. Cooper, 'The "New" Nietzsche', p. 860. He further indicates that 'Hume, who was as dismissive of that realm [realm of fixed entities] as Nietzsche, thought we could know truths and appreciate beauty. The interesting questions, for both of them, are how we are to understand such notions once transcendental pretensions have been put to rest' (ibid.). For a detailed comparative analysis of Hume's and Nietzsche's views see Nicholas Davey, 'Nietzsche and Hume on Self and Identity'.
[30] Gemes is referring to GM I 13 but this applies also to the fragment quoted above. Ken Gemes, 'Postmodernism's Use and Abuse of Nietzsche', p. 340.
[31] In *Daybreak*, he offers a variation on the notion of the little reason as a tool and relates it to the drives: 'our intellect is only the blind instrument of *another drive* which is a *rival* of the drive whose vehemence is tormenting us: whether it be the drive to restfulness, or the fear of disgrace and other evil consequences, or love. While "we" believe we are complaining about the vehemence of a drive, at bottom it is one drive *which is complaining*

but rather the will is the expression of a commanding affect or sensation: 'In all willing it is absolutely a question of commanding and obeying, on the basis, as already said, of a social structure composed of many "souls"' (BGE §19). This brings to the person exercising volition 'feelings of delight as commander' (BGE §19). These feelings of delight lead to a mistaken view of oneself as being an 'I' that chooses consciously to exercise one's will one way or another and entertains the illusion according to which we have choice. A closer examination into the nature of human subjectivity, however, shows how this view is mistaken. Commenting on BGE §12, Robert C. Miner says that 'there is no autonomous "I" standing behind the drives, capable of constructing their order. There is only the play of drives.'[32] He distinguishes between four different notions of the self in Nietzsche and what he identifies as the 'deep self' 'is constituted by a multiplicity of drives, of which Nietzsche thinks we have only the dimmest knowledge'.[33] He concludes that the question of what or who it is that masters the drives is unanswered. I take it, however, that it is the deep self, as identified by Miner, that does the volition and commands the drives.

Commenting on the notion of the 'soul as subjective multiplicity' (BGE §12), Susan West emphasises the anti-dualistic view of the self that it entails. She sees it in terms of a description of an intra-relation between body and soul: 'soul belongs to body, but reflective soul, as its interpretive organ, so to speak, creates meanings beyond the body's unconscious, automatic, instinctual processes'.[34] I would argue that this reading is missing the point that the body's own thinking is also

> *about another*, that is to say: for us to become aware that we are suffering from the *vehemence* of a drive presupposes the existence of another equally vehement or even more vehement drive, and that a *struggle* is in prospect in which our intellect is going to have to take sides' (D §109).

[32] Robert C. Miner, 'Nietzsche's Fourfold Conception of the Self', p. 355.
[33] Ibid. p. 353. Miner thinks there is a strange blend of essentialism and anti-essentialism in Nietzsche. This may have to do with Nietzsche's equivocations on the notion of consciousness that I have referred to above.
[34] Susan West, 'When Nietzsche's Texts "disappear under the interpretation"', p. 101.

interpretive, as we have seen. In fact, West's characterisation misses the intra-relation she herself posits. It is not the case that the body has a soul, rather: the body is grand reason. The way she portrays Nietzsche's view risks falling back into dualism.[35] However, I agree with her when she says: 'Bodily interpretations create, as it were, a new form of being alive within itself, and such a new form of being, in turn, assumes a life of its own: we are the creature who re-creates itself.'[36] As she goes on to explain, 'we can say that the activity of body and its soul constitutes an on-going, most productive tension: it constitutes a metaphor creating meaning from out of its own embodied affective-experience'.[37] Christophe Colera, who understands Nietzsche as offering a reconceptualised individual in the form of a corporeal subjectivity, claims that the world in Nietzsche is understood in terms of a text that has not been written by an author but of which the body, as corporeal subjectivity, is both the author and the interpreter.[38] Again, this is the phenomenological relation between the corporeal subjectivity and the world as the bidirectional constitutive relation of intentionality. This leads me to the notion of being-in-the-world that I want to tackle via an analysis of the very famous aphorism 36 of *Beyond Good and Evil* in which Nietzsche declares the world to 'be "will to power" and nothing else. –' (BGE §36).

'The World Viewed from Inside'

The subjective multiplicity that we are constitutes itself and the world via its experiencing as the bundle of drives that it is.

---

[35] I will grant that I may be misreading her in the same way that Gerhardt misread the child's statement in 'Of the Despisers of the Body' (see note 11 in this chapter) and perhaps West means it as the body/soul. If this is the case, then my disagreement with her vanishes.
[36] West, 'When Nietzsche's Texts "disappear under the interpretation"', p. 101.
[37] Ibid. p. 102.
[38] He says: 'Le monde est présenté par Nietzsche comme un "texte." Un texte non pas écrit par un auteur, mais dont le corps serait l'auteur et l'interprète' (Christophe Colera, *Individualité et subjectivité chez Nietzsche*, p. 102).

The encounter with the world is radically different than it was in rationalist dualistic philosophies that conceive of a subject as completely separated from the world, perceiving it and storing its perceptions in its mind, conceived as a receptacle, a blank slate. Given Nietzsche's view of the body, a rereading of the 'orthodox' interpretation of the will to power as expressed in BGE §36 is in order. This one holds that there is a force in the world that pushes life to overcome itself. This force is the will to power. Zarathustra says: 'Where I found a living creature, there I found will to power' (TSZ 'Of Self-Overcoming'). The will to power is a cosmological force as well as a force that is active within the microcosm that the individual is. Zarathustra says so much when he adds: 'And life itself told me this secret: "Behold," it said, "I am that *which must overcome itself again and again*"' (TSZ 'Of Self-Overcoming').[39] Thus, there is a deep connection between the individual and the world as both are 'moved' by the same force.[40]

While it may be tempting to dismiss this as yet another poetic and somewhat mysterious account offered by Zarathustra in the prophetic mode characteristic of the book, it can be explained along with BGE §36 and fragments of the same period as an expression of Nietzsche's phenomenological commitments regarding consciousness and its relation to the world. As we have seen, Nietzsche is concerned with investigating the experience of the embodied individual. What, then, does he really mean when he talks of the will to power and the world? This is what he says in *Beyond Good and Evil*:

> Suppose, finally, we succeeded in explaining our entire instinctive life as the development and ramification of *one* basic form of the will – namely, of the will to power, as

---

[39] Commenting on this passage in light of his understanding of will to power, Bernd Magnus claims that 'Will-to-power is form-giving, articulation; [. . .]' (*Nietzsche's Existential Imperative*, p. xiv). It is what allows for the co-constitutive process I have been discussing to unfold.

[40] This is another point at which Nietzsche stands very close to Spinoza's monism.

my proposition has it; suppose all organic functions could be traced back to this will to power and one could also find in it the solution of the problem of procreation and nourishment – it is *one* problem – then one would have gained the right to determine all efficient force univocally as – *will to power*. The world viewed from inside, the world defined and determined according to its 'intelligible character' – it would be 'will to power' and nothing else. (BGE §36)

Recall what has been said of the human intellect as the colourist of the world. Reading the above quoted passage in this light, it becomes clear why the world must be will to power, 'and nothing else'. Taking into consideration Günter Abel's analysis and what he suggests about the human being, namely that the interpreting human, as an interpretive bodily organisation, is the boundary of its own world and meaning,[41] further reinforces my view: Nietzsche is not proposing a cosmological theory as has sometimes been suggested. He is explaining what the world is as 'viewed from inside', that is, from the point of view of the human, of the little reason within the great reason that the body is. Again, the world is created by the encounter of the human consciousness with reality. This human mind interprets what it encounters, and its interpreting is the equivalent of a creation. We make the world as we encounter it. Because humans are will to power, the world is then will to power, and nothing else. The world is in fact the creation of the will to power that the human is. Nietzsche talks about being, as being in-itself, as being irrelevant for humans; what really matters is the world as it exists for us. In this case, the world is necessarily the world of the will to power. Since human beings are fundamentally an embodiment of will to power, and since they make the world

---

[41] He says: 'The interpreting human being is, as the interpretive bodily organization it is, the boundary of its world and meaning.' (My translation of 'Der interpretierende Mensch ist als die Interpretative Leib-Organisation, die er ist, die Grenze seiner Welt und des Sinns' (Günter Abel, 'Interpretatorische Vernunft und menschlicher Leib', p. 122).)

in accordance with themselves, the world is necessarily a world of will to power.[42]

What are we to make of this mighty commander, the self that the body is (though not to be equated with the 'I', which is its own tool as we discussed)? Is the embodied intentional consciousness the will to power?

> Suppose nothing else were 'given' as real except our world of desires and passions, and we could not get down, or up, to any other 'reality' besides the reality of our drives – for thinking is merely a relation of these drives to each other: is it not permitted to make the experiment and to ask the question whether this 'given' would not be sufficient for also understanding on the basis of this kind of thing the so-called mechanistic (or 'material') world? (BGE §36)

What is it that 'causes' thinking?[43] The mutual relation of instinctual activity – of the body's activity. This is the *Selbst* at work, the grand reason of the body. The consciousness of this body in the world constitutes itself through its encounter

---

[42] In my book on Nietzsche and Sartre (*Le nihilisme est-il un humanisme?*), I have explained how their philosophies are very close in relation to nihilism, the quest for meaning, and ethics. However, despite the many parallels I uncovered between the two thinkers, the drawing together stopped at this major hurdle: I thought that the Sartrean notion of freedom which pushes us towards our self-overcoming was very similar to the will to power of Nietzsche that performs the same function. However, there was no way one could say that Sartrean freedom also held for the world. Where in Nietzsche the will to power was a notion that served to explain both the individual and the world, Sartrean freedom was restricted to the individual. But now that I understand that the will to power is not a cosmological principle, rather that it is the human that feeds the will to power into the world it creates, it seems that Nietzsche and Sartre would be even closer together than I initially thought. If this is the case, we would thus be dealing with the same ontological setting in both Nietzsche's and Sartre's philosophy. Hence, what I had identified previously as a fundamental divergence would vanish.

[43] I am using this verb with extreme caution because Nietzsche is far from adopting a causalist view.

with the world and constitutes the world at the same time as will to power. This is the bidirectional process of intentionality. The will to power – this grand reason that the body is – shapes the world as will to power since this intentional consciousness constitutes and creates the world for itself as phenomenon. The world as phenomenon is nothing else but will to power.

In a notebook entry from the period during which he was working on *Beyond Good and Evil*,[44] Nietzsche offers a slightly different take on this, emphasising the nature of the will to power as unfolding force:

> And do you know what 'the world' is for me? . . . This world: a monster of force, without beginning, without end, a fixed, iron quantity of force which grows neither larger nor smaller, which doesn't exhaust but only transforms itself . . . as force everywhere, as a play of forces and force-waves simultaneously one and 'many' . . . as a becoming that knows no satiety, no surfeit, no fatigue – this, my *Dionysian* world of eternal self-creating, of eternal self-destroying, this mystery world of dual delights, this my beyond good and evil, without goal, unless there is a goal in the happiness of the circle, without will, unless a ring feels good will towards itself – do you want a *name* for this world? . . . *This world is the will to power – and nothing besides!* And you yourselves too are this will to power – and nothing besides! (NF-1885 p. 38[12])

---

[44] This is the notebook entry published as the concluding aphorism of the edition of *The Will to Power* that was edited by Walter Kaufmann and published in English in 1967. It has been shown that WP §1067, correctly referenced now as NF-1885 p. 38[12], was in fact a draft for BGE §36. One of my pet peeves is that some commentators still prefer to quote WP §1067 when in fact Nietzsche finalised it in the form of BGE §36 and crossed it out in his own notebook. I am not saying that one ought not to examine the notebook entry, which is what I am going to do just now because it has interesting elements, but that if one does, it should not be at the expense of an analysis of the published aphorism in *Beyond Good and Evil*. There is no philological or philosophical reason to prefer WP §1067 over BGE §36 but there is to prefer BGE §36 over WP §1067: it was Nietzsche's authorial choice to go with this version of his claim of the world as will to power.

The first thing to note is that this draft does not refer to the 'intelligible character' or the 'view from inside'. The passage reads as a description of the nature of the world and the human being in it. It obscures the constitutive work of human consciousness in focusing on the work of force as self-creating. It is understandable that commentators using mostly this passage would come up with a cosmological interpretation of the will to power.[45] However, I see this passage as complementing BGE §36 in that it explains the inner movement of the reality of the drives and the organic functions, pointing to the vitalism and dynamism of these processes and thereby further distancing us from any understanding of 'will' in the phrase 'will to power' as the conscious, rational choice of a direction to give to one's organism or the world.

Far from eliminating the self as has been suggested by some, Nietzsche offers us a rich and complex view. If the traditional notion of the self is rejected so vehemently by him, it is because it is damaging in its deceiving simplicity. To believe that one is a rational thinking subject separated from its body, the world and others, is a misconception that fails to capture the intricate inner workings of consciousness as well as the intersubjective and interworldly fabric of which we are made. The next chapter examines how Nietzsche's multi-layered embodied consciousness is also a being-in-the-world and a being-with-others in the phenomenological sense.

---

[45] This is a point Linda L. Williams also makes indicating that it is possible to hold a view of will to power as Nietzsche's metaphysics only by focusing on the notebook entry. As she sees it, Nietzsche is rather interested in the will to power as a behavioural and moral principle. She says: 'The relationships among language, grammar, concepts, and truth are complex in Nietzsche's writings ... but they are all tools for the human being's construction of a sensible world, a world in which the person can exist and, ideally, thrive. It is this thriving, this flourishing of humanity, or, more specifically, certain members of humanity ('great' humans), that interests Nietzsche' (*Nietzsche's Mirror*, pp. 99–100).

4
Being-in-the-World—Being-with-Others

The analyses provided above show that Nietzsche held a view of human subjectivity as intentional embodied consciousness. This consciousness is a manifold that constitutes itself and the world via its experiences. The problem of truth and knowledge is what leads Nietzsche to this discovery through an exercise of historical philosophising akin to a phenomenological reduction. The task now is the following:

> Seeing things as they are! The means: to be able to see them from a hundred eyes, by many people! It was the wrong way to emphasize the impersonal and to describe as moral the point of view of the other. The right way is to see through many others and many eyes and through all sorts of personal eyes.'[1]

---

[1] My translation of '*die Dinge sehen, wie sie sind*! Mittel: Aus hundert Augen auf sie sehen können, aus vielen Personen! Es war ein falscher Weg, das Unpersönliche zu betonen und das Sehen aus dem Auge des Nächsten als moralish zu bezeichnen. *Viele* Nächste und aus *vielen* Augen und aus lauter persönlichen Augen sehen – ist das Rechte' (NF-1881 p. 11[65]). Jocelyne Lebrun considers this passage as the key to a reading of Nietzsche that would bring him close to Husserl's call, 'back to the things themselves', '*zu der Sachen selbst*'. As she points out, Nietzsche uses '*Ding*' while Husserl uses '*Sache*', but the concept referred to is the same and the point is for the subject to dismiss any metaphysical interpretation and let seeing happen, allowing for constitutive consciousness and its work to be unearthed. She discusses this as part of her project to read Nietzsche as engaged in a phenomenology of poetic imagination in the same vein as Ricœur and Bachelard. See her 'Pour une phénoménologie de l'imagination poétique', p. 206.

Things as they are: that is precisely the construct we have created in our encounter with being. We have to see things for what they are. Looking at them with the right perspective, we will also see ourselves. Nietzsche later says:

> One has to learn to *see*, one has to learn to *think*, one has to learn to *speak* and *write*: the end in all three is a noble culture. Learning to *see* – habituating the eye to repose, to patience, to letting things come to it; learning to defer judgment, to investigate and comprehend the individual case in all its aspects. This is the *first* preliminary schooling in spirituality: *not* to react immediately to a stimulus, but to have the restraining, stocktaking instincts in one's control. Learning to *see*, as I understand it, is almost what is called in unphilosophical language 'strong will-power': the essence of it is precisely *not* to 'will', the *ability* to defer decision. (TI 'What the Germans Lack' §6)

As an intentional consciousness, the human being is conscious *of* objects that are given in the world. As we have seen, the relation between consciousness and the world is a creative one insofar as the human head perceives the world and colours it. Thereby, consciousness – as a subjective multiplicity of the body as grand reason – is the creator of the world on the basis of the pre-given world. For Nietzsche, not only is the hypothetical realm of the in-itself irrelevant for us, but a consciousness without or prior to its encounter with the pre-given world is also irrelevant and, in fact, inconceivable. Consciousness only exists in virtue of its relationship to what is external to it.

According to Nietzsche, then, embodied consciousness is a being-in-the-world. That phrase with its meaningful hyphens, famously elaborated upon by Heidegger in *Being and Time*, captures that the human being is always and ever of and in the world and cannot be conceived separated from it. Heidegger claims that '*Being-in is thus the formal existential expression* of the being of Da-sein which has the essential constitution of being-in the-world.'[2] In the same section, he adds:

---

[2] Martin Heidegger, *Being and Time*, p. 51.

According to what we have said, being-in is not a 'quality' which Da-sein sometimes has and sometimes does not have, *without* which it could *be* just as well as it could with it. It is not the case that human being 'is,' and then on top of that has a relation of being to the 'world' which it sometimes takes upon itself. Da-sein is never 'initially' a sort of a being which is free from being-in, but which at times is in the mood to take up a 'relation' to the world. This taking up of relations to the world is possible only because, as being-in-the-world, Da-sein is as it is.[3]

Likewise, the Nietzschean subject cannot be disentangled from the world. It constitutes itself through its encounter with the world and, as intentional consciousness, it is constituted by the world. It is a worldly being. The world is filled with objects and the subject's being conscious of these objects allows for consciousness to emerge. The world and its objects are the conditions of possibility for consciousness: if there was nothing external to consciousness, it could not be. It is clear that the human being thus conceived is a being-in-the-world.[4] Nietzsche says: 'Only when he has attained a final knowledge of all things will man have come to know himself. For things are only the boundaries of man' (D §48). He pursues the same thought in *The Gay Science* as he says: 'as we describe things and their one-after-another, we learn how to describe ourselves more and more precisely' (GS §112).[5] In the same way that it is constituted by

---

[3] Ibid. pp. 53–4.
[4] For this reason, it becomes imperative to be mindful of 'the question of *place* and *climate*. No one is free to live everywhere' (EH 'Clever' §2). There are many remarks in Nietzsche's corpus about nutrition and the influence of climate on one's physiology and, therefore, on one's consciousness. While it is clear that someone with such poor health would be concerned for such for himself, there is also a theoretical grounding to such concern. Being a permeable polyp-being, an embodied consciousness that is a being-in-the-world, paying close attention to such questions is indeed crucial since they will impact our being in its core.
[5] In the same aphorism, he also says that 'we first turn everything into an image, our image!' (GS §112), which takes us back to the claim that the human being stands in the way of things (D §438) that I discussed previously. Here, however, his claim intends to refute the notion of causality.

the objects it encounters through the intentional process, it is also constituted by the others it meets. Indeed, one is not only constituted by objects, material or immaterial, but also by others who populate the world. Therefore, the human being is necessarily a being with-others and just as we are ontologically dependent on the world, we are ontologically dependent on others.[6]

As we have seen, Nietzsche explains the origin of consciousness in aphorism 354 of *The Gay Science*, titled 'On the "genius of the species"'. He asks the question, '*For what purpose*, then, any consciousness at all when it is in the main *superfluous?*' (GS §354) Indeed, he just explained that it is not necessary to our *animal life* (i.e., the biological, physiological) to be conscious. He answers: '*consciousness has developed only under the pressure of the need for communication*: . . . it was needed and useful only between human beings . . . Consciousness is really only a net of communication between human beings' (GS §354).[7] The being of the human being as conscious is therefore directly dependent on its relation to others. Not only is the individual's very being dependent on the other but on its sensations as well. There is an interesting passage in *Human, All Too Human* to that effect. He says:

> From his relations with other men, man adds a new species of *pleasure* to those pleasurable sensations he derives from himself . . . To feel sensations of pleasure on the basis of human relations on the whole makes men better; joy, pleasure, is enhanced when it is enjoyed together with others . . . (HH I §98)

---

[6] In *The Visible and the Invisible*, Merleau-Ponty writes 'Thought is a relationship with oneself and with the world as well as a relationship with the other; hence it is established in the three dimensions at the same time' (p. 145).

[7] It is important to keep in mind, as Constâncio, Mayer Branco and Bartholomew remark, that 'We may call this a world of "intersubjectivity", but we have to bear in mind that part of Nietzsche's point is that the perspectival world of social communications – or the world constituted by a non-solipsistic consciousness, which is in fact a social *Verbindungsnetz*, "a net connecting one person with another" (GS 354) – should not be seen as an aggregate of fixed, permanent, unifying "subjects"' (João Constâncio, Maria João Mayer Branco and Bartholomew Ryan, 'Introduction', p. 4).

This is a clear indication that the presence of others and our interaction with them affects how we experience the world and therefore our own conscious (and unconscious) being. The being of others is part of our own being. This is another facet of the ambiguous multiplicity that we embody and it has important ethical implications as we will see.[8] In *Daybreak*, he says:

> That is why I go into solitude – so as not to drink out of everybody's cistern. When I am among the many I live as the many do, and I do not think as I really think; after a time it always seems as though they want to banish me from myself and rob me of my soul – and I grow angry with everybody and fear everybody. I then require the desert, so as to grow good again. (D §491)[9]

What this is pointing to is the permeability of the human being. Rebecca Bamford examines this from the point of view of empathy and defends Nietzsche's views against those interpreters who understand him as championing cruelty and welcoming human suffering when he ought to reject it wholesale. She uses the notion of intersubjective fluidity that Henry Staten put forward in his *Nietzsche's Voice*[10] and says:

---

[8] It is interesting to note that in his *Introduction to Phenomenology* and in discussing classical phenomenology, Robert Sokolowski explains that 'The identity that is given through its manifold of appearances belongs to a dimension different from that of the manifold. The identity is not one member of the manifold' (*Introduction to Phenomenology*, p. 30), and 'When we introduce the presence of other persons, when we include the dimension of intersubjectivity, a much richer array of manifolds comes into play' (Ibid. p. 31). This aligns well with my discussion of the impact of conceiving of the human being as being-in-the-world that is a being-with-others.

[9] A passage like this is reminiscent of Heidegger's analyses of authenticity and the they-self. There is a risk for Da-sein, caught inauthentically in the Mit-sein, to dissolve in the they by simply thinking as *they* think, valuing as *they* value, etc. As Heidegger says, 'The they, which is nothing definite and which all are, though not as a sum, prescribes the kind of being of everydayness' (*Being and Time*, p. 119). Nietzsche's musings here are evocative of this they-self that is a daily inauthentic trap.

[10] See Henry Staten, *Nietzsche's Voice*.

intersubjective fluidity not only allows for the interchange of subject positions, it also allows for an authentic intersubjective merger on the ground of power, which offers a challenge to an individuated conception of pure subjective awareness as well as to the classical subject positions of sadist and masochist.[11]

The being-with-others of the human being is what allows for this intersubjective fluidity. This fluidity will also take an interesting form in Nietzsche's discussion of friendship, free spiritedness, and *Übermenschlichkeit*. However, before getting into these and looking into how they are related to self-constitution, I wish to look into the structuralist undertones at work in Nietzsche's view of being-in-the-world. Conceiving, of the human being as such, entails that the individual is also constituted by structures of the intersubjective, social-political world, such as morality, social codes, laws, beliefs and culture. I wish to examine some parallels that can be drawn with the later Foucault's views with regard to how one relates to the immaterial power structures in the world via an aesthetics of the self. While the attention paid to Foucault in this chapter may be considered surprising and perhaps even excessive, I see it as extremely helpful in order to disambiguate the tension emphasised in Nietzsche studies between the hard determinism supposedly embraced by Nietzsche on the one hand and his emphasis on self-liberation on the other. It is important to discuss these before tackling Nietzsche's ethical figures of the free spirit and the *Übermensch*.

A Nietzschean 'Structuralism'?

The Nietzschean subject as being-in-the-world is entirely permeable. As we have seen, our polyp-being is constituted by the experiences it has and those are never had in a vacuum and

---

[11] Rebecca Bamford, 'The Virtue of Shame', p. 254.

in isolation. With such an understanding of the subject, self-knowledge is a genuine challenge. He says:

> Direct self-observation is not nearly sufficient for us to know ourselves: we require history, for the past continues to flow within us in a hundred waves: we ourselves are, indeed, nothing but that which at every moment we experience of this continued flowing ... In many families, indeed in individual men, the strata still lie neatly and clearly one on top of the other. (AOM §223)

What Nietzsche is identifying here is the way in which each individual is the bearer of the historical becoming of human beings, of culture, and of everything therein including morality. As he puts it, one always suffers from one's cultural past (HH I §249). For Nietzsche, culture is both a macro- and a microcosm. He says:

> The finest discoveries concerning culture are made by the individual man within himself when he finds two heterogeneous powers ruling there ... Such a hall of culture within the single individual would, however, bear the strongest resemblance to the cultural structure of entire epochs and provide continual instruction regarding them by means of analogy. For wherever grand cultural architecture has developed, its purpose has been to effect a harmony and concord between contending powers through the agency of an overwhelming assemblage of the other powers, but without the need to suppress them or clap them in irons. (HH I §276)

The opposing powers Nietzsche is referring to here are those of arts and science. He explains that the strategy to accommodate this tension is to make oneself larger as to accommodate the tension with various mediating powers in between. This discussion anticipates BGE §12 and its proposal to conceive of the 'soul as social structure of the drives and affects' for such a structure would be 'regulated' by mediating powers and tensions that each drive would exert upon itself and others. In addition, what the passage above from *Human, All Too Human* indicates is that the social structure of the soul is also a hall of culture, that it is permeated by the cultural setting in which the soul exists.

Aphorism 276 is part of a *Gedanken-kette* of the chapter 'Tokens of higher and lower culture' with aphorisms 272 and 274 in which he further explains this view. In 272, he refers to 'rings of individual culture', explaining that cultural progress is tied to individual progress and how individuals enter the realm of culture. In the closing aphorism of the chapter, he explains that by exercising one's historical sense, one can understand that one is the product of one's culture and one can set oneself as a goal,

> to become a necessary chain of rings of culture and from this necessity to recognize the necessity inherent in the course of culture in general. When your gaze has become strong enough to see at the bottom of the dark well of your nature and your knowledge, perhaps you will also behold in its mirror the distant constellations of future cultures. (HH I §292)

This clearly indicates the intermingling of the individual in one's culture, and such intermingling is constitutive of the individual's character. In fact, an examination of individual characters can give insight in the culture and historical periods in which they find themselves. Discussing historical sense, he explains:

> It is in this ability rapidly to reconstruct such systems of ideas and sensations on any given occasion, as for example the impression of a temple on the basis of a few pillars and pieces of wall that chance to remain standing, that the historical sense consists. The first result of it is that we comprehend our fellow men as being determined by such systems and representatives of different cultures, that is to say as necessary, but as alterable. (HH I §274)

Nietzsche is here clearly indicating how individual selves are constituted by the structures he refers to and yet they are also alterable. This is pointing to a degree of freedom for the self in its relation to itself as this product of the power of structures. Criticising the notion of an 'unalterable character', he says, 'this favourite proposition means rather no more than that, during the brief lifetime of a man, the effective motives are unable to scratch deeply enough to erase the imprinted script of many millennia' (HH I §41).[12] That imprinted script comprises beliefs and valuations that are independent of and yet deeply affect the individual. 'This fog of habits and opinions lives and grows almost independently of the people it envelops; it is in this fog that there lies the tremendous effect of general judgments about "man"' (D §105). The individual existence is impacted in its core by this. Again, it is as a permeable polyp-being that one stands to be constituted by what is exterior to oneself. Immediately following aphorism 119 in which he put forward this analogy, Nietzsche exclaims, 'be sure of this: you will be acted upon! at every moment! Mankind has in all ages confused the active and the passive: it is their everlasting grammatical blunder' (D §120).

Nietzsche also famously claims that morality, our whole set of valuations and prescriptions, 'is herd instinct in the individual' (GS §116; see also §117). When an individual chooses or judges

---

[12] As pointed out in a note to this aphorism, the notion of unalterable character was one that Schopenhauer held on to and so this is a critique of Schopenhauer's views. It is a rejection of a hard determinism that is sometimes attributed also to Nietzsche. What confuses matters for readers of Nietzsche is that aphorisms 106 and 107 seem to endorse it. Aphorism 106 titled 'By the waterfall' argues for the absence of free will. The title itself could be a reference to Baron d'Holbach's *System of Nature* in which he compares the life of the human to the flowing of a river as a necessary unfolding. Likewise, he also rejects free will saying that while a person swims in a river they fail to see that their movement is necessitated by the flow. However, and as I will be arguing, Nietzsche's repeated calls to his readers to transform themselves contradict the view according to which he would entirely reject free will. In any case a close reading of HH I §107 also shows that he does not embrace such hard determinism. What aphorism 107 does, rather, is free the individual from moral judgement that would impute complete responsibility for one's actions. He does hint to the possibility for oneself to determine one's actions in relation to the inherited order of ranks that one must deal with. This is what allows for morality to fluctuate.

a course of action, they are in fact carrying forward the values that have been imprinted in them by morality and religion. These grand discourses pervade and shape individual thought and valuing. In a similar vein and focusing on the mechanics of the herd, Nietzsche claims that it is the common experiences had by human beings of one people, shared in a common sphere of language, that ease communicability that make up the herd. Sharing 'similar conditions (of climate, soil, danger, needs, and work), what results from this is people who "understand one another" – a people' (BGE p. 268). When one is of 'one people', one shares in the experiences, the language to refer to them, and the valuing that occurs. However, these are not entirely determining either. Nietzsche's numerous calls to his readers to free themselves from such shackles are an indication of this as well as his analysis of human progress and the role free spirits play therein. I believe that in this respect, he stands very close to the later Foucault's take on the relation between the subject and power.[13]

[13] Jill Hargis has argued that 'Given Nietzsche's earlier compelling and important insight that *all* people are constrained by history, his hope for a distinctly different and elite type of human was a contradictory and even desperate shift in his thought' ('(Dis)embracing the Herd', p. 477). However I find this statement surprising since she also acknowledges that Nietzsche and Foucault are close, especially with regard to the proposals of *Human, All Too Human*. I think precisely this closeness allows us to dismiss what appears to be a contradiction. Hargis further indicates that Foucault and Nietzsche shared a view of history that was in opposition to 'the scientific genealogical approach of Darwin and other positivists because they refuse to acknowledge their own role in the creation of morals and values' (Ibid. p. 491 n58). She thinks that their views on how to use the knowledge garnered by history diverges in the later works of Nietzsche at the point where he focuses on the will to power. I would disagree with this since I see both as proposing that one must engage in self creation on the basis of relating to oneself as dynamic becoming, which is the expression of the will to power.
One may want to argue that the parallels between Foucault and Nietzsche go against my claim that Nietzsche is engaged in phenomenology since Foucault himself explained that he turned to Nietzsche in an effort to distance himself from phenomenology. However, this distancing was motivated by a rejection, on Foucault's part, of a sovereign founding subject that he saw as essential to phenomenology. Phenomenology, however, does not have to rest on such a foundation and certainly Nietzsche's own wild phenomenology does not.

In the essay 'The Subject and Power', Foucault declares that the general theme of his research is the notion of the subject and not that of power.[14] From a genealogical point of view, it is important that we gain 'a historical awareness of our present circumstance'.[15] It is imperative to look into the constitution of the subject, and this necessarily leads us to an uncovering of the workings of power both on and within the subject. Foucault has been explicit about the fact that it was Nietzsche's notion of genealogy as philosophical method that inspired him in that regard.[16] Foucault offers the following:

> It is a form of power which makes individuals subjects. There are two meanings of the word *subject*: subject to someone else by control and dependence, and ties to his own identity by a conscience or self-knowledge. Both meanings suggest a form of power which subjugates and makes subject to.[17]

Here, Foucault indicates two ways in which the subject is constituted (the 'two meanings' he has in mind): while human beings are constituted by relations of power (subject to those forces), they are also engaged in a relation to themselves that makes them subject of their existence. This is the process of subjectivation that Foucault proposes and which I see as akin to Nietzsche's view.

Quoting Foucault in Volume 2 of *The History of Sexuality*, Ansell-Pearson points out that 'The task is to break with accustomed habits of knowing and perceiving, so that one has the chance to become something different than what one's history

---

[14] Michel Foucault, 'Afterword', p. 209. About this, Keith Ansell-Pearson comments 'Whatever we think of the status of Foucault's thinking on the subject, it is clear that the topic is at the centre of his concerns. What is difficult to work through and make cohere is the changing fate of the subject in his corpus' ('Questions of the Subject in Nietzsche and Foucault', p. 414). I agree wholeheartedly with Ansell-Pearson and will not attempt to resolve this difficulty here.
[15] Michel Foucault, 'Afterword', p. 209.
[16] See Foucault's 'Nietzsche, Genealogy, History'.
[17] Michel Foucault, 'Afterword', p. 212.

has conditioned one to be, to think and perceive directly.'¹⁸ This task is possible because of the relation to oneself the subject can have as a subject of power. Christopher Cordner explains,

> Everyone is enmeshed in networks of power ... In his later work Foucault highlighted the contingency of these determinations of 'who we are.' Rapport à soi [relation to oneself] is the way in which contingency and history are recapitulated into the free expression of who we are.¹⁹

What this is pointing to is a distancing from oneself which is crucial to the subjectivation process. One must, through the relation to oneself, take a distance from oneself, and reflectively re-apprehend oneself. To talk about a process of subjectivation is to presuppose that there is no such thing as a subject that is already there and given to the self; we must construct it.²⁰ Indeed, there is a subject which is the result of the action of power, but this subject is not the moral subject or, as we shall see below, the authentic self. That situated, worldly and embodied subject will be consolidated as such only after the free consciousness has exercised its reflective practice on it.

Valérie Daoust explains this process of subjectivation in the following helpful way. She points out that it is impossible for the individual to free oneself from power and that the best one may do is to articulate strategies for exercising one's freedom within power. Whatever liberation there is would not be one 'from an exterior that oppresses me but rather a liberation of

---

¹⁸ Keith Ansell-Pearson, 'Questions of the Subject in Nietzsche and Foucault', p. 416.
¹⁹ Christopher Cordner, 'Foucault, Ethical Self-concern and the Other', p. 595.
²⁰ About this, Frédéric Gros says, 'To talk of subjectivation presupposes that the subject is not given to itself, that it builds itself, it elaborates itself.' (My translation of: 'Parler de subjectivation suppose d'abord que le sujet ne soit pas donné à lui-même, mais qu'il se construise, s'élabore ...' ('Sujet moral et soi éthique chez Foucault', p. 232).) I have discussed these issues at greater length in my 'Authenticity and Distantiation from Oneself', where I discuss Foucault in relation to Beauvoir and Sartre, key existential phenomenologists who also stand close to Nietzsche.

the self by the self and through practices of freedom'. Thus, she says, 'The transformation of subjectivity is not to discover "who I am," but to reject first "who I am" in resisting power and knowledge.'[21] Clearly then, the subject must engage in this process of discovering who one is. Taking a distance from oneself after having gained an understanding of one's passive subjectivation through the effect of power, the subject must engage in a creative process of subjectivation, appropriating oneself through practices of freedom. This would constitute what Daoust refers to as 'identitarian authenticity' ('authenticité identitaire').[22] This is what Nietzsche calls for as well. We have seen that he considers it essential to seek to know oneself and to thereby engage in a relation to oneself. In *Daybreak*, he says:

> Out of damp and gloomy days, out of solitude, out of loveless words directed at us, *conclusions* grow up in us like fungus: one morning they are there, we know not how, and they gaze upon us, morose and grey. Woe to the thinker who is not the gardener but only the soil of the plants that grow in him! (D §382)

While this is directed specifically at thinkers, it does apply to any human being in his view. One must be active in one's becoming and not merely passive like a puppet at the mercy of whatever shapes it.

Ansell-Pearson further notes that the conception of the self in Foucault results in conceiving of the self as 'activity' rather than 'substance' which, again, points to a Nietzschean understanding of the self as dynamic becoming. He explains: 'Here we now have a subject, as Deleuze appreciates, capable of turning back on itself and of critically examining the processes of its

---

[21] My translation of 'il ne s'agit pas tellement d'une libération définitive d'un dehors qui m'opprime, mais surtout d'une libération de soi par soi par des pratiques de liberté. La transformation de la subjectivité n'est pas de découvrir "qui je suis," mais de rejeter d'abord "qui je suis" en résistance au pouvoir et au savoir' (Valérie Daoust, 'Foucault et Taylor sur la vérité', p. 14).

[22] Ibid. p. 14.

own constitution and bringing about changes in them.'²³ This ethics of care of the self takes the form of a social practice in Foucault, since no individual lives in isolation, and 'It's only by establishing and maintaining the right relation to oneself that we have the basis for forming full relations with others.'²⁴ So while this caring for oneself might be conceived as a solitary – and even solipsistic – exercise, this is not what Foucault has in mind. In fact, and as Frédéric Gros puts it, the 'care of the self, far from excluding the other, rather presupposes him or her . . . On the other hand, care of the self also intensifies the relation to political action rather than hindering it.'²⁵ The techniques of the self that will be employed by the free subject to care for oneself through a process of distanciation are varied. But the goal is to care for oneself via these processes. This is the goal Foucault sees the virtue ethicists of ancient Greece as pursuing. For Ansell-Pearson, it is clear that both Nietzsche and Foucault are engaged in this project of understanding processes of subjectivation for a self that is also subject to power. He also sees both thinkers as focusing on how this self may relate to itself to avoid being completely subjected to power (*assujetti*). From that, Ansell-Pearson concludes that 'We can describe both Nietzsche and Foucault as modern-day virtue ethicists who seek to "liberate the capacity of individual self-choice and personal self-formation from oppressive conformism . . ." (Ingram 2003: 240).'²⁶

[23] Keith Ansell-Pearson, 'Questions of the Subject in Nietzsche and Foucault', p. 419.
[24] Ibid. p. 420.
[25] Frédéric Gros, 'Le Souci de soi chez Michel Foucault', p. 702. Alain Beaulieu notes that the care of the self has two aspects to it: it is valuable insofar as it makes an individual a potentially good social/political agent, one who may act in a leadership role, and it is also valuable in itself. (See 'Étude critique: *Le gouvernement de soi et des autres* et *Le courage de la vérité*', p. 166.)
[26] Keith Ansell-Pearson, 'Questions of the Subject in Nietzsche and Foucault', p. 425. Ansell-Pearson reads *Daybreak* as containing a clear socio-political backdrop (see Ibid. p. 422). My argument here is that the wild phenomenology emerging in the middle period works, including *Daybreak*, provides the ground for this virtue ethics and politics to be elaborated. To me, there is a socio-political backdrop to all of Nietzsche's works, even those that appear to be less obviously concerned with the ethical and the political.

Human beings are worldly social beings. As such, they are subject to power relations and the subject of their own relation to themselves as an expression of power. This gives another sense to Nietzsche's statement in his notebooks '*This world is the will to power – and nothing besides! And you yourselves too are this will to power – and nothing besides!*' (NF-1885 p. 38[12]). This passage can now be read under a Foucauldian light or, rather, as anticipating the Foucauldian take on the subject and power. Human beings are not merely puppets of those plays of forces, they are able to reflectively – and non-reflectively as a bundle of drives – re-apprehend themselves. In both Nietzsche and Foucault, this points to the being-in-the-world of the individual that is also a being-with-others. This leads Foucault to suggest that the subject is no longer individual but a collective or trans-individual.[27] Being permeated by power relations, we are social beings; we are being-with-others. Therefore, for Foucault, and as already indicated by Ansell-Pearson, individual existence always has an ethical and a political dimension. As Gros indicates, 'what interests Foucault in the care of the self, is the manner by which it is integrated in the social fabric and constitutes a motor for political action'.[28] As suggested by Judith Revel, the aesthetics of existence, insofar as it constitutes in part a resistance to the effects of power on oneself as subject, constitutes an eminently political act in Foucault.[29] This also applies to Nietzsche for whom the aesthetic creation of oneself as a subject of one's life is also key, even though he does not put the political implications of it at the forefront of his discussion. Clearly, though, one's authentic becoming will impact the socio-political realm of which one is always a part.

As I explained in the introduction, phenomenologists often prefer to dwell on the descriptive, but many engage in phenomenological descriptions in the first place in order to provide themselves with the firm grounding needed to engage in ethical

[27] Michel Foucault, *Dits et écrits I*, p. 841.
[28] Frédéric Gros, 'Le Souci de soi chez Michel Foucault', p. 701.
[29] See Revel's entry on 'Esthétique (de l'existence)' in her *Dictionnaire Foucault*, p. 51.

and political reflections. This is certainly the case for Nietzsche for whom ethical flourishing is a lifelong preoccupation. Having established that the human being is the manifold which he has described, and which is connected with others and the world as we have seen, he pursues his ethical reflections by considering how one may escape the yoke of traditional alienating moralities and institutions that stifle growth. This leads him to the figure of the free spirit, the first of Nietzsche's ethical ideal figures.

5
Fettered and Free Spirits

Because we are beings-in-the-world and subjects of power, because 'Nietzsche's self is the product of both nature (*physis*) and culture',[1] fettered spirits are the rule and free spirits are the exception. Indeed, as someone who can think differently, shed a critical eye on the world around them, and create their own values, the free spirit possesses and exercises the rare strength of self-mastery[2] that allows them to relate to their subjection to power in a different way. As multi-layered embodied subjectivities, they are still permeated by the world and their self is still constituted as a being-in-the-world and a being-with-others. However, they are not herd-like and relate to others and the world differently. As we will see, this entails that they will seek and engage in different types of relations with others, friendships that are agonistic in nature, in order to bring out the best potential in themselves and others. The whole pursuit is that of ethical flourishing.

The Ethical Ideal of the Free Spirit

The figure of the free spirit is Nietzsche's ethical ideal in his middle period works. I have mentioned earlier how Nietzsche conceived of his middle period works, *Human, All Too Human*,

---

[1] Keith Ansell-Pearson, 'In Search of Authenticity and Personality', p. 285.
[2] We could give a new meaning to the master/herd morality by considering that the free spirit is the master of the herd of instincts and drives that constitute him. The ethical ideal of the free spirit posits that one must be such a self-aware master of oneself.

Daybreak and *The Gay Science*, as his *ganze Freigeisterei*; literally: his whole free spiritedness. On the back cover of the first edition of *The Gay Science*, Nietzsche indicates that his book completes a series of works which started with *Human, All Too Human*. The overall goal of these works was to draw a new portrait and ideal of the free spirit.³ However, Nietzsche will later reject this ideal as too moral. He says, 'Morality is vanquished and overcome through free-spiritedness' ('Die Moral ist durch die Freigeisterei auf ihre Spitze getrieben und überwunden' (NF-1882, p. 4[16])). But despite this important role, the free spirit is itself moral.⁴ In a letter from that period, he admonishes Lou Salomé: 'Do not let yourself be fooled about me – Certainly you do not believe that the Free Spirit is my ideal?' ('Lassen Sie sich nicht über mich täuschen – Sie glauben doch nicht, daß, der "Freigeist" mein Ideal ist?' (BVN-1882, p. 335)) and again in a letter to Köselitz, he says: 'What is certain is that with it, I have stepped over into another world – the "Free Spirit" is *fulfilled*' ('Gewiß ist, daß ich damit in eine andere Welt hinübergetreten bin – der "Freigeist" ist *erfüllt*' (BVN-1883)). This other world in which he just stepped is that of the *Übermensch* since he is writing *Thus Spoke Zarathustra* at the time. I will turn to that concept later but for now I want to examine closely the concept of the free spirit which is definitely a precursor for the later ethical ideal and serves a key function in the development of Nietzsche's thought.

In his 1886 preface to *Human, All Too Human*, Nietzsche famously says:

> – Thus when I needed to I once also invented for myself the 'free spirits' . . . 'free spirits' of this kind do not exist, did not exist – but as I have said, I had need of them . . . as brave companions and familiars with whom one can laugh and chatter when one feels like laughing and chattering, and whom one can send to the Devil when they become tedious – as compensation for the friends I lacked. (HH I 'Preface' §2)

---

³ See section 'Questions of Method' in Chapter 1 (pp. 25–6).
⁴ In a notebook entry he claims 'However we now recognize that free-spiritedness is itself moral' ('Aber jetzt erkennen wir die Freigeisterei selber als Moral' (NF-1882, p. 6[4])).

Given his views on being-with-others and how the others we interact with impact our self-constitution, it is indeed necessary to create for oneself the friends one needs, should those be lacking. As we will see when I broach the topic of friendship, only agonistic friendships serve an ethical purpose and one ought to pursue them. Thinking of himself as a free spirit, Nietzsche has a need for the type of spirits that will help him further elevate himself, which means returning to his own self. The Preface is interesting in that regard in that it provides us an explanation as to why he qualifies as a free spirit himself. Recall that he refers to *Human, All Too Human* as 'the memorial of a crisis' (EH 'HH' §1).[5] The crisis is his own, having suffered from nihilism and recovered from it. The 'great liberation' that he associates with free spiritedness is not an easy nor painless one. As he puts it, 'It is at the same time a sickness that can destroy the man who has it, this first outbreak of strength and will to self-determination, to evaluating on one's own account, this will to *free* will' (HH 'Preface' §3). This sickness is borne out of suspicion or, as we have discussed earlier, a sceptical stance that is adopted by the free spirit, the free thinkers referred to as 'we children of the Enlightenment' (HH I §55). Exercising doubt and investigating the origins of various discourses, beliefs and cultural practices, one is led to wonder if there is any truth, if any value may still hold, whether there is any ground to stand on save for the one that one creates for oneself. Hence the question he asks, '*must* we not be deceivers?' (HH 'Preface' §3), which I relate to his view of the world as fiction that was discussed earlier.

Recovery is possible for the strong individual but goes through various stages where one acquires '*mature* freedom of spirit' (HH I 'Preface' §4) and thereby great health. One experiences 'birdlike freedom, bird-like altitude, bird-like exuberance' that allows one to put things beneath one (HH I 'Preface' §4) and finally see oneself and the things closest to oneself. He says: 'to become sick in the manner of these free spirits, to remain sick for a long time and then, slowly, slowly, to become healthy, by which I mean "healthier", is a fundamental *cure* for all pessimism' (HH I 'Preface' §5). The great health allows one to master oneself and embrace perspectivism (HH I 'Preface' §6) and requires that one

---

[5] I discussed this in the introduction.

tackles the problem of order of rank (HH I 'Preface' §7). The free spirits are experimenters that have also been 'adventurers and circumnavigators of that inner world called "man"' (HH I 'Preface' §7). They have acquired a knowledge of themselves that allows them to return to themselves. Collating these claims with what he says in *Ecce Homo* about the book makes clear that he takes himself as an exemplar of becoming a free spirit: 'Human, All Too Human, this memorial of a rigorous self-discipline with which I made a sudden end of every sort of "higher swindle", "idealism", "beautiful feelings" and other womanishnesses that I had been infected with' (EH 'HH' §5) and,

> I have never been so happy with myself as in the sickest and most painful periods of my life: one has only to look at "Daybreak" or perhaps the "Wanderer and his Shadow" to grasp what this "return to myself" was: a highest kind of *recovery* itself! (EH 'HH' §4)

And finally, in the section 'Why I am so wise', he says 'My humanity is a constant self-overcoming. But I need solitude – which is to say, recovery, return to myself, the breath of a free, light, playful air' (EH 'Wise' §8).[6] Nietzsche takes himself as a

---

[6] The theme of solitude is an interesting one in Nietzsche. As Burnham notes, it occurs both literally and figuratively in his works. Nietzsche himself engaged in practices of solitude such as preferring to live in smaller towns and going for extended hikes by himself. Figuratively, this solitude is valued as a practice that allows for ideas to emerge as well as for keeping the necessary distance with others with whom it may not be desirable to interact for fear of being tainted by the herd instinct. Solitude is conceived as a counterweight to the power of the herd on the individual (see Burnham's *The Nietzsche Dictionary*, p. 306). Personally and philosophically, then, for Nietzsche solitude is a good experience that one must seek actively in order to realise one's free spiritedness. To be a free spirit also entails to be free from others who bring one down rather than elevate. However, and as Burnham also points out, solitude ought not to be a permanent state. Episodes of solitude are to be followed with episodes of interacting actively with others. Thus, in the first section of 'Zarathustra's Prologue', Zarathustra explains that he is like a cup that overflows after ten years of solitude in a cave and, 'This cup wants to be empty again, and Zarathustra wants to be man again' (TSZ 'Prologue' §1). Solitude has allowed him to recharge, so to speak, but while by himself he was not fully a man. To be so, one must also exist as a being-with-others.

case study and it allows him to create the concept of free spiritedness. After all, as he puts it in *Beyond Good and Evil*, 'Gradually it has become clear to me what every great philosophy so far has been: namely, the personal confession of its author and a kind of involuntary and unconscious memoir' (BGE §6).

The figure of the free spirit emerges as one who frees oneself from the shackles of traditional discourses and the supposed truths they offer. The free spirit is a critic and a nihilist in the sense mentioned above. They are such because of their search for truth and authenticity. This search is the driving force of the free spirit. As Amy Mullin puts it, 'one of the most striking features of the free spirit is his passion for knowledge – his need for reasons rather than faith'.[7] This fundamental need is what leads the free spirit to embrace her critical stance. While the free spirit makes a quick appearance in HH I §30, where Nietzsche mentions that adopting a contrarian stance is not the right path for the free spirit, it is really in Chapter 5, 'Tokens of higher and lower culture', that the notion is fleshed out by Nietzsche. This is interesting if one considers the theme of this chapter: cultural evolution. This chapter discusses how cultures and societies evolve through a dialectic of regression/progression. The free spirit and the genius are figures that trigger change and help the movement forward to occur. This movement forward is not straightforward however: it comprises many backward steps. Nietzsche views progress as a circular movement forward that entails a stepping back. However, progress is not strictly circular; rather, it takes the form of a series of loops. The backward movement of the circle (when drawn from right to left) propels us forward to a point that is beyond the starting point. He also thinks that higher culture does not reject older forms but rather seeks to accommodate them.[8] Importantly, Nietzsche explains in the opening aphorism of that chapter that progress

---

[7] Amy Mullin, 'Nietzsche's Free Spirit', p. 398.

[8] This view of cultural progress, or what could also be called in Nietzschean terms 'cultural self-overcoming', could be understood under the light of a Hegelian dialectic of progress. Walter Kaufmann interprets Nietzsche as offering such dialectical thinking with regard to the individual's ethical becoming (see *Nietzsche: Philosopher, Psychologist, Antichrist*). However,

is parallel in the individual and in the social or cultural group. Further, he insists on the dialectical relation between fettered and free spirits since both are needed for progress to happen. Nietzsche says that two things must come together:

> firstly the augmentation of the stabilizing force through the union of minds in belief and communal feeling; then the possibility of the attainment of higher goals through the occurrence of degenerate natures and, as a consequence of them, partial weakenings and injuring of the stabilizing force; it is precisely the weaker nature, as the tenderer and more refined, that makes any progress possible at all. (HH §224)

The degenerate natures in this quote refer to the free spirits as those who think differently. This description follows in the next aphorism. Referring to this, Ken Gemes points out that 'Nietzsche is near unique in claiming that degeneration is in fact a precondition of progress'.[9] What is key is that all elements are required for progress to occur. No being is left out or ought to be left out from the realm of interaction that produces the movement forward.[10]

---

and as I have argued in my *Le Nihilisme est-il un humanisme?*, as much as the overcoming propelled by the will to power may resemble a Hegelian dialectic of progress there are three reasons why it cannot be understood as such: (1) Hegel posits that becoming is driven by logos; (2) Hegel's view is a teleology; and (3) one of Hegel's goals is the preservation of Christianity. Nietzsche would disagree with all three and his thinking is actually in direct contradiction to those. I agree with Gilles Deleuze's statement to the effect that 'we must take seriously the resolutely anti-dialectical character of Nietzsche's philosophy' (*Nietzsche and Philosophy*, p. 8). For my argument in the context of an analysis of will to power, see my *Le Nihilisme est-il un humanisme?*, p. 59.

[9] Ken Gemes, 'Postmodernism's Use and Abuse of Nietzsche', p. 355.

[10] This in itself should be sufficient to dismiss the interpretations of Nietzsche that understand him as proposing to radically segregate the social realm between nobles and slaves and prevent any interaction between them. In aphorism 76 of *The Gay Science*, Nietzsche says 'We others are the exception and the danger – and we need eternally to be defended. – Well, there actually are things to be said in favour of the exception, provided that it never wants to become the rule' (GS §76). I will come back to this later.

Aphorism 225 of *Human, All Too Human I* offers us a first definition of the concept of the free spirit: the free spirit is a relative concept. Nietzsche explains, 'He is called a free spirit who thinks differently from what, on the basis of his origin, environment, his class and profession, or on the basis of the dominant views of the age, would have been expected of him' (HH I §225). The free spirit is an exception as opposed to the rule, which is to be a fettered spirit, a creature of habits who has faith in institutions and supports them. Because the free spirit thinks differently and defies commonly held beliefs, they are perceived as evil and as a threat by the fettered spirits (HH I §241). The free spirit is a threat because she makes use of her intellect, which is of superior quality and sharpness, to question things and embody a sceptical outlook, to pursue the goals of the Enlightenment in herself (WS §221), which is to say to dare think on one's own and for oneself without recourse to authority. Nietzsche says that her spirit of enquiry remains light-hearted against the age of seriousness, thus anticipating the gay science that will be the object of the book concluding the *Freigeisterei* series (HH I §240).

In *The Gay Science*, he revisits this view of the free spirit, this time referring to it as *der Irrsinnigen*, the madman.[11] This one constitutes the 'greatest danger' because of how they think differently and initiate changes that fettered spirits, by their nature, resist. Nietzsche says, 'Not truth and certainty are the opposite of the world of the madman, but the universality and the universal binding force of a faith' (GS §76). This 'madman' combats the universalising approach of the fettered spirits, the herd. It is their longing for truth that makes them exceptional: 'Continually, precisely the most select spirits

---

[11] 'The madman' is the title of aphorism 125 in which the death of God is proclaimed by the madman. However, in German, aphorism 125 is referring to 'Der tolle Mensch', so more precisely 'the great human being'. Kaufmann's choice of translating this phrase as 'the madman' is consistent with an interpretation of the madman of GS §76, discussed here, as being the free spirit, that is an exceptional spirit, one that is strong enough to sustain the death of God.

bristle at this universal binding force – the explorers of truth above all. Continually this faith, as everybody's faith, arouses nausea and a new lust in subtler minds' (GS §76). Nietzsche proposes that the free spirit is superior, but the strength of her intellect does not entail that she possesses the truth. Instead, Nietzsche says:

> what characterizes the free spirit is not that his opinions are the more correct but that he has liberated himself from tradition, whether the outcome has been successful or a failure. As a rule though, he will nonetheless have truth on his side, or at least the spirit of inquiry after truth: he demands reasons, the rest demand faith. (HH I §225)

The free spirit is presented as a seeker, one who searches for truth on her own and refuses to accept authoritative discourses. This will eventually allow her to uncover the truth about herself and will prepare the ground for one's own valuing.[12] Authenticity is here hinted at as the longing for truth. In aphorism 292, Nietzsche appeals to the reader to try to make of herself a free spirit. He indicates how to achieve this: by not looking down on past experiences, such as religion and art which, despite being a bad soil have born great fruits (HH I §292), and by embracing historical thinking and making oneself an instrument of knowledge since knowledge frees the spirit (HH I §288). In aphorism 252, the acquisition of knowledge is described as a form of overcoming – every pursuit of truth is considered worthwhile. Knowledge makes one 'conscious of one's strength' and allows one to go 'beyond former conceptions' (HH I §252). Nietzsche explains that the free spirit will be a mindful spirit, one who will suspend one's own internal eye every now and then in order to better experiment and, therefore, better know oneself

---

[12] The truth that is being sought is not only about oneself and the world but also about morality. As a fettered spirit, one remains blind to the lies told by a Christian morality that rests upon the metaphysical understanding of the world. The task, however, is to uncover those lies, see through them and build anew. More on this below.

(WS §236). He indicates that it is crucial to focus on experiences before analysing them.[13]

It is primordial for the free spirit to avoid any inertia of one's spirit which may lead to a stiffening of one's thoughts. Exercising scepticism, the free spirit will be the enemy of convictions and will be on the path of truth, a special path which will also entail error. The free spirit is an ever-evolving concept and error is an integral part of its progress (AOM §4). Its own progress parallels cultural progress with periods of progression and periods of regression. The concluding two chapters of Book I of *Human, All Too Human* provide us with a portrait of the free spirit and his philosophy of the morning. It follows a series of aphorisms on truth and convictions. In aphorism 637, Nietzsche says of the free spirit that 'even if he should be altogether a thinking snowball, he will have in his head, not opinions, but only certainties and precisely calculated probabilities' (HH I §637). Further, he says that the way of the free spirit is to 'advance from opinion to opinion, through one party after another, as noble *traitors* to all things that can in any way be betrayed' (HH I §637). Thus, free spirits are presented as seeking 'spiritual nomadism' (AOM §211). This is part of the obligation for free spirits to become masters of themselves. To be such, one must have freed oneself from alienating beliefs and convictions. This means adopting the critical sceptical stance that Nietzsche champions. One must free oneself from 'conceptions of morality, religion, and metaphysics. Only when this sickness *from one's chains* has also been overcome will the first great goal have truly been attained: the separation of man from the animals' (WS §350).[14] But this freedom from constraints and received dogma carries with it an implicit ought. As Gemes explains it, 'this is not to say that they

---

[13] This amounts to a recommendation to use phenomenological bracketing. It can be argued that the herd mentality is the equivalent of the natural attitude that needs to be bracketed in order to achieve genuine knowledge. The free spirit is the one that dismisses the natural attitude and seeks a deeper – better – knowledge of herself and the world. I thank an anonymous reviewer of my manuscript for raising this point.

[14] It ought to be noted that the first four chapters of *Human, All Too Human* which precede the emergence of the free spirit consist in this endeavour.

[free spirits] are free of the constraint of a self imposed form. Their play is the serious play of self-creation.'[15] The noble freed spirit's motto shall be: 'Peace all around me and good will to all things closest to me' (WS §350). The Wanderer who eventually comes to wish to pay attention to the things closest to him pleases the Shadow. This is the final discussion of 'The Wanderer and his Shadow' and one that closes the investigation on what it means to be a free spirit in *Human, All Too Human*. More needs to be said now about how this figure functions as an ethical ideal of authenticity.

The Virtuous, Authentic Free Spirit

Nietzsche asks, 'is there anything more beautiful than *looking* for one's own virtues?' (BGE §214). This is part of what the virtue of authenticity entails, which is paramount for Nietzsche, and it is embodied by the ideal of the free spirit. A fundamental virtue of the free spirit is her capacity to be true to the strength of her intellect and to have the will to use it. Once she has done so, she will engage in spiritual nomadism. Nietzsche writes:

> He who has attained to only some degree of freedom of mind cannot feel other than a wanderer on the earth – though not as a traveller to a final destination: for this destination does not exist. But he will watch and observe and keep his eyes open to see what is really going on in the world; for this reason he may not let his heart adhere too firmly to any individual thing; within him too there must be something wandering that takes pleasure in change and transience. (HH I §638)

> These chapters dismiss as illusory and alienating human-made discourses such as metaphysics, morality, religion and art that have been established as transcendentally grounded and therefore absolutely true. These chapters thus pave the way for the emergence of the free spirit, the one who sees these discourses for what they are: human fabrications. These chapters and their use of historical philosophising as identified as the proper method in HH I §2 chronicle Nietzsche's own emancipation and becoming a free spirit. The implicit aim is to also take the reader on this path of liberation.

[15] Ken Gemes, 'Postmodernism's Use and Abuse of Nietzsche', p. 346.

While this may seem to speak against the notion of authentic becoming – becoming what one is – I would argue that it is rather the key to authenticity.[16] As Golomb aptly explains, 'Nietzsche makes it clear that becoming one's true self is a perpetual movement of self-overcoming, a free creation of one's own values and perspectives. These presuppose the persistent overcoming of any "higher self"'.[17] Starting with the middle period writings the notion of *Einheit*, the unity of the self, is less and less discussed. Gemes has noted that while Nietzsche valorised unity and spoke about it positively in his early works, he tends to speak about it negatively in the later works. However, as he explains, the valorisation of unity in fact does not change. What happens instead is that while he continues to valorise 'unity as a goal . . . he rejects certain false notions of unity and this rejection comes to dominate his use of the term "Einheit"'.[18] I agree with Gemes and think that this goal is precisely what the free spirit aims for. This unity of the self, towards which one aims, is not the actualisation of one's essence but, rather, the actualisation of oneself as this perpetual movement of overcoming, as the dynamic becoming that one is as a multi-layered embodied consciousness. As Daniel Breazeale points out, Nietzsche does not hold an essentialist (naturalist) or an anti-essentialist view of the self. He says that Nietzsche:

> refuses to accept either as wholly adequate for understanding what it means to 'be a self.' On the one hand, he recognizes that in order to 'become who one is,' one always requires a sufficient amount of self-knowledge to insure that what one

---

[16] Jacob Golomb notes that while Nietzsche does not make use of the term 'authenticity' it is what he has in mind when he discusses 'Wahrhaftigkeit' (see 'Nietzsche on Authenticity', p. 243).

[17] Ibid. p. 246.

[18] Ken Gemes, 'Postmodernism's Use and Abuse of Nietzsche', p. 351 n22. In the previous note, Gemes provides a count for the number of occurrences of the term *Einheit* in the *Nachlass*. Comparing text samples of similar sizes (some 93,000 to 100,000 words), he notes that the usage of the term goes from fifty occurrences between 1869 and 1872 to five occurrences only between 1880 and 1881 and seventeen between 1888 and 1889 (see p. 350 n21).

is striving to become is really consistent with what one is (though, to be sure, the 'knowledge' in question does not have to be propositional in character or fully explicit)... Mere 'knowledge' – no matter how indirect or tacit – is not enough; in order to 'be yourself' you have to act. This is the kernel of truth in all anti-essentialist theories: the self is something constructed, indeed, it is always 'under construction.'[19]

As he further points out, there are times in his writings where Nietzsche will affirm both positions within the same work without adjudicating between them. Breazeale's discussion of this pertains to his analysis of the theory of selfhood introduced in *Schopenhauer as Educator* to which I turn further below as it pertains to the virtue of authenticity.

It is important to emphasise that the highest self one can become is still an ambiguous multiplicity as described previously. Part of becoming authentic, which is Nietzsche's ethical worry, is to know oneself as this ambiguous multiplicity that one is and further, and most importantly, to will oneself to exist as this ambiguous multiplicity. Nietzsche says: 'Active, successful natures act, not according to the dictum "know thyself", but as if there hovered before them the commandment: *will* a self and thou shalt *become* a self' (AOM §366). As Nuno Nabais indicates, 'since individuality is not a primary datum to be found by each individual within himself, it has to be reconceived as a task to be accomplished'.[20] The free spirit is the one who has the strength to do this. Coming to the realisation that one is this ambiguous multiplicity, the free spirit will resist the reification of itself in a unified, fixed identity – which is what metaphysical, moral and religious views have traditionally tried to superimpose on the human being – and will nurture herself as the embodied dividuum she is. Actually, the relation to the Other also provides that challenge to reification. Being-with-others entails being divided and multiple. But one must be authentic about it. One must will to be

---

[19] Daniel Breazeale, 'Becoming Who One Is', pp. 14–15.
[20] Nuno Nabais, 'The Individual and Individuality in Nietzsche', p. 82.

what one is. The free spirit, as authentic, will opt for embodying the dividuum and will thus be on the path of *Übermenschlichkeit*. The free spirit is none other than this embrace of oneself as ambiguous multiplicity: a dynamic state of being *qua* becoming, not the end goal to a linear progress of being, rather the process of individuation itself if and only if it is embraced authentically.

In the middle period works, Nietzsche offers a list of ends and excellences that the free spirit ought to pursue: self-mastery, self-sufficiency, self-discipline and self-reverence.[21] All of these are means to become an authentic self. They also entail self-knowledge. As Nietzsche understands it, learning about things and the world is important but the most important undertaking is to learn about oneself. In fact, these endeavours are one and the same: to learn about the world is to learn about oneself as intentional embodied consciousness that constitutes the world and itself in its being conscious of it. It is subject to and subject of the world and the forces therein. Speaking of becoming and how one may be impatient once on that path, Nietzsche says:

> He learns much in the process [of attaching oneself to a philosopher's or poet's teachings]: but often a youth forgets while doing so what is most worth learning and knowing: himself; he remains a partisan all his life. Alas, much boredom has to be overcome, much sweat expended, before we discover our own colours, our own brush, our own canvas! – And even then we are far from being a master of our own art of living – but at least we are master in our own workshop. (WS §266)[22]

---

[21] I am indebted to Simon Robertson's comprehensive list which also lists occurrences of such ends and excellences in mature works. See 'Normativity for Nietzschean Free Spirits', p. 594.

[22] Note the painting analogy here again, this time employed to refer to the creation of oneself. This takes us back to the notion of aesthetic reason discussed above (see Chapter 2, note 50). Also note the emphasis on self-mastery: to be 'master in our own workshop', which amounts to being the subject of power identified by Foucault in his aesthetics of the self (discussed in the previous chapter).

The most important piece of knowledge one can acquire is of oneself. To fully know what one is, is the key to this authentic becoming. As Simon Robertson puts it,

> To master oneself, though, one must understand oneself. This involves uncompromisingly honest scrutiny (GS p. 335; BGE p. 39; A p. 50; EH IV p. 7): [a] veridical assessment of the kind of person one already is . . . the ends a free spirit sets himself reflect both the *particularities* of who he already is, as embodied in his motives, and what he realistically believes he can make of himself.[23]

This uncovers the virtue of honesty, being true to one's self, which is the overarching virtue for the free spirit. In other words: authenticity is paramount to free spiritedness.[24]

It is in the third *Untimely Meditation, Schopenhauer as Educator*, that the notion of authentic striving alongside the notion of selfhood is first presented. Nietzsche's ethical concern with it predates the emergence of the free spirit in *Human, All Too Human*, but prepares the way for it and is certainly worth paying attention to. I find Breazeale's arguments on the status of this work convincing. Breazeale provides a very useful and comprehensive analysis of the history of the work which demonstrates its importance in the Nietzschean corpus. As part of that analysis, Breazeale gathers evidence from Nietzsche's letters and notes, and he considers *Schopenhauer as Educator* as a source of information on the programme set out for his mature philosophy to come. Specifically, Nietzsche thought that it laid out promises fulfilled in his later works. Breazeale quotes a letter from 21 April 1883 to Peter Gast where Nietzsche says, 'It is curious: I wrote the commentary prior to the text! Everything was already promised in Schopenhauer as Educator. But there was still a long way to go from Human All-Too-Human to the Übermensch.'[25] Breazeale argues the following on the philosophical import of

---

[23] Simon Robertson, 'Normativity for Nietzschean Free Spirits', p. 601.
[24] I discuss the connection between honesty and authenticity in what follows.
[25] Quoted in Breazeale, 'Becoming Who One Is', p. 7.

the work: 'From a strictly philosophical point of view, the most interesting feature of *Schopenhauer as Educator* is perhaps the complex theory of the self that is sketched – or rather, presupposed – in the first few sections of that work', and he explains that *Schopenhauer as Educator* contains, in compressed form, 'one of the earliest expositions of a distinctively Nietzschean theory of selfhood, one that directly anticipates many of the features found in his later remarks on the subject, while possessing a clarity that the latter sometimes lack'.[26] While I agree with Breazeale that this is the most interesting aspect of the work, I would insist on the fact that this theory is presupposed rather than elaborated at great length. With that said, let us consider what Nietzsche proposes in section 1.

Nietzsche claims 'We are accountable to ourselves for our own existence;[27] consequently, we also want to be the real helmsmen of our existence and keep it from resembling a mindless coincidence' (SE §1). Further, he adds, 'your true being does not lie deeply hidden within you, but rather immeasurably high above you, or at least above what you commonly take to be your ego' (SE §1). It is important to unpack these statements. In the first one, Nietzsche posits that we are responsible for our own being and for what we make of it. It is not enough to be born with a certain set of qualities, we must endeavour to actualise them. Indeed, as Robertson remarks, 'there may be people who, having relinquished morality's grip, either do not pursue the highest excellences [as the free spirits will do] or else do but fail to realize them'.[28] These have an important presence in *Thus Spoke Zarathustra* under the guise of the last men, for example. What this statement entails is that we must take our own becoming in our hands, making it our responsibility. The term 'helmsmen'

---

[26] Ibid. p. 13. Breazeale's arguments about this work point again to the difficulty related to dividing the Nietzschean corpus into neatly separated periods. Things are messier than this in the elaboration of Nietzsche's philosophy. I have made that point earlier in relation to the pursuit of truth.

[27] The German has 'Dasein'. While I see a connection here with Heidegger's usage, see note 56 in Chapter 2 above for Kaufmann's comments on Nietzsche's usage.

[28] Simon Robertson, 'Normativity for Nietzschean Free Spirits', p. 611 n33.

(*Steuermänner*) which is used here indicates that we can gear our existence in certain ways and, thus, we can be held responsible for the direction we give ourselves.[29] In *Human, All Too Human*, Nietzsche writes,

> Everyone *possesses inborn talent*, but few possess the degree of inborn and acquired toughness, endurance and energy actually to become a talent, that is to say to *become* what he *is*; which means to discharge it in works and actions. (HH I §263)

It is presumably the free spirits who will have that strength.

In the second statement, Nietzsche introduces the notion of authenticity with the term 'true being' (*eigentliche Selbst*). It is not deeply hidden within oneself, as the metaphysical tradition would have it. When Nietzsche speaks of self-knowledge, it is not a matter of introspecting in order to uncover what one is and do nothing with it. Instead, it is a matter of discovering oneself through one's actions and the steering of one's existence. This is expressed in the later imperative found in *The Gay Science*: '*What does your conscience say?* – "You shall become the person you are"' (GS §270). That self, *das eigentliche Selbst*, the one that we must become, is our ethical goal.[30] But the key to authenticity, as said before, is to know oneself. To understand what one is, is the key to one's authentic ethical becoming. And, as Nietzsche says,

> No one can build for you the bridge upon which you alone must cross the stream of life, no one but you alone . . . There is one single path in this world on which no one but you can travel. (SE §1)

---

[29] Note that this image is close to that offered by Descartes with regard to the connection between mind and body in the sixth meditation wherein he explores the possibility that the mind is in a body 'as a sailor is in a ship'. There, he rejects the view that they would be radically separated and offers instead that the mind is intermingled with the body (see Descartes, *Meditations on First Philosophy*). In Nietzsche's case, it is interesting to note that this view allows for the tension between essentialism and anti-essentialism, that is, between a self that is already what it is and a self that is self-created.

[30] Golomb points out that 'To become "what we are" is not to live according to our so-called "innate nature," but to create ourselves freely' ('Introductory Essay', p. 13).

Knowing oneself is the key to becoming oneself. However, in order to know oneself, one must be freed from traditional understandings of morality and the moral self. Which is why, in *Ecce Homo*, Nietzsche seems to refute the importance of self-knowledge by saying:

> To become what one is, one must not have the faintest notion what one is. From this point of view even the blunders of life have their own meaning and value – the occasional side roads and wrong roads, the delays, 'modesties,' seriousness wasted on tasks that are remote from the task. All this can express a great prudence, even the supreme prudence: where *nosce te ipsum* would be the recipe for ruin, forgetting oneself, misunderstanding oneself, making oneself smaller, narrower, mediocre, become reason itself. (EH 'Why I am so Clever' §9)

However, rather than dismiss the importance of self-knowledge, I would argue that what Nietzsche is emphasising here is the experimental aspect of self-discovery as well as the notion that we make ourselves through our deeds. We must do so while being free from preconceived notions of who or what we are. In any case, the free spirit may possess this virtue; she has freed herself from traditional understandings.[31] Nietzsche explains further the meaning of this imperative to become the person one is by saying:

> We, however, *want to become those we are* – human beings who are new, unique, incomparable, who give themselves

---

[31] As Ken Gemes puts it, 'Before he can construct an ideal of the future unified active self of the Overman he must destroy the idol of the unified Cartesian self' ('Postmodernism's Use and Abuse of Nietzsche', p. 354). While Gemes refers specifically to the *Übermensch*, I believe this applies equally to the free spirit. Gemes also indicates that the postmodernists have misunderstood the point of Nietzsche's rejection of the notion of a unified Cartesian self. He says: 'the problem with the notion of a unified free Cartesian soul is not that it is a metaphysical error but that it covers up the problem of becoming' (Ibid. p. 353). As I am arguing here, the unity of the self that ought to be pursued by the free spirit is the unity of the dynamic becoming of a subjectivity that is conceived as multiple and as intentional consciousness as described in earlier chapters.

laws, who create themselves. To that end we must become the best learners and discoverers of everything that is lawful and necessary in the world: we must become physicists in order to be able to be *creators* in this sense – while hitherto all valuations and ideals have been based on *ignorance* of physics or were constructed so as to *contradict* it. Therefore: long live physics! And even more so that which *compels* us to turn to physics – our honesty! (GS §335)

Here again, the virtues of honesty and authenticity are emphasised, as are the related virtues of creativity, self-mastery and knowledge, understood as both self-knowledge and knowledge of the world. In fact, Nietzsche associates authenticity, being who one is, with knowledge to such an extent that it is as much an ethical virtue as it is an epistemological one. The free spirit engages in lawgiving, in norm creation, as a result of having freed herself from metaphysical and moral discourses. Nietzsche says,

> Insofar as the individual is seeking happiness, one ought not to tender him any prescriptions as to the path to happiness: for individual happiness springs from one's own unknown laws, and prescriptions from without can only obstruct and hinder it. (D §108)

What matters for the free spirit is not which norm she will create for herself but, rather, the manner in which these norms are adopted; namely, through a process of critical enquiry commanded by the virtue of authenticity and its correlate, honesty.[32] As Golomb puts it, it is not the content of the norms adopted by the free spirit that matter but rather the manner in which they are adopted.[33]

The free spirit will engage in a transvaluation of values as a result of their constructive nihilism. Taking themselves as

---

[32] This is why the virtue ethics offered by Nietzsche revolves around the individual and its own virtues rather than resting on universal principles.
[33] See Jacob Golomb, 'Nietzsche on Authenticity', p. 247.

the measuring stick, they will reject any morality that consists in negating the human as it is. Any morality that represses the body and the instinctual, that praises its repression and harsh control for fear of sin, is a morality that is detrimental to the flourishing of the human as the embodied consciousness that it is. The free spirit who knows themselves as such will reject a morality that wants to turn them into an ascetic, a being who, with only their mind and faith, would control and crush their body. Christian morality is replete with commandments that are alienating for a being of flesh like the human. The Kantian categorical imperative is another refinement of this disembodied view of the human by emphasising the power of reason and wilful determination in practical deliberation and moral action. However, this is resting on a distorted view of the human which does not consider it as what it is: an embodied consciousness that is a bundle of drives and instincts, the subjective multiplicity and the grand reason of the body that we discussed. The free spirit therefore rejects any morality that does not take into account the human being as it is. This nihilism is based on her own understanding of the human, established through a sceptical and phenomenological enquiry devoid of metaphysical biases. It is a constructive nihilism because, as Nietzsche claims and I have quoted earlier, 'We negate and must negate because something in us wants to live and affirm – something that we perhaps do not know or see as yet' (GS §307). In *Ecce Homo*, he specifies again that 'denial and destruction is a condition of affirmation' (EH 'Destiny' §4). This constructive nihilism opens the pathway to a virtue ethics grounded on the phenomenological positions adopted.[34] 'I contradict as has never been contradicted and am nonetheless the opposite of a negative spirit' (EH 'Destiny' §1).

---

[34] For an analysis of the different types of nihilisms in Nietzsche, the ones he rejects and the one he embraces, see my *Le Nihilisme est-il un Humanisme?* See also my 'Sartre and Nietzsche: Brothers in Arms'. It is interesting that Nietzsche takes himself as an exemplar of this nihilistic attitude: 'I contradict as has never been contradicted and am nonetheless the opposite of a negative spirit' (EH 'Destiny' §1). As mentioned, he is the one who has unveiled the truth about metaphysics and morality, the one in whom the

Nietzsche speaks of the *homo poeta* as the one who has 'slain all gods' (GS §153). Having rejected morality and declared the death of God (GS §125), one is in a position to create both oneself and the world anew. He repeats that 'we want to be the poets of our life – first of all in the smallest, most everyday matters' (GS §299). This is another admonition to pay attention to the things closest to us and the world around us. Aphorism 270, quoted above, summarises the virtue of authenticity: 'You shall become the person you are' (GS §270). It is part of an interesting *Gedanken-kette* that closes Book III of *The Gay Science*. Book III is the culmination of Nietzsche's critique of morality in that it declares the death of God and opens with a call for a naturalisation of humanity 'in terms of a pure, newly discovered, newly redeemed nature' (GS §109), the redeemed nature praised in aphorism 335, among others.[35] Aphorisms 269 to 275 summarise in very short format what is required for the

revaluation of values has become flesh. This is what makes him dynamite (EH 'Destiny' §1, see also note 45 in Chapter 1 above). Further, in the last sections of *Ecce Homo*, he asks three times as a means to open the aphorisms whether he has been understood. He says: 'Have I been understood? – What defines me, what sets me apart from all the rest of mankind, is that I have unmasked Christian morality' and what horrifies him in it 'is the lack of nature, it is the utterly ghastly fact that anti-nature itself has received the highest honours as morality, and has hung over mankind as law, as categorical imperative!' (EH 'Destiny' §7). Further again, 'Have I been understood? – . . . The unmasking of Christian morality is an event without equal, a real catastrophe. He who exposes it is a *force majeure*, a destiny – he breaks the history of mankind into two parts' (EH 'Destiny' §8). It is a matter of health for the human being as embodied multiple subjectivity, for himself as such, for himself as a free spirit who has sought and exposed the truth about himself and the world, to expose the lies of Christian morality and other rationalist avatars. Finally, he wraps up the book with 'Have I been understood? – *Dionysos against the Crucified . . .*' (EH 'Destiny' §9). By taking himself as an example, by making his philosophy personal and the story of his recovery, he is indicating that such pursuits will always be individual projects. My thanks go to Daniel W. Conway for bringing up this point._

[35] It should be noted that this naturalisation does not make of Nietzsche the naturalist thinker some commentators have wanted to make him. Recall the arguments presented earlier to reject this reading.

free spirit to become the person they are. It is worth quoting this part as a whole.

> *In what do you believe?* – In this, that the weights of all things must be determined anew. (GS §269)
> *What does your conscience say?* – 'You shall become the person you are.' (GS §270)
> *Where are your greatest dangers?* – In pity. (GS §271)
> *What do you love in others?* – My hopes. (GS §272)
> *Whom do you call bad?* – Those who always want to put to shame. (GS §273)
> *What do you consider most humane?* – To spare someone shame. (GS §274)
> *What is the seal of liberation?* – No longer being ashamed in front of oneself. (GS §275)[36]

Those who put to shame are deemed bad because they erected moralities that made being good always impossible for individuals and set up ideals that were negations of the 'nature' of human beings. However, one may become what one is now that morality has been vanquished along with the metaphysical views that were alienating for human beings, leading them to be ashamed of themselves. This entails that one must create values for oneself. Indeed, dismissing metaphysical views means that one has a renewed access to things themselves and can engage in an interpretation and valuation of things and of oneself since, as I have explained, this is always a bidirectional process of constitution. With regard to what he says about pity as dangerous, this relates to his view on the necessity to associate with individuals that can contribute to elevate oneself. The process of becoming what one is requires agonistic friendships, as we will see shortly. Pity towards oneself or towards others is possible only when one associates with weaker individuals but

---

[36] In a note, Kaufmann remarks that this ties back to the last sentence of the concluding aphorism of Book II where he says, 'And as long as you are in any way *ashamed* before yourselves, you do not yet belong with us' (GS §107).

also when one is entrapped in moral thinking.[37] Those relationships are unhealthy for all concerned as they do not allow for the growth towards oneself that Nietzsche is looking for. One must be able to engage with others in whom one can see one's hopes. Finally, this *Gedanken-kette* may be said to extend to the first aphorism of Book IV where Nietzsche says,

> I want to learn more and more to see as beautiful what is necessary in things: then I shall be one of those who make things beautiful. *Amor fati*: let that be my love henceforth! ... Looking away shall be my only negation. And all in all and on the whole: some day I wish to be only a Yes-sayer. (GS §276)

The free spirit who has freed themselves from the shackles of metaphysics, religion and morality must overcome nihilism by being an affirmative spirit. In *Daybreak*, Nietzsche warns the thinker, and I would say that his warning applies to the free spirit and to all: 'Woe to the thinker who is not the gardener but only the soil of the plants that grow in him!' (D §382). Indeed, it is key for one to relate to oneself and create oneself and not merely be the passive subject of one's experiences, as discussed above. As Ansell-Pearson points out, the genuine ego that one ought to put in place 'is a construction and work in progress, centred on the cultivation of drives'.[38] He is referring to an aphorism I have already quoted in part where Nietzsche is criticising those who let themselves be fully constituted by the 'fog of habits and opinions'. He says: 'no individual among this majority is capable of setting up a real ego [*ergründetes ego*], accessible to him and fathomed by him, in opposition to the

---

[37] Rebecca Bamford notes that 'Reading Nietzsche's critique [of pity] as a part of his broader cultural concern with the problem of nihilism underlines the active need which Nietzsche has to challenge our moral intuitions about the phenomenon of *Mitleid*' ('The Virtue of Shame', p. 245).

[38] Keith Ansell-Pearson, 'Questions of the Subject in Nietzsche and Foucault', p. 427. In another essay, Ansell-Pearson notes that 'There is a kind of "core" for Nietzsche, but this is simply the potential for a self' ('In Search of Authenticity and Personality', p. 285).

general pale fiction and thereby annihilating it' (D §105). And yet, this is precisely the task that lays ahead.[39]

The Free Spirit and Agonistic Friendship

One of the most important obligations to fulfil for the free spirit is to be master of oneself. Self-mastery entails self-knowledge. Learning about things is important but it is of most importance to learn about ourselves (WS §266) – perhaps through knowing things as discussed earlier. In 'The Wanderer and his Shadow', Nietzsche emphasises the importance of the other who can assist one in knowing oneself. He explains that it is important to have friends who will give us access to our own fortress (WS §491), that we need others as railings for our own development (WS §600), and that we must be open to the voice of others and the situation. We are not rigid single individuums (WS §618) and we are certainly not autarkic entities. Everyone needs a complement, a shadow (WS §258).

One must be one's own lawgiver, be a free spirit who embodies all the characteristics and virtues mentioned. But it remains that the very being of the human, the fact that we are ontologically dependent on others and always in their presence, requires that this becoming happens in relation to others. Rosalyn Diprose has pointed this out from a different angle while comparing Nietzsche and Merleau-Ponty. She explains that Nietzsche's philosophy comprises an openness to the other that is often disregarded. She claims that 'The distance necessary to self-overcoming is given in proximity to others'.[40] Her point is that

---

[39] Relating this to what Nietzsche says later in D §119 about the fully-grown polyp and how its nature is contingent, Ansell-Pearson notes that 'The ethical task in Nietzsche, it would seem, is not to allow oneself to be this mere happenstance' ('Questions of the Subject in Nietzsche and Foucault', p. 428). He also notes that 'The philosophical and ethical therapy Nietzsche is proposing in *Daybreak* appears to be directed at those solitary free spirits who exist on the margin of society and seek to cultivate or fashion new ways of thinking and feeling, attempting to do this by taking the time necessary to work through their experiences' (Ibid. p. 432).

[40] Rosalyn Diprose, *Corporeal Generosity*, p. 27.

if one was caught in a solipsistic trap, there would be nothing pushing one to overcome oneself. For self-overcoming to be possible, therefore, interaction with the other is required. But not just any other. If it is true that the subject is ontologically dependent on others – if it is constituted by the others with whom it is in relation as a being-with-others – it becomes imperative that the individual be in the company of the 'right' individuals. In a way, a member of the herd cannot help but share in the herd mentality: the herd permeates them as they permeate it. Likewise, a noble soul will be noble in virtue of being permeated by the noble mentality if they associate with likewise noble individuals.[41] To reiterate with Diprose, 'it is because my body is given to others and vice versa that I exist as a social being. Hence, corporeal identity is never singular, always ambiguous, neither simply subject nor object.'[42] In this context, who one associates with is crucial for the being-with-others one is. Nietzsche understands so much when he says: 'Are you a slave? If so, you cannot be a friend. Are you a tyrant? If so, you cannot have friends' (TSZ 'Friend'). As Robert C. Miner explains, 'there are human types with whom it is *unhealthy* to be friends'.[43]

This is why free spirits need to find other free spirits to keep company and why Nietzsche's views of friendship imply an agonistic relation. Simply put: one must engage in relations with others that will bring the best out of oneself.[44] As we have seen, in his preface to *Human, All Too Human*, Nietzsche explained that he invented the free spirits when he had a need for them, 'as compensation for the friends I lacked' (HH I 'Preface' §2). However, those free spirits *qua* friends have to serve an important ethical

---

[41] In this context, Zarathustra's ten-year retreat in a cave in the company of his animals (each representing higher virtues) may be read as a way to ensure that he is not 'infected' by the lower men and last men. Interestingly, when he emerges out of his retreat and goes back to men, he does become sick! But he does feel the urge to go back to men and come down from his cave, 'to be man again'. However, 'Thus began Zarathustra's down-going' (TSZ 'Prologue' §1). Also consider note 9, Chapter 4 above.
[42] Rosalyn Diprose, *Corporeal Generosity*, p. 4.
[43] Robert C. Miner, 'Nietzsche on Friendship', p. 49.
[44] See Daniel I. Harris, 'Friendship as Shared Joy in Nietzsche', pp. 199–221.

function beyond keeping one's good company. Nietzsche speaks of a 'refined concept of friendship' belonging to noble morality.[45] Others with whom we engage will serve as role models if they are higher types, in Nietzsche's case, free spirits/friends. But, more deeply, being in the presence of such individuals should entice us to overcome ourselves which is the Nietzschean ethical imperative that he put forward as '"You shall become the person you are"' (GS §270). Nietzsche explains, 'In your friend you should possess your best enemy. Your heart should feel closest to him when you oppose him . . . You cannot adorn yourself too well for your friend: for you should be to him an arrow and a longing for the [Overhuman]' (TSZ 'Friend' translation modified). The friend should pull us upwards, should serve as that stepladder towards our highest self.

This agonistic relation affects our very being. The ontological relation to the other that I have described earlier implies that, in such relations, our being-in-the-world is modified ontologically but that also, as a result, our ethical being is shaped and modified by these relations. In his article on the Nietzschean notion of friendship, Miner emphasises the ethical role of friendship if it is established on an agonistic relation with the other.[46] He further suggests that friendship, for Nietzsche, rests upon a search for truth. When it aims at such, it must be construed in agonistic terms, otherwise: 'If friendship becomes content with the mere tolerance of difference or otherwise loses its oppositional character, it becomes a counterfeit of itself.'[47]

---

[45] See Robert C. Miner, 'Nietzsche on Friendship', p. 69. In this passage, he is referring to what Nietzsche proposes in BGE §260. This is the aphorism in which Nietzsche famously distinguishes between the master morality and the slave morality.

[46] Ibid.

[47] Ibid. p. 49. Miner further explains that friendship among higher types requires a balancing of qualities and that 'The highest friendships are difficult to maintain. This is true, I have shown, because they require their participants to hold at least three pairs of opposed qualities in a delicate balance. These are love of self, along with dissatisfaction with self; candor toward the friend, along with appropriate reserve and perhaps even the occasional deception; and solitude and companionship' (Ibid. p. 56).

Relations with others need to be nurtured so that they can put the individual on the path of self-overcoming. Only agonistic relations will serve that purpose for oneself and for the friend. Ontologically, my relation to the other is fundamentally constitutive of myself. Ethically, it determines whether I will engage on the path of self-overcoming. Politically, it will be the determining factor of whether social groups flourish and bring humanity closer to Overhumanity. As Rosalyn Diprose puts it, in Nietzsche, 'The political is ontological, but only insofar as it is always intersubjective.'[48] The ontological grounds the ethical and the political. We are being-with-others ontologically, ethically and politically. Individually, we need others to push us on the path of self-overcoming. Friendship is thus essential to one's flourishing. However, genuine friendship is possible only among equals who are willing to engage in agonistic relations. Following what was said above we need to keep in mind that 'equals' here does not entail a strict equality. Indeed, if two individuals were the same, they could not engage in this dynamic agonistic relation.

As Nietzsche continues to deal with the concept of the free spirit in the writings that follow the *Freigeisterei*, he gradually feels the limitations of this concept. He claims that the concept may have put morality on its head but is itself moral in the end. Saying that the free spirit is 'accomplished', he claims that it is not his ideal.[49] While the concept morphs and evolves and is eventually replaced by the *Übermensch* as the ethical ideal we must strive for, Nietzsche retains the concept of the free spirit and discusses it again in *Beyond Good and Evil*. There are some significant differences between the free spirit of *Human, All Too Human* and the later iteration, not so much as to the nature of the concept itself as to the role Nietzsche attributes it.[50] In

---

[48] Rosalyn Diprose, *Corporeal Generosity*, p. 176.
[49] See pp. 000 above for this discussion.
[50] For more details on the free spirit as it occurs in *Beyond Good and Evil* and *Human, All Too Human*, one can consult the essays by Christa Acampora, Katrina Mitcheson and Richard Schacht in Rebecca Bamford (ed.), *Nietzsche's Free Spirit Philosophy*.

Part Two of *Beyond Good and Evil*, Nietzsche still advocates for adopting a critical stance towards knowledge, one of the key features of the free spirit. He also revisits the idea that the world is erroneous and has been created by us and anticipates the sections of *Twilight of the Idols* where he rejects both the real and the apparent world.[51] The free spirit is again considered to be the one who sees clearly into what is, that is '*voir clair dans ce qui est*' (to see clearly into what is; BGE §39). Nietzsche is quoting Stendhal's description of a good philosopher as a definition of 'A final trait for the image of the free-spirited philosopher' (ibid.). To see clearly into the being of things, into what is, is an important trait and one that has been indicated in previous works as we have seen. But Nietzsche also indicates that, 'A new species of philosophers is coming up' (BGE §42). These philosophers of the future, as he calls them, will be experimenters (*Versuchers*). He conceives of them as related to the free spirits and yet different. He says:

> they, too, will be free, *very* free spirits, these philosophers of the future – though just as certainly they will not be merely free spirits but something more, higher, greater, and thoroughly different that does not want to be misunderstood and mistaken for something else. (BGE §44)

Whether the philosopher of the future, as *very* free spirit, is an improvement over the ideal of the free spirit as conceived in *Human, All Too Human* is a question I do not wish to settle.[52] It is clear that the free spirit has paved the way for the later figures of the *Übermensch* and philosopher of the future and that they share a lot of the same characteristics. In *The Gay Science*, he speaks of the free spirits in terms of 'preparatory human

---

[51] See in particular the series of aphorisms 34, 35 and 36 in BGE as we discussed them in the last section of Chapter 3.

[52] Here I only want to gesture towards the distinctions that Nietzsche envisions and not dwell on a detailed analysis of them. The reader will refer to the essay by Jacob Golomb, who has explored the subtle differences between the concepts of 'we free spirits' and 'free spirit par excellence' in his 'Can One Really Become a "Free Spirit Par Excellence" or an Übermensch'.

beings'. With their strength and various qualities, they pave the way for Overhumanity. Nietzsche claims that they are:

> human beings who know how to be silent, lonely, resolute, and content and constant in invisible activities; human beings who are bent on seeking in all things for what in them must be *overcome*; human beings distinguished as much by cheerfulness, patience, unpretentiousness . . . The secret for harvesting from existence the greatest fruitfulness and the greatest enjoyment is – to *live dangerously*! Build your cities on the slopes of Vesuvius! Send your ships into uncharted seas! Live at war with your peers and yourselves! Be robbers and conquerors as long as you cannot be rulers and possessors, you seekers of knowledge! (GS §283)

We recognise in this description some of the characteristics that Nietzsche has been attributing to the free spirit. The admonition to live dangerously goes hand in hand with the call for free spirits to have courage and will to truth. The call to send 'ships into uncharted seas' refers back to aphorism 124 of the same book, immediately preceding that of 'The madman' (GS §125). In it, Nietzsche says:

> We have left the land and have embarked. We have burned our bridges behind us – indeed, we have gone farther and destroyed the land behind us. Now little ship, look out! Beside you is the ocean: to be sure, it does not always roar, and at times it lies spread out like silk and gold and reveries of graciousness. But hours will come when you will realize that it is infinite and that there is nothing more awesome than infinity . . . Woe, when you feel homesick for the land as if it had offered more freedom – and there is no longer any 'land'. (GS §124)[53]

---

[53] As Kaufmann notes, this relates directly to one of the poems in the appendix 'Songs of Prince *Vogelfrei*' (free as a bird or a freedom bird as described in GS §294 and akin to the free spirit). The poem goes: 'That way is my will; I trust / In my mind and in my grip. / Without plan, into the vast / Open sea I head my ship'.

Free spirits who have exercised their critical enquiries into traditional discourses have 'burned the bridges' and made the land disappear. The ship is left to explore and wander according to its own will. One must become a creator and affirm the infinite possibilities laying ahead of one. The free spirit is conceived as having that strength in the middle period writings. In addition, Nietzsche calls for them to 'live at war', that is to say, to engage in agonistic relationships that will allow them to flourish and overcome themselves.

The free spirit as a preparatory human being is a very strong figure. But new figures and variations on that ideal move us towards the *Übermensch*. These may be conceived as fine-tuning and improvement of the ethical ideal embodied by the free spirit. Notwithstanding the later improvements, I believe we can consider the concept of the free spirit as introduced in *Human, All Too Human* as a viable ethical ideal. It is the ethical ideal of authenticity and search for truth that we should all aim for, an ethical ideal grounded in the phenomenological positions adopted. That ideal is also pursued through a re-evaluation of values which lead one to be the creator of one's own values. And, as Nietzsche himself puts it, the free spirit is a preparatory human being for what is yet to come, a necessary stage for human beings' progress towards themselves. The Overhuman will represent the last 'stage' in this progress. As the embodiment of the dynamic becoming one is, the Overhuman supersedes the earlier ideal of the free spirit but maintains the features of the multi-layered embodied consciousness in the world and with others that Nietzsche has established.

6
Becoming Overhuman

The figure of the Overhuman is a key concept in Nietzsche's philosophy and, yet, it is one that still lacks clarity. Why is that? As we will see, Nietzsche's language around that key notion is highly metaphorical and evocative rather than descriptive. This leaves room for much interpretation. But if we are to be the careful readers Nietzsche wants us to be, we need to pay attention to key features that cohere with his description of the human being and its relations to the world and others. This requires that we do not construe the Overhuman as a state to be achieved, some kind of fixed outcome of a process of ethical improvement and flourishing. Rather, the Overhuman is itself a dynamic ideal, one that continually unfolds through a process of self-overcoming, thereby embodying the will to power and manifold conscious being that it is. It is a being that, out of necessity, is a becoming. At the risk of offering a *contradictio in adjecto* to describe the Overhuman, it is a being whose essence is to perpetually become. As we will see, for this to be possible one must embrace an ethics that is affirmative through and through. This entails turning one's back resolutely to moralities and ascetic points of view that alienate the human. We will also see that the only ethics that can lead to Overhumanity is a free-spirited virtue ethics that seeks the affirmation of life.

The Figure of the Overhuman

In her essay on Nietzsche's type of naturalism, Christa Davis Acampora defines the Nietzschean subject as an agonistic subject.

This subject is the embodiment of the tensions that it is as a bundle of drives and subjective multiplicity that I have described in Chapter 3. Acampora also uses the phrase 'agonized subject' which I find more resonant with what Nietzsche proposes given that it conveys the dynamic becoming that this subject is and must be, also being constituted by external forces. She says:

> Nietzsche's agonistic subject is at war with himself – or, to be more precise, is a war himself – but unlike Nietzsche's predecessors, who also grant that the human is subject to conflict and who have sought to eliminate this struggle as a way of gaining mastery over the self, Nietzsche often suggests it is the maintenance and sustenance of such discord that constitutes the best life as he sees it. What kind of morality could possibly be generated from this disharmony and dissonance? ... Nietzsche conceives a possibility of deriving values out of conflict in such a way that it both cultivates the subject characterized in the manner described above, which is to say it provides some organization (without elimination) of conflicting forces, and supplies a mechanism for deriving values that can be flexible and responsive to the becoming constituents of the communities such values bind and define.[1]

The morality that ensues is an 'ethos of the agonized subject'. I contend that this agonised subject is none other than the Overhuman.

It is in *Thus Spoke Zarathustra* that the figure of the Overhuman is most extensively and most famously discussed. In other works, one may find only a few occurrences and oblique references to the concept. In *Ecce Homo* again, however, Nietzsche refers to it quite a bit, in the section on *Zarathustra*, in particular, but also in the section 'Why I write such excellent books' where he laments that the concept has been repeatedly misinterpreted (EH 'Books' §1), as well as in the section 'Why I am

---

[1] Acampora, Christa Davis, 'Naturalism and Nietzsche's Moral Psychology', p. 326.

a destiny', in which he refers back to Zarathustra's determination that even the highest men he has encountered would call his Overhuman a devil (EH 'Destiny' §5). This is, of course, reminiscent of how free spirits are perceived by fettered spirits as evil and as a threat (HH I §241). The Overhuman is the first element of Zarathustra's teaching once he encounters people on the market square of the town nearest from the mountain he just left at the beginning in section 1 of the Prologue. He says: '*I teach you the Overhuman. Man is something that should be overcome*' (TSZ 'Prologue' §3).² Again, he says that:

> Man is a rope, fastened between animal and Overhuman – a rope over an abyss ... What is great in man is that he is a bridge and not a goal; what can be loved in man is that he is a *going-across* and a *down-going*. (TSZ 'Prologue' §4)

And again, 'What is the ape to men? A laughing-stock or a painful embarrassment. And just so shall man be to the Overhuman: a laughing-stock and a painful embarrassment' (TSZ 'Prologue' §3). I have said that it is of prime importance for the individual to know oneself. But this knowledge of oneself ought to be a prompter to overcome oneself. Indeed, knowing oneself as the embodiment of will to power and the field of tensions generated by the bundle of drives one is should be followed by the desire to embrace dynamic becoming for oneself. The Overhuman is such a wilful dynamic becoming. In his analysis of the notion of the self in Nietzsche, Miner explains that it is 'a matter of both construction and discovery ... A person who "discovers

---

² In all quotations referencing the concept of the *Übermensch*, from *Thus Spoke Zarathustra, Ecce Homo* and *The Anti-Christ*, I will replace the term chosen by Hollingdale to translate *Übermensch*, 'superman', with the more appropriate and accurate 'Overhuman'. The 'über' (over) in *Übermensch* is meant to convey the dynamic process of becoming that Nietzsche sees at work in human beings and wants them to embrace actively. Simply put, then, to translate it as 'superman' indicates an augmentation or perfection of the type 'man' that Nietzsche in fact rejects in favour of a radical transformation, as this quote readily indicates from the get-go by saying that 'man' must be overcome.

himself" has not completed the task of becoming what he is. On the contrary, Nietzsche says, it marks the point at which the task begins.'³ For Ansell-Pearson, becoming Overhuman is a becoming what we are. He says, 'We will grow and become the ones that we are, however, only by experiencing dissatisfaction with ourselves and assuming the risk of experimenting in life, even to the point of living unwisely, freely taking the journey through our wastelands, quagmires, and icy glaciers.'⁴ This again points to the notion of embracing oneself as dynamic becoming.

Nietzsche claims that:

> The Overhuman is the meaning of the earth. Let your will say: The Overhuman *shall be* the meaning of the earth! I entreat you, my brothers, *remain true to the earth*, and do not believe those who speak to you of superterrestrial hopes! (TSZ 'Prologue' §3)

While this is a clear call to move away from metaphysical and moral theories that dismiss the immanent in favour of the transcendent realm, it also relates to the notion of a human world that we have discussed as a phenomenological concept. Indeed, in the section 'Of the Bestowing Virtue', he says:

> Stay loyal to the earth, my brothers, with the power of your virtue! May your bestowing love and your knowledge serve towards the meaning of the earth! ... Lead, as I do, the flown-away virtue back to earth – yes, back to body and life: that it may give the earth its meaning, a human meaning! ... May your spirit and your virtue serve the meaning of the earth, my brothers: and may the value of all things be fixed

---

[3] Robert C. Miner, 'Nietzsche's Fourfold Conception of the Self', p. 349. In his essay, Miner distinguishes between the deepest self, the 'I', the higher self and the true self. The true self would be one that knows itself in all of its aspects and refuses stagnation by embracing its being as this dynamic inner multiplicity.

[4] Keith Ansell-Pearson, 'In Search of Authenticity and Personality', p. 304.

anew by you. To that end you should be fighters! To that end you should be creators! (TSZ 'Bestowing Virtue' §2)

It is crucial to return to the earth and to the body and this is what the Overhuman, as the meaning of the earth, will embody. This entails not only seeking truth but also embracing it. As Ansell-Pearson puts it, 'Proving equal to the task of "incorporating" truth and knowledge constitutes an essential dimension of what it means for us to become the overhuman ones that we paradoxically are.'[5] He believes that perspectivism plays a key role in this exercise of incorporating truth. However, not just any perspective will do: 'There is, in fact, a principal "perspective" at work in Nietzsche's thinking which is that of "life".'[6] Recall what Zarathustra says about this: 'Where I found a living creature, there I found will to power' (TSZ 'Of Self-Overcoming') and 'And life itself told me this secret: "Behold," it said, "I am that *which must overcome itself again and again*"' (TSZ 'Of Self-Overcoming').

The incorporation of truth that Ansell-Pearson discusses is a manifold process and entails the acceptance and embrace of a number of things. Among those is the acceptance of life and of oneself as will to power as well as *amor fati* and the accompanying ethical proposal of the eternal recurrence. As we have seen, Nietzsche declares in *The Gay Science* that he wants 'to be only a Yes-sayer' (GS §276). This is expressed many times in *Thus Spoke Zarathustra*. In the section 'Of Redemption', it is connected with the idea of human beings as fragmented. He says:

> I walk among men as among the fragments and limbs of men! The terrible thing to my eye is to find men shattered in pieces and scattered as if over a battle-field of slaughter ... I walk among men as among fragments of the future: of that future which I see ... To redeem the past and to transform

[5] Keith Ansell-Pearson, 'The Incorporation of Truth', p. 241.
[6] Ibid. p. 243.

every 'it was' into an 'I wanted it thus!' – that alone do I call redemption!' (TSZ 'Of Redemption')[7]

For human beings to be authentic and no longer fragmented there is a need to affirm life and oneself. To be clear: the fragments he is referring to here are not the same as the inner multiplicity of the subject that we have discussed. Rather, he sees human beings as fragmented and alienated by metaphysical and religious views that introduce splits and hierarchies between the mind and the body, between the individual and the world, between individuals themselves. Superimposing these erroneous distinctions on the lived reality of the human causes them to be alienated and fragmented, to be the fragments of what they could be, were they allowed to authentically thrive as the beings they are. For this to happen, some radical transformation is needed in that, beyond rejecting alienating views, one must embrace a novel view on life and oneself.

Transforming oneself is not easy, to say the least. This difficulty is well-illustrated in the famous passage 'Of the Vision and the Riddle': 'I saw a young shepherd writhing, choking, convulsed, his face distorted; and a heavy, black snake was hanging out of his mouth. Had I ever seen so much disgust and pallid horror on a face?' Zarathustra tries to help the shepherd by pulling on the snake, in vain. He finally entreats him to bite the snake's head off:

> Who is the shepherd into whose mouth the snake thus crawled? Who is the man into whose throat all that is heaviest, blackest will thus crawl? The shepherd, however, bit as my cry had advised him; he bit with a good bite! He spat far away the snake's head – and sprang up. No longer a shepherd, no longer a man – a transformed being, surrounded with light, laughing! Never yet on earth had any man laughed as

---

[7] I have altered Hollingdale's translation of 'jener Zukunft, die ich schaue' as 'of that future which I scan' to 'of that future which I see'. Zarathustra observes the sorry state in which human beings find themselves, thanks to the alienation suffered at the hand of the metaphysical-religious tradition.

he laughed! O my brothers, I heard a laughter that was no human laughter—. (TSZ 'Of the Vision and the Riddle' §2)

This passage is to be related to 'The Greatest Weight' in *The Gay Science* in which the demon announces the eternal recurrence of all things, great and small. That thought experiment will leave one either gnashing one's teeth and cursing the demon or accepting the thought and calling him a god. Nietzsche says: 'If this thought gained possession of you, it would change you as you are or perhaps crush you.' Having it hang over one's thinking in every act of deliberation would be the greatest weight. And he adds: 'how well disposed would you have to become to yourself and to life *to crave nothing more fervently* than this ultimate eternal confirmation and seal?' (GS §341). This is the 'heaviest' that has crawled in the shepherd's throat and which he must, without Zarathustra's or anyone else's help, accept and embrace himself in order to be radically transformed. This is the overcoming of nihilism that is required in order to become an Overhuman, one who can laugh with such roaring laughter, a laughter that goes well beyond the cheerfulness of *The Gay Science*.[8]

The transformation that has to occur from the human being to the free spirit and then to the Overhuman is pretty radical. Nietzsche explains the process on various occasions, more or less directly and more or less poetically. Two passages are particularly illuminating. 'How the "Real World" at last Became a Myth. History of an Error' explains the emergence of the metaphysical worldview and how it came to alienate human beings from reality. This history comprises six different steps with the

---

[8] As Bernd Magnus puts it, 'Recurrence (and its real or possible truth) is a representation of a particular attitude toward life ... The attitude toward life Nietzsche wishes to portray is the opposite of decadence, decline of life, world-weariness. The attitude he wishes to portray is the attitude of affirmation, of overfulness; the attitude which expresses ascending life, life as celebration, life in celebration ... Simply put, again, eternal recurrence expresses the attitude of *Übermenschlichkeit* and is the being-in-the-world of *Übermenschen*' ('Perfectibility and Attitude in Nietzsche's *Übermensch*', p. 646). Accepting eternal recurrence and embracing life as it is, is the fundamental attitude proper to the Overhuman.

last one being the overcoming of metaphysics. The fifth step is that of the critique and rejection of the idea of the 'real world'. It is that of the 'return of cheerfulness and *bon sens* . . . all free spirits run riot' (TI 'Myth'). The sixth step, that of the abolition of both the 'real' and the 'apparent' world, is that of 'Mid-Day; moment of the shortest shadow; end of the longest error; zenith of mankind; INCIPIT ZARATHUSTRA' (TI 'Myth'). This is the great noon, the moment of emergence of truth and of the Overhuman, as we will see below. Zarathustra begins and the Overhuman enters the scene: 'a shadow came to me – the most silent, the lightest of all things came to me! The beauty of the Overhuman came to me as a shadow: what are the gods to me now! . . .' (EH 'Zarathustra' §8). This last step, however, still lies ahead. As Zarathustra says, 'There has never yet been an Overhuman. I have seen them both naked, the greatest and the smallest man. They are still all-too-similar to one another. Truly, I found even the greatest man – all-too-human!' (TSZ 'Priests').[9] This is because they are not capable of the great health yet: 'the great health – that one does not merely have but also acquires continually, and must acquire because one gives it up again and again, and must give it up' (GS §382). The Overhuman is the one capable of great health, the ideal that 'runs ahead of us, a strange, tempting, dangerous ideal . . . the ideal of a human, Overhuman well-being and benevolence that will often appear *inhuman*' (GS §382). The Overhuman surpasses the human being to such a great extent that, just like the free spirit is considered a threat and evil by the fettered spirits, it would be fearful to the higher men:

> Your souls are so unfamiliar with what is great that the Overhuman would be *fearful* to you in his goodness! And you wise and enlightened men, you would flee from the burning sun of wisdom in which the Overhuman joyfully bathes his nakedness! You highest men my eyes have encountered!

---

[9] Many times Nietzsche refers to historical figures as approximations to the Overhuman but they are merely a 'sort of Overhuman' (A §4). See also TI 'Expeditions' §37.

This is my doubt of you and my secret laughter: I think you would call my Overhuman – a devil!' (TSZ 'Of Manly Prudence')[10]

The second passage of interest with regard to transformation is the section 'Of the Three Metamorphoses' in *Thus Spoke Zarathustra*. There Nietzsche describes the transformation from the camel to the lion and then to the child. The camel is the equivalent to the fettered spirit and accepts the burden of the metaphysical worldview and its associated morality. The spirit undergoes a metamorphosis and becomes a lion, 'it wants to capture freedom and be lord in its own desert'. It is the enemy of the 'thou shalt' and it says, 'I will!' However, 'To create new values – even the lion is incapable of that: but to create itself freedom for new creation – that the might of the lion can do.' This metamorphosis of the spirit is the equivalent of the free spirit, it can say no, it has the strength to say no to the greatest 'thou shalt'. However, the lion must still become a child: 'The child is innocence and forgetfulness, a new beginning, a sport, a self-propelling wheel, a first motion, a sacred Yes. Yes, a sacred Yes is needed, my brothers, for the sport of creation: the spirit now wills its own will, the spirit sundered from the world now wins its own world' (TSZ 'Three Metamorphoses'). One must not only 'speak like children'[11] (TSZ 'Of the Despisers of the Body'), but one must also become a child, a yes-sayer, a creator of values, a creator of its own world. Annemarie Pieper suggests that the choice of the name 'child' for this last metamorphosis is indicative of the fact that it is only at this stage that one may be deemed fully human. It is only at this stage of one's development that one begins to live as an individual. The child is the embodiment and expression of the aesthetic reason that allows it to construct values and oneself in a playful manner. To become a child, to become an Overhuman, entails overcoming oneself. The overcoming of oneself allows one to be human in

---

[10] We have seen above that he refers to the Overhuman as evil in EH 'Destiny' §5.
[11] Recall the analysis of this passage in Chapter 3.

an authentic sense.[12] Overcoming oneself does not entail rejecting what one is. It means, instead, actualising one's full being. Nietzsche says: 'Behold, I am a prophet of the lightning and a heavy drop from the cloud: but this lightning is called Overhuman' (TSZ 'Prologue' §4), and further: 'I want to teach men the meaning of their existence: which is the Overhuman, the lightning from the dark cloud man' (TSZ 'Prologue' §7). This is clearly indicative that the Overhuman is an outgrowth of the human being; namely, that it emerges from the depth of the human being and, as an overcoming, an incorporation and fulfilment of its potentiality, 'that future that I see' (TSZ 'Of Redemption'). What is coming is the great noontide:

> And this is the great noontide: it is when man stands at the middle of his course between animal and Overhuman and celebrates his journey to the evening as his highest hope: for it is the journey to a new morning. Then man, going under, will bless himself; for he will be going over to Overhuman, and the sun of his knowledge will stand at noontide. '*All gods are dead: now we want the Overhuman to live*' – let this be our last will one day at the great noontide! (TSZ 'Of the Bestowing Virtue' §3)

The Overhuman is an incorporation of truth and of oneself. It is a fully embodied human being which is as much a body as it is a soul and there is no clear-cut delineation between these 'parts' of itself. It is the embodied, multi-layered consciousness we discussed earlier. The Overhuman is an agent who acts in order to fulfil their own being as an instance of will to power with the aim to flourish as an individual. This means that the Overhuman makes itself the creator of its own values and that they set themself on the path of overcoming. Indeed, being an instance of will to power, the moral agent constantly strives to

---

[12] See Annemarie Pieper, 'Die große Vernunft des Leibes', pp. 66–71. She says, 'The name "child" signifies that it is first with this stage that the human becomes human.' (My translation of 'Der Name "Kind" deutet an, dass erst auf dieser Stufe der Mensch zum Menschen wird' (Ibid. p. 68).)

overcome oneself but also creates the world, oneself, and one's values. Since this valuation happens from the point of view of the situated embodied consciousness, a return to the body is necessary.

Interestingly, Nietzsche's rejection of the alienating morality of the metaphysical-religious tradition leads him to elaborate a new ethics which fosters the flourishing of fully embodied agents, an entirely affirmative ethics. He says:

> At bottom I abhor all those moralities which say: 'Do not do this! Renounce! Overcome yourself!' But I am well disposed toward those moralities which goad me to do something and do it again, from morning till evening, and then to dream of it at night, and to think of nothing except doing this well, as well as *I* alone can do it ... I do not wish to strive with open eyes for my own impoverishment; I do not like negative virtues – virtues whose very essence it is to negate and deny oneself something. (GS §304)

Being affirmative in this sense, his ethics is also a reversal of any morality that rejects any positive role of the body and tries to make of the moral agent a purely rational agent. Many passages in his writings explain what Nietzsche considers objectionable in the traditional view. His attacks on asceticism are informative in this respect. Chapter 3, 'The Religious Life', of *Human, All Too Human* contains a *Gedanken-kette* that presents an early and sustained critique of this aspect of the metaphysical-religious tradition (HH I §§136–44). Herein, he explains that asceticism is a sublimated expression of a defiance of oneself. Asceticism reveals itself as a division of oneself where one part is valued over the other: 'man takes a real delight in oppressing himself with excessive claims and afterwards idolizing this tyrannically demanding something in his soul. In every ascetic morality man worships a part of himself as God and for that he needs to diabolize the other part. –' (HH I §137). Interestingly, the ascetic is also will to power in that they *too* need to wage war (i.e., to overcome). But instead of using this force as a way to overcome oneself as an embodied being, the ascetic wages war against oneself. Christianity, for example, demonised sexuality and thus provided the ascetic with an enemy within. Nietzsche says:

> It is easy to see how designating the ineluctably natural as bad, and then invariably finding it so, makes men themselves worse than they need be. The artifice practised by religion and by those metaphysicians who will have man evil and sinful by nature is to make him suspicious of nature and thus *make* him himself bad: this being a consequence of his inability to divest himself of nature's garb. (HH I §141)

The metaphysical-religious tradition demands that the human being disregards one's embodied being. This demand is impossible to fulfil as one *is* an embodied consciousness, as one's self (the ego, one's consciousness) is body. Nietzsche's critique of this tradition and his ultimate rejection of it stems from his understanding of the human being as fundamentally embodied and multi-layered that we have analysed in earlier chapters.

Nietzsche's human being is not only embodied but *must* be embodied in order to be a truly positive moral agent. One might want to ask how it is possible for a human being to 'have to be' embodied while one is always embodied from the get-go. There is no point X where a human being can be said to be disembodied. As we have seen, consciousness is embodied, of necessity. However, the human being may not be cognizant of the embodied nature of their consciousness. Therefore, the individual must work towards this realisation, i.e., they must make it a reality for them that yes, indeed, they are an embodied consciousness, with all that that entails. This is the process of incorporation of truth discussed above. Nietzsche's arguments against asceticism are aimed at asceticism in an attempt to completely deny the embodied nature of human consciousness. Through seeking self-knowledge, individuals may come to this realisation and, with sufficient strength, embrace the being they are.

In his ethical proposals, Nietzsche is busy trying to posit the body itself as the unity of grand reason in the human being. Nietzsche's morality, which follows his re-evaluation of values, presents us with a moral agent who is the Overhuman, that is, a person who acts according to their unified self. This being is the expression of the will to power that it is. An embodied consciousness at work in the world, creating oneself, creating the world and, most importantly, creating its own values: human immanent values. Are these embodied values? In fact, if we consider the fundamental moral principle one can derive from Nietzsche's philosophy, it is tempting to call his morality an 'embodied morality'. In *The Anti-Christ*, he says 'What is good? – All that heightens the feeling of power, the will to power, power itself in man. What is bad? – All that proceeds from weakness. What is happiness? – The feeling that power *increases* – that a resistance is overcome' (A §2). The fundamental moral principle that can be derived from this reads: 'Anything that affirms, creates and augments life is good.'[13] Individuals who are engaged in ethical processes of value creation and decision-making must operate under that principle. Doing so, human beings will promote themselves as instances of will to power, of life overcoming itself. The human being will be true to oneself as an embodied consciousness, as a self that is a body, a body that is will to power. Only then can one be said to truly flourish as a human being and be an Overhuman.

With the figure of the Overhuman, Nietzsche presents us with an exacerbated phenomenological ethical ideal,[14] one that goes beyond the free spirit. Bernd Magnus challenges this notion of an ideal and wants to distinguish between the

---

[13] This moral principle could easily be related to Spinoza's positions in the *Ethics*. This task, however, remains insufficiently explored, by me and other commentators. Promising pathways are opened by Kim André Jacobsen's master's thesis, *Nietzsche and Spinoza*, Aurelia Armstrong's 'The Passions, Power, and Practical Philosophy', and David Wollenberg's 'Nietzsche, Spinoza, and the Moral Affects', among a few others.

[14] By this phrase, I want to capture the idea that this is the ethical ideal emerging from the phenomenological views Nietzsche espouses. This is my ongoing claim in this book: that the ethical – and the political – are firmly grounded in the views he elaborated about the human being.

Overhuman as an ideal type and what he calls an 'attitudinal reading'. He says:

> what I have in mind when I refer to the attitudinal interpretation is that it does not necessarily emphasize the Übermensch as a human ideal of perfectibility . . . Instead, I take the Übermensch to be the nonspecific representation, the underdetermined embodiment if you will, of a certain attitude toward life and world – the attitude which finds them worthy of infinite repetition.[15]

What Magnus is rejecting here is the idea of a type that would be set and fixed. He wants to emphasise that the Overhuman is a process, a being that is moved by a certain specific attitude that allows it to exist as dynamic becoming. As he further indicates, those lamenting the lack of specificity of character traits or of a specific method to attain Overhumanliness miss the point that the Overhuman is not an ideal type but an illustration, a gesturing towards what adopting the 'right' attitude (or perspective as Ansell-Pearson would have it[16]) would entail in terms of the radical transformation and overcoming of the human being. I agree with Magnus but still wish to characterise the Overhuman as an ideal, albeit a dynamic ideal of becoming Overhuman. Nietzsche has claimed that the Overhuman is the meaning of the earth. By this he means that the Overhuman is a being of this world but more: as the 'meaning of the earth', the Overhuman creates the world for itself and makes itself via its intentional embodied consciousness. It is crucial for Nietzsche that we become free spirits and understand the power of our grand reason and the role played by our little reason. We will be free spirits when we are freed from the weight that has been tied to our body and freed from the illusory harmful division introduced between body and soul by the metaphysical-religious tradition. Understanding the kind of being that we are and understanding that we are the creators of ourselves via our situated bodies

---

[15] Bernd Magnus, 'Perfectibility and Attitude in Nietzsche's *Übermensch*', p. 643.
[16] See above note 6, this chapter.

is liberating for the spirit. Becoming creators on that basis and adopting and embracing the right attitudes and perspectives will allow for the becoming Overhuman which is ultimately the ideal Nietzsche upholds.[17]

A Free-Spirited Virtue Ethics for Overhumans

The connection between Nietzsche's moral agent who creates her own self through lawgiving creativity and the moral agent of ancient virtue ethics has been discussed by a few commentators.[18] It has been suggested by Michael Ure, among others,

---

[17] Jacob Golomb would disagree with this position. In an essay on the notion of the free spirit par excellence in relation to the free spirit and the Overhuman, Golomb argues that the Overhuman is not the pinnacle of Nietzsche's ethical thinking and that in fact it is the free spirit par excellence. However, he believes both to be untenable and therefore considers that there is 'an inherent flaw in Nietzsche's existential philosophy: namely, the nonviability of its most sublime ideals' ('Can One Really Become a "Free Spirit Par Excellence" or an Übermensch', p. 22). What Golomb is emphasising here is the distinction that I see between the occurrence of the free spirit in the middle period works and in later works such as *Beyond Good and Evil*. I do not see those as two separate types of free spirits but rather as a modulation and evolution of the concept. Further, Golomb denies that the Overhuman is a viable concept because he sees that figure as inevitably tied to a social setting. As such, 'the processes of social conditioning and the assault from within on one's "pure power" will continue to exert their antiauthenticating and weakening effects' (Ibid. p. 37). However, as Nietzsche has explained, the Overhuman is precisely this creature that can become sick and heal itself again thanks to its strength and attitude towards oneself and life. Being exposed to a social setting would not be an impediment to being realised but rather, according to my interpretation, a precondition for the ideal to be fulfilled.

[18] The following is an extensive – but not exhaustive – list of studies that investigate, one way or another, the connection between Nietzsche's philosophy and ancient virtue ethics in its Aristotelian, Stoic or Epicurean form: Keith Ansell-Pearson, 'Care of Self in Dawn' and 'True to the Earth'; Jessica Berry, 'The Pyrrhonian Revival in Montaigne and Nietzsche'; Thomas H. Brobjer, 'Nietzsche's Affirmative Morality'; Christine Daigle, 'Nietzsche: Virtue Ethics ... Virtue Politics?'; Lester H. Hunt, *Nietzsche and the Origin of Virtue*; Horst Hutter and Eli Friedland (eds), *Nietzsche's Therapeutic Teaching*; Bernd Magnus, 'Aristotle and Nietzsche'; Michael Slote, 'Nietzsche and Virtue Ethics'; Christine Swanton, 'Outline of a Nietzschean Virtue Ethics'; Michael Ure, 'Nietzsche's Free Spirit Trilogy and Stoic Therapy'.

that Nietzsche understood himself as developing a new philosophical therapy. As I have discussed, Nietzsche's philosophy is, in many ways, an account of his own recovery. Ure says that Nietzsche 'shares with the Hellenistic schools the belief that the central motivation for philosophizing is the urgency of human suffering and that the goal of philosophy is human flourishing, or *eudaimonia*'.[19] There is some debate, however, as to which Hellenistic school may have influenced him or even whether it was Aristotle's views on the development of one's character in the *Nicomachean Ethics* that served as a source of inspiration. This is a question that arises from Walter Kaufmann's suggestion that we should understand Nietzsche's opposition to Christianity and Christian religion in view of the influence Aristotle exerted on him. His claim rests on the connection he makes between Aristotle's concept of pride, or 'greatness of soul' (*megalopsychia*), and Nietzsche's notion of the *Übermensch*.[20]

I agree instead with Magnus's critique of Kaufmann and think that Aristotle's understanding of *eudaimonia* and *phronesis* are at odds with Nietzsche's ideals. Aristotelian *eudaimonia* is linked to the exercise of one's rationality in thought and in action. The good life is that of the individual who lives a rational life, i.e., one that is guided by practical wisdom, *phronesis*. Aristotle's practically wise person, the *phronemos*, possesses the wisdom necessary to determine virtue, understood as the means between a vice by excess and a vice by default. Briefly put, virtues are the means by which a *phronemos* will attain *eudaimonia*, the happy life of intellectual activity. Human beings need virtues as such character traits allow them to flourish. The *phronemos* chooses her own virtues in view of her own maturation as a rational being. This emphasis on the rational nature of the human being and the Aristotelian definition of happiness as the life of reason clashes with Nietzsche's own views. Indeed, Aristotle does not mean it as the grand reason

---

[19] Michael Ure, 'Nietzsche's Free Spirit Trilogy and Stoic Therapy', p. 62.
[20] For Kaufmann's argument, see his *Nietzsche: Philosopher, Psychologist, Antichrist*.

of the body and certainly does not have in mind a subjective multiplicity as Nietzsche conceives. As Magnus and others have pointed out, Nietzsche would see in this yet another iteration of the metaphysical-religious view of the human that prevents flourishing rather than fostering it.

Even if we cannot understand Nietzsche's ethical ideals in Aristotelian terms,[21] I think there are interesting aspects of the programme set out in the *Nicomachean Ethics* that resemble what Nietzsche puts forth in the figure of the free spirit. Interestingly, the *phronemos*, like the free spirit, is her own master and lawgiver. One could even offer that the *phronemos* is also a relative concept, which is how Nietzsche defines the free spirit. Indeed, while there is extensive discussion of virtues and their related vices by excess or by default in the *Nicomachean Ethics*, it is interesting to note that they are all relative to circumstances and to individuals. One must be virtuous but the exact way in which one must be virtuous is not specified. What matters throughout is the moral development and flourishing of the agent. Because Aristotle conceives of the human being as essentially a rational animal, this flourishing is linked to the exercise of reason. But if one conceives of the human in a different way, the concern with flourishing will not ultimately rest with the development of one's intellectual abilities but rather with the development of the individual as a subjective multiplicity, which is how Nietzsche conceives of the human being. Flourishing remains paramount despite its diverging expression and content.

Scholars who examine the connection between Nietzsche's ethics and ancient virtue ethics agree that Nietzsche is concerned with the good life and the means to attain it. However, this good life differs from that described by Aristotle. For example, Michael Ure argues that Nietzsche was embracing a form of Stoicism in which *eudaimonia* amounts to 'freedom from

---

[21] This here is a short rendition of a more detailed argument in my 'Nietzsche: Virtue Ethics . . . Virtue Politics?'

emotional disturbance'.[22] On the other hand, Keith Ansell-Pearson argues that it was Epicurus's understanding of *eudaimonia* as simple and modest living that appealed to Nietzsche. Indeed, Ansell-Pearson thinks that it was Epicurus who was the main source of inspiration in the middle period works as Nietzsche was working to liberate himself 'from the metaphysical need, to find serenity within his own existence, and to aid humanity in its need to now cure its neuroses'.[23] It would be in Epicurus that Nietzsche finds the inspiration to focus on the closest things rather than on metaphysical-religious first and last things. This relates to what Nietzsche says of the free spirit's renewed attention to the things closest to her which I have discussed earlier. Speaking of the free spirit's convalescence, Nietzsche writes:

> It seems to him as if his eyes are only now open to what is *close at hand*. He is astonished and sits silent: where *had* he been? These close and closest things: how changed they seem! What bloom and magic they have acquired! . . . He had

---

[22] While Ure thinks that it was Stoicism that was a major source of influence on Nietzsche, he also thinks that Nietzsche parted ways with Stoicism to a degree: 'by the early 1880s he began to express strong misgivings about Stoic therapy, in particular about its conception of the foundations of human flourishing and *eudaimonia*' ('Nietzsche's Free Spirit Trilogy and Stoic Therapy', p. 72). He explains that the view according to which *eudaimonia* would amount to a 'complete freedom from emotional disturbance' is one Nietzsche rejects (Ibid. p. 73). However, Ure argues that in order for Nietzsche to be in a position to put forward the notion of *amor fati* and the correlate eternal recurrence he must embrace a cosmic Stoicism which entails an affirmation of natural necessity and fate (see Ibid. pp. 74–80). I have discussed earlier the naturalistic interpretation of Nietzsche and its limitations. I think that *amor fati* and the eternal recurrence can be adopted as ethical tools for flourishing without having to embrace a corresponding cosmological view.

[23] Keith Ansell-Pearson, 'True to the Earth', p. 104. Keith Ansell-Pearson points out that Epicurus becomes a prominent influence in 1879 ('True to the Earth', p. 102). According to him, Nietzsche appreciates the 'refined asceticism' of Epicureanism (Ibid. p. 103; this is a phrase that Ansell-Pearson takes from Richard Roos, 'Nietzsche et Épicure', p. 298).

been *beside* himself: no doubt of that. Only now does he see himself – and what surprises he experiences as he does so! (HH I 'Preface' §5)

Interestingly this passage ends with Nietzsche referring to the notion of practical wisdom: 'There is wisdom, *practical wisdom*, in for a long time prescribing even health for oneself in small doses' (HH I 'Preface' §5; my emphasis). The practical wisdom of the free spirit consists in looking at the world differently, in thinking differently, and re-evaluating things thanks to her new gaze. Having freed herself from metaphysical-religious discourse, the free spirit may pay attention to the things closest to her and may discover herself anew.

In *Ecce Homo*, the book which tells the story of 'How One Becomes What One Is', Nietzsche wonders, half ironically, 'why on earth I've been relating all these small things', and answers:

> small things – nutrition, place, climate, recreation, the whole casuistry of selfishness – are inconceivably more important than everything one has taken to be important so far. Precisely here one must begin to *relearn*. What mankind has so far considered seriously have not even been realities but mere imaginings – more strictly speaking, lies prompted by the bad instincts of sick natures that were harmful in the most profound sense – all these concepts, 'God,' 'soul,' 'virtue,' 'sin,' 'beyond,' 'truth,' 'eternal life.' (EH 'Clever' §10)

Paying attention to the small things, the things closest to us, turning one's gaze away from harmful illusions and imaginings, that is, freeing oneself from them, will lead one to become who one is. This is the path to truth, a re-evaluated notion of truth, one which is to be gained through self-knowledge and knowledge of the world or of the closest things, that is, of the immanent realm of existence as opposed to the transcendent realm which has been rejected. This knowledge is the (re)discovery of oneself as situated embodied intentional consciousness, as being-with-others and being-in-the-world. This path to truth is the path to authenticity for the self.

Nietzsche's concern with the moral development and flourishing of the agent is what aligns him with virtue ethics. The focus on the character of the individual and her flourishing, specifically, is what aligns him with ancient virtue ethics, be they of Aristotelian, Stoic, or Epicurean leanings. Each emphasise that the agent must be concerned with her own flourishing and all views hold that one must actualise one's nature. This means that they all adhere to an ideal of authenticity. Nietzsche's focus on authenticity and the free spirit's search for authenticity as well as the Overhuman's incorporation of truth entitles us to claim that he presents a virtue ethics, a free-spirited one. This ethics and the ethical ideal one must aim for emerge from the phenomenological understanding of the human being that Nietzsche offers as soon as he engages in his critique of otherworldly metaphysical and moral systems, starting in earnest with *Human, All Too Human*. This ethical stance grounded in his wild phenomenology is one that allows the human being to become what it is. This becoming, however, does not occur in isolation. To complete this enquiry, some reflections on the political are in order.

Conclusion: From the Ethical to the Political

Recall Nietzsche's ethical principle as can be derived from aphorism 2 of *The Anti-Christ*: 'Anything that affirms, creates and augments life is good.' He says that good is: 'All that heightens the feeling of power, the will to power, power itself in man.' And bad is 'All that proceeds from weakness.' This leads him to say: 'The weak and ill-constituted shall perish: first principle of *our* philanthropy. And one shall help them to do so' (A §2). Such a call for the elimination of the weak certainly does not seem to cohere with a virtue ethics that aims for the advancement and flourishing of human beings, such as we discussed in the previous chapter. What can Nietzsche mean by that and what is his take on the political? Siemens and Roodt quite rightly say that:

> Nietzsche's significance for political thought has become the single most hotly contested area of Anglophone Nietzsche research: Is Nietzsche a political thinker at all – or an antipolitical philosopher of values and culture? Is he an aristocratic political thinker who damns democracy as an expression of herd mentality – or can his thought, especially his thought on the Greek *agon*, be fruitfully appropriated for contemporary democratic theory?[1]

---

[1] Herman Siemens and Vasti Roodt, 'Introduction', p. 1. Their volume contains essays that address these two questions as well as questions pertaining to the relation between Nietzsche and Arendt, Nietzsche and biopolitics, and Nietzsche and rights.

Even if the nature of Nietzsche's political thought is of such importance, the number of answers to the questions posed by Siemens and Roodt is great and there is no agreement as to what position he adopted and which political regime, if any, he favoured.[2] There is also the possibility, evoked by some perhaps out of sheer puzzlement as to the wildly divergent claims he makes in his works, that he was something like a suprapolitical thinker, one who 'takes the very meaning of the political beyond familiar or traditional terms of reference, continually transforming our understanding of politics'.[3] In what follows I will not attempt to solve these questions. My aim is more humble; and I want to offer a reflection on the political as it relates to my reading of Nietzsche as a phenomenologist, and what I see as a coherent position given what he has said about free spirits, the Overhuman and their ethical stance.

A Virtue Politics?

As I have discussed above, Nietzsche's concern is with the flourishing of human beings. This is what motivates his critique and proposals for the new ideals of the free spirit and the Overhuman. Likewise, his critique of politics and his 'anti-political' stance are driven by his concern for human flourishing. Simply said, he is not satisfied that the political regimes he observed or read about nor the way politics was conducted are conducive to such flourishing. Foremost, he wishes for a politics that will at best foster human flourishing and at least not be an impediment to it. Such a politics, which we could call a 'virtue politics' in relation to his 'virtue ethics', would be concerned with the flourishing of individuals in a group. A virtue politics would want to build a social structure in which every individual would have an equal chance at flourishing. No one would be placed in such a position of oppression or dire need that they would be incapable

---

[2] For an efficient summary of these different views, see Nathan Widder, 'The Relevance of Nietzsche to Democratic Theory', pp. 188–90.
[3] Herman Siemens and Vasti Roodt, 'Introduction', p. 1.

of pursuing their own development. A virtue politics that looks after the flourishing of all individuals within a group would advocate an equality of opportunities. This does not necessarily entail that an equality of results would follow. The idea is that society or the political order should not play a determining role in deciding whether the individual will flourish or not. This begs the question, which is so hotly debated in Nietzsche studies, of what kind of regime Nietzsche would have to embrace as the virtue ethicist he is.

A democratic regime would seem to be appropriate in that democracy claims to provide equal opportunities to all. However, in many passages he is very critical of many aspects of this type of political regime. For example, in *Beyond Good and Evil* he rejects both democracy and socialism as equally problematic and on the same count, claiming: 'to us the democratic movement is not only a form of the decay of political organization but a form of the decay, namely the diminution, of man, making him mediocre and lowering his value' and further:

> The *over-all degeneration of man* down to what today appears to the socialist dolts and flatheads as their 'man of the future' – as their ideal – this degeneration and diminution of man into the perfect herd animal (or, as they say, to the man of the 'free society'), this animalization of man into the dwarf animal of equal rights and claims, is *possible* there is no doubt of it. Anyone who has once thought through this possibility to the end knows one kind of nausea that other men don't know – but perhaps also a new *task!*—(BGE §203)

This is in no way a one-time outburst in Nietzsche's writings. For example, in the later text *Twilight of the Idols* he says:

> Democracy has always been the declining form of the power to organize: I have already, in *Human, All Too Human*, characterized modern democracy, together with its imperfect manifestations such as the 'German *Reich*', as the *decaying form* of the state. (TI 'Expeditions' §39)

He is referring to this passage from *Human, All Too Human* where he says, 'modern democracy is the historical form of the decay of the state.-' (HH I §472).[4] Opening the chapter titled 'A Glance at the State', he quotes Voltaire as saying: '*quand la populace se mêle de raisonner, tout est perdu*' (HH I §438; 'When the people mingles into reasoning, all is lost').[5] As for nationalism and socialism, they are also undesirable in that they are not conducive to the flourishing of higher individuals and culture (see HH §480, WS §285, §289, §§292-3).

However, democracy is not entirely bad and may even be unavoidable (WS §§275-6). As he explains in *Beyond Good and Evil*, the conditions we find in democratisation 'are likely in the highest degree to give birth to exceptional human beings of the most dangerous and attractive quality' (BGE §242). As we have seen, this is desirable for Nietzsche since exceptional human beings are the drivers of human progress. And yet, only a few aphorisms later, he claims that:

> Every enhancement of the type 'man' has so far been the work of an aristocratic society – and it will be so again and

---

[4] Interestingly, this whole aphorism is about the way in which religion and government come to control people and each in their own way, and sometimes in collaboration, maintain the herd. He explains that religion provides government with 'a calm, patient, trusting, disposition among the masses' (HH I §472). He explains that the rise of democracy entails a relegation of religion to the private sphere and even a certain degree of irreligiosity that may lead to the withering away of the state. While he has advocated for as little state as possible because it is a waste of one's spirit to devote time and energy to it (D §179), this outcome is not a desirable one. This leads Lester H. Hunt to say 'The evil of the state is that it prevents us from doing the work which would replace it as a source of values; that work not being done, the destruction of the state would do us less than no good. The point is to turn our backs on issues of state policy altogether and take up the neglected task. In this quite literal sense of the word, Nietzsche is "anti-political"' ('Politics and Anti-Politics', p. 463).

[5] This is my own translation of Voltaire's phrase. Hollingdale translates it as 'when the mob joins in and adds its voice, all is lost', which is less than accurate.

CONCLUSION: FROM THE ETHICAL TO THE POLITICAL

again – a society that believes in the long ladder of an order of rank and differences in value between man and man, and that needs slavery in some sense or other. (BGE §257)[6]

In the following aphorism, he claims that 'The essential characteristic of a good and healthy aristocracy ... accepts with a good conscience the sacrifice of untold human beings who, *for its sake*, must be reduced and lowered to incomplete human beings, to slaves, to instruments' (BGE §258).[7] He concludes this *Gedanken-kette* by saying:

> Even the body within which individuals treat each other as equals, as suggested before – and this happens in every healthy aristocracy – if it is a living and not a dying body, has to do to other bodies what the individuals within it refrain from doing to each other: it will have to be an incarnate will to power, it will strive to grow, spread, seize, become predominant – not from any morality or immorality but because it is *living* and because life simply *is* will to power ... 'Exploitation' does not belong to a corrupt or imperfect and primitive society: it belongs to the *essence* of what lives, as a basic organic function; it is a consequence of the will to power, which is after all the will to life. (BGE §259)

---

[6] David Owen argues that 'the claim that political hierarchy is a necessary condition of the elevation of human beings ... may seem harder to avoid. Fortunately, however, while Nietzsche holds this position at the time of writing *Beyond Good and Evil*, it is dropped by the time of *On the Genealogy of Morality*. I say it is dropped not because Nietzsche explicitly disavows it but because it is not compatible with the argument of the latter book' ('Equality, Democracy, and Self-Respect', p. 122). Owen suggests that Nietzsche's analysis of the human being that can promise and its ideal of sovereignty as described in *On the Genealogy of Morality* is incompatible with an oppressive aristocracy.

[7] See also *Beyond Good and Evil* §61 and the whole section 'What is noble' of the same book.

One finds a milder version of this already in *Human, All Too Human* where he says:

> *My utopia.* – In a better ordering of society the heavy work and exigencies of life will be apportioned to him who suffers least as a consequence of them, that is to say to the most insensible, and thus step by step up to him who is most sensitive to the most highly sublimated species of suffering and who therefore suffers even when life is alleviated to the greatest degree possible. (HH I §462)

How do we reconcile these different claims and how do we also make them cohere with what else he says about the noble, self-affirming spirits who, being powerful enough so that their power can overflow, can treat less noble individuals with commiseration? Indeed, Nietzsche goes so far as to make it a higher individual's duty to be gentle towards weaker ones. He says: 'When an exceptional human being handles the mediocre more gently than he does himself or his equals, this is not mere politeness of the heart – it is simply his *duty*' (A §57). Now, unless one thinks that weaker human beings will flourish on their own terms under the wise guidance and gentle oppression of higher individuals, it seems impossible to reconcile the aristocratic politics delineated above with a virtue ethics concerned with human flourishing.

I said that virtue politics is concerned with the flourishing of individuals within a group. Could we have another kind of virtue politics that would be concerned with the flourishing of individuals *as a* group? In this case, it seems that a society that would have oppression as one of the conditions for the flourishing of stronger individuals would be acceptable if it was to lead to the flourishing of the group. Individual flourishing would not matter but rather it would be the flourishing of the whole that would be of primary focus. In a way, one can say that the ancient Greek society was organised in such a way that the oppression of a large portion of inhabitants of the city-state was a condition for the well-being of that state. It has been stressed that ancient Greek democracy was able to flourish as it did only because of the large number of slaves it relied upon to take care of the menial tasks while the higher individuals were involved in higher tasks. However, while Nietzsche certainly admired some features of the ancient Greek city-states, it is difficult to imagine him in agreement with this given what he has said of the Overhuman.[8] From the point of view of his ethical proposals, there is nothing in Nietzsche's position that justifies advocating a system that would favour the flourishing of only a group of individuals. In my opinion, it is impossible to talk about a virtue politics in the second sense, i.e., a virtue politics that would promote the flourishing of individuals as a group, because it would imply that some individual's flourishing would be discarded in favour of that of others.

I find myself in agreement with Lawrence J. Hatab's and David Owen's views on this matter and think that Nietzsche is more of a democrat than he might have thought and that his thinking is highly relevant to our democratic lives. As Hatab points out, 'Nietzsche indeed is anti-egalitarian but that egalitarianism may not be the *sine qua non* of democratic politics ... many elements of democratic practice and performance are more Nietzschean than he suspected (or we have suspected).'[9] He further explains that democracy and excellence are fully compatible

---

[8] One of the ancient Greek political models Nietzsche could relate to would be that of Plato. In the *Republic*, Plato talks about an ideal city-state that would be organised in three classes: the guardians, the warriors, and the artisans and farmers. Plato explains that the children of the warriors will undergo a very strict educational programme where their capacities will be tested so that only the best of them will complete the programme and become guardians. One could argue that there is some equality of opportunities for the children of the warrior class. All of them have an opportunity to become guardians. However, this opportunity still depends on the existence of the lower strata of the pyramid – the artisans and farmers. Consequentially, we still don't have a system that favours the flourishing of all but, rather, we find ourselves with a system that favours the flourishing of a select group of individuals.

[9] Lawrence J. Hatab, 'Prospects for a Democratic *Agon*', p. 133. The subtitle of Hatab's essay, 'Why We Can Still Be Nietzscheans', is a pun on the title of a collection of essays edited by Luc Ferry and Alain Renaut, *Why We Are Not Nietzscheans*, and against which he maintains a democratic Nietzsche.

'as long as excellence is understood in a contextual and performative sense, rather than a substantive sense of permanent, pervasive, or essential superiority'.[10] There is no need for fixed notions of excellence and, therefore, the opportunities can be given to all to excel each in their own way. This leads Hatab to say that 'as long as opportunities are open in a democratic society, a meritocratic, contextual apportionment of different roles and performances need not seem undemocratic'.[11] This meritocratic and contextual attribution of roles is what Nietzsche is advocating. David Owen's take on this provides a very cogent argument and one I wholeheartedly embrace given what I have discussed earlier.[12] He says:

> modern democracy can avoid the pitfalls that Nietzsche identifies in 'the democratic movement of our times' to the extent that it cultivates an agonal political culture in which citizens strive to develop their capacities for self-rule

---

[10] Lawrence J. Hatab, 'Prospects for a Democratic *Agon*', p. 139.
[11] Ibid. p. 140.
[12] As I have said above, Owen's argument rests on his analysis of *On the Genealogy of Morality*. In discussing the sovereign individual, he explains that 'Nietzsche's argument is that the vice of servility is the failure to recognize oneself as a being who can stand to oneself as a sovereign individual – it is to *surrender* one's entitlement by failing to acknowledge oneself as an autonomous individual, it is to disown one's humanity. In this respect, the servile man is derelict with regard to what is the *first* duty to oneself on Nietzsche's account, namely, to recognise oneself as a being who can stand to oneself as a sovereign individual. Moreover, we should note that if my reconstruction of Nietzsche's position is accurate, one's grounds of recognition self-respect cannot be separated from one's grounds of recognition other-respect. To fail to recognise others as beings who can stand to themselves as sovereign individuals is to undermine the grounds of my own recognition self-respect, *i.e.*, that I am, *qua* human being, a being who can stand to myself as a sovereign individual' ('Equality, Democracy, and Self-Respect', pp. 115–16). As we will see shortly, the 'nature' of the human being as embodied consciousness, as a bundle of drives and a subjective multiplicity in dynamic becoming also commands that we engage in agonistic relations with others, and this means with others of all types of strength.

in competition with one another, a culture that honors exemplary democratic citizens as setting standards that we should seek to match and surpass. The point of this Nietzschean argument is that if democracy is to meet its own best aspirations, it requires citizens who cultivate those political virtues (e.g., independence of mind) which are necessary to this task. This is a central purpose of the democratic *agon*: to cultivate citizens who stand to themselves politically as sovereign individuals.[13]

Owen makes this point in relation to an early essay in which Nietzsche discusses the notion of the *agon*, 'Homer's Contest' (1872). Nietzsche praises this feature of Athenian society according to which all citizens strive to excel according to their own individual talent. The socio-cultural setting in which they live requires that they contribute to Athens to the best of their abilities. This entails that individuals constantly seek to overcome and improve themselves, actualising their full potential. As we have seen earlier in relation to the free spirit and friendship, Nietzsche considers agonistic relations essential to the flourishing of individuals. Also, it is the social extension of internal processes of strife and resistance among the competing drives in the individual. Hatab summarises this neatly in saying, 'The self is constituted in and through what it opposes and what opposes it; in other words, the self is formed through agonistic relations.'[14] This is because the human being is a being-in-the-world as I have described. The *agon* examined by Nietzsche in 'Homer's Contest' is an activity reserved to the elite, as Hatab points out. However, as he also indicates, 'agonistics can be seen as a fundamentally social phenomenon. Since the self is formed in and through tensional relations with others, then any annulment of my Other would be an annulment of myself. Radical agonistics, then, discounts the idea of sheer autonomy

---

[13] Ibid. p. 126.
[14] Lawrence J. Hatab, 'Prospects for a Democratic *Agon*', p. 135.

and self-constitution.'[15] This is the case because we are fundamentally being-with-others, as we discussed earlier.

What type of equality, if any, does Nietzsche want? This is an important question given his critique of democracy as precisely that type of regime that, by bringing about equality among people, constitutes a levelling down of human beings. Recall that this is his argument to dismiss democracy. In *Human, All Too Human* he identifies two kinds of equality: 'The thirst for equality can express itself either as a desire to draw everyone down to oneself (through diminishing them, spying on them, tripping them up) or to raise oneself and everyone else up (through recognizing their virtues, helping them, rejoicing in their success)' (HH I §300). Considering this passage in conjunction with Nietzsche's critique of democracy, a critique he finds akin to that of other, more conventional, political thinkers, like John Stuart Mill for example,[16] Owen concludes that Nietzsche endorses the second type of equality and that it 'makes clear that he is not, as commonly supposed, an antiegalitarian thinker, but an advocate of, what we might call, the perfectionist view of equality in which *everyone* is called on, *and aided*, to develop their capacities for self-government'.[17]

---

[15] Ibid. p. 142. Hatab thinks that this is a better model than a subject-based freedom. He also adds that 'the structure of an *agon* conceived as a contest can readily underwrite political principles of fairness. Not only do I need an Other to prompt my own achievement, but the significance of any "victory" I might achieve demands an able opponent' (ibid.). Note that the opponent must be able and not necessarily an equal. As I have discussed previously in relation to friendship, equality is to be loosely understood since perfect equality would not be generative of the desire to overcome oneself (see pp. 139–41). Paul van Tongeren has also argued for a renewed view of democracy under the light of Nietzsche's understanding of the human being in agonistic terms. See his 'Esprit libre et démocratie'. See also his essay, 'Nietzsche as "Über-Politischer Denker"'.

[16] This is something he takes from James Conant who, in his essay 'Nietzsche's Perfectionism', relates Nietzsche's critique to the notion of the 'tyranny of the majority' and the 'despotism of conformity' that worried such thinkers as John Adams, William James, Thomas Jefferson, John Stuart Mill and Alexis de Tocqueville (quoted in David Owen, 'Equality, Democracy, and Self-Respect', p. 119).

[17] David Owen, 'Equality, Democracy, and Self-Respect', p. 120.

I agree with Owen that this is the equality that Nietzsche is seeking. This requires a re-evaluation of politics in the same way that a re-evaluation of values was needed for ethics. It does not necessarily entail, however, a rejection of democracy. In fact, and as I have indicated earlier, a re-evaluated democracy, one which would be perfectionist and engage in radical agonistics, would provide us with the right political setting in which to flourish.

Nathan Widder goes further than this notion of a re-evaluated democracy and claims that Nietzsche, along with Foucault and Deleuze, is more profoundly democratic than any democracy ever encountered. He says that because our politics stick to notions of identity and identity striations, 'we are not yet democratic enough'.[18] He points out that, for Nietzsche – and Foucault and Deleuze reading him on this matter – the essence of the political is to move away from identity. As he points out,

> It is an ethics [the ethics 'beyond good and evil'] that, rather than seeking to secure the identity of oneself and another through mutual recognition and respect – a view containing the hidden proviso that the other may be different only insofar as he/she is also the same – presses beyond such traditional oppositions of self and other.[19]

And further, 'Nietzsche's political contribution thus comes in his presentation of an ontological dynamic in which identity and opposition appear only as reductive misinterpretations. A political or social theory that puts primacy on identity is therefore necessarily missing something.'[20] It is in fact alienating since it is forcing unitary identity on beings that are everything but that. Indeed, as we have seen, one's identity is always in flux, constituted via one's being-in-the-world and via one's

---

[18] Nathan Widder, 'The Relevance of Nietzsche to Democratic Theory', p. 206.
[19] Ibid. p. 195.
[20] Ibid. p. 196.

relation to oneself as such. Hatab refers to the notion of identity of conventional politics as

> the fantasy of self-sufficient, fully free, uncontested occurrences born in Western conceptions of divine perfection and continued in various philosophical models of demonstrative certainty and theoretical governance ... As radically open, an agonistic politics [such as Nietzsche's] has the virtue of precluding the silencing of any voice, something especially important when even purportedly democratic dispositions are comfortable with exclusions.[21]

Thus, Nietzsche's thinking has great potential to enrich our political lives by providing us with tools to improve our democracies so that we may flourish as the types of beings we are. In order for all individuals to have the possibility to engage in agonistic relations – and thus to engage on the path of flourishing – it is clear that an oppressive political regime is out of the question. For Nietzsche, it is imperative that whatever political regime we have, it does not interfere with our individual and social overcoming. Some regimes will be stumbling blocks – aristocratic, monarchic, imperial regimes as well as some economic systems such as the exploitative capitalism he sees emerging in the nineteenth century (interestingly, a critique he shares with Marx, despite his contempt for socialists). Democratic regimes that are permeated by Christian values make people equal through a process of levelling down. What Nietzsche has in mind, however, is another type of democracy that rests upon a perfectionist view of equality that would generate the right conditions for all individuals to flourish, a kind of levelling up.

With all of this said, I am not sure we can think of Nietzsche as a political theorist. His thinking about politics is more encompassing than a specific concern for institutions and types of regimes, even though he has many things to say about them. As I have repeated a few times, his concern is more fundamentally

---

[21] Lawrence J. Hatab, 'Prospects for a Democratic *Agon*', p. 145.

with the flourishing of individuals and how to make that flourishing possible. While he engaged in criticism of political institutions and contemporary and past regimes, he did not really engage in an elaboration of what the proper political regime would be. He was more interested in moral agents and, insofar as those live together, he had concerns for politics. One can derive, from what he has said about his moral ideals, some sense of what he would prefer politically, but this necessarily must be a somewhat creative exercise governed by rules of coherence: one must arrive at a proposal for politics that would allow for the moral ideal that Nietzsche elaborates on the basis of his phenomenological views to thrive. This means that he is neither anti-political nor apolitical. Conceiving of the human being in the way he does entails that he has political views even if he does not fully elaborate them.

In *Ecce Homo*, Nietzsche claims that 'Only after me will there be *grand politics* on earth-' (EH 'Destiny' §1).[22] This closes the aphorism in which he announces that 'I am not a man I am dynamite' (EH 'Destiny' §1). He explains that his discovery of the truth, his seeing through the lies that have oppressed us for centuries, has led him to his re-evaluation of all values, to criticise and reject in order to affirm. And in relation to that, he explains, 'The concept politics has then become completely absorbed into a war of spirits, all the power-structures of the old society have been blown into the air – they one and all reposed on the lie' (EH 'Destiny' §1). This lie being exposed opens the way for his grand politics. In this aphorism, he connects all aspects of his philosophy. The grand politics that he talks about here is to be understood in the same terms as we understand the notion of subjective multiplicity. Grand politics is the macrocosmic

---

[22] As Burnham points out, Nietzsche is critical of the notion of 'grand politics' (*große Politik*) as proposed by Bismarck in that it is self-serving to the extent that it eradicates the people as 'people' (HH I §481, D §189). Burnham explains that in the later works, '"great politics" means the task of free spirits or good Europeans – and the strategies or instruments employed in that task – of taking "comprehensive responsibility" for the future of humankind' (Douglas Burnham, *The Nietzsche Dictionary*, p. 264).

expression of the processes unfolding within the microcosm of the soul as 'subjective multiplicity' and 'soul as social structure of the drives and affects' (BGE §12).

Understanding oneself as embodied intentional consciousness, as being-in-the-world, as grand reason, as being-with-others, and as subject to those as well as subject of one's own self-making (in an authentic pursuit), the free spirit and Overhuman are able to engage in a *große Politik* of themselves, one that fosters their flourishing as the beings they are as well as the flourishing of others. Engaging in such politics is the means by which one can fully become what one is.

At the term of this enquiry, we are confronted with a very different and better Nietzsche.[23] As expected, taking a close look at the proposals he elaborates in the middle period works, at a time when he is freeing himself from various theoretical and personal influences and rediscovering himself, allows for a different perspective to be taken on the concepts that emerge in later works. Being careful readers, as I hope to have been, we can unearth the threads of coherence and systematicity that were always there but were often ignored. This is also made possible by taking into consideration how concepts stay the same or gain new meaning as they recur in later works. Understanding Nietzsche as offering a phenomenology, albeit a 'wild' one, shifts perspective sufficiently to shed new light on key concepts of his thinking. This in turn may allow us to take a different approach to our own philosophising and tackle contemporary ethical and political problems with new tools. Individual and collective flourishing certainly needs rethinking in this day and age. Nietzsche's ethical ideal, grounded as it is in his wild phenomenology, has the potential to take us in new directions that are worth exploring. We certainly cannot do worse than we are doing currently. With Nietzsche's views and a better understanding of who and what we are, there is great potential. Like the little ship of aphorism 124 of *The Gay Science*, we

---

[23] This was the claim put forward by Ruth Abbey and Paul Franco, namely that focusing on the middle period works and the concepts emerging therein would allow for a better Nietzsche to emerge. See Chapter 1.

must set out on that adventure, recognise that we are faced with infinite possibilities, and that 'there is nothing more awesome than infinity' (GS §124). In doing so, we will follow Nietzsche's own path from illness to recovery, from critique to constructive philosophising, from alienation to flourishing. However, and let the last word be Nietzsche's:

> *Vademecum – Vadetecum*
> Lured by my style and tendency,
> you follow and come after me?
> Follow your own self faithfully –
> take time – and thus you follow me.
> (GS, 'Joke, Cunning, and Revenge' §7)

Bibliography

Abbey, Ruth, *Nietzsche's Middle Period* (Oxford: Oxford University Press, 2000).
Abel, Günter, 'Interpretatorische Vernunft und menschlicher Leib', in Mihailo Djuric (ed.), *Nietzsches Begriff der Philosophie* (Würzburg: Königshausen & Neumann, 1990), pp. 100–30.
Acampora, Christa Davis, 'Naturalism and Nietzsche's Moral Psychology', in Keith Ansell-Pearson (ed.), *A Companion to Nietzsche* (Oxford: Wiley-Blackwell, 2009), pp. 314–33.
Allison, David B., 'Introduction', in David B. Allison (ed.), *The New Nietzsche: Contemporary Styles of Interpretation* (Cambridge, MA: The MIT Press, 1985), pp. xi–xxviii.
Anderson, R. Lanier, 'Nietzsche on Truth, Illusion, and Redemption', *European Journal of Philosophy* 13(2), 2005: pp. 185–225.
Ansell-Pearson, Keith, 'Care of Self in Dawn: On Nietzsche's Resistance to Bio-political Modernity', in M. Knoll and B. Stocker (eds), *Nietzsche as Political Philosopher* (Berlin and New York: Walter de Gruyter, 2014), pp. 269–86.
Ansell-Pearson, Keith, 'In Search of Authenticity and Personality: Nietzsche on the Purifications of Philosophy', *American Catholic Philosophical Quarterly* 84(2), 2010: pp. 283–312.
Ansell-Pearson, Keith, 'The Incorporation of Truth: Towards the Overhuman', in Keith Ansell-Pearson (ed.), *A Companion to Nietzsche* (Oxford: Wiley-Blackwell, 2009), pp. 230–49.
Ansell-Pearson, Keith, 'Questions of the Subject in Nietzsche and Foucault: A Reading of *Dawn*', in João Constâncio, Maria

João Mayer Branco, and Bartholomew Ryan (eds), *Nietzsche and the Problem of Subjectivity* (Berlin and New York: Walter de Gruyter, 2015), pp. 411–35.

Ansell-Pearson, Keith, 'True to the Earth: Nietzsche's Epicurean Care of Self and World', in Horst Hutter and Eli Friedland (eds), *Nietzsche's Therapeutic Teaching* (London: Bloomsbury, 2013), pp. 97–116.

Armstrong, Aurelia, 'The Passions, Power, and Practical Philosophy: Spinoza and Nietzsche Contra the Stoics', *Journal of Nietzsche Studies* 44(1), Special Issue: Nietzsche and the Affects (2013): pp. 6–24.

Bamford, Rebecca, '*Ecce Homo*: Philosophical Autobiography in the Flesh', in Nicholas Martin and Duncan Large (eds), *Nietzsche's 'Ecce Homo'* (Berlin and New York: Walter de Gruyter, forthcoming).

Bamford, Rebecca (ed.), *Nietzsche's Free Spirit Philosophy* (Lanham: Rowman & Littlefield, 2015).

Bamford, Rebecca, 'The Virtue of Shame: Defending Nietzsche's Critique of *Mitleid*', in Gudrun von Tevenar (ed.), *Nietzsche and Ethics* (Bern: Peter Lang, 2007), pp. 241–61.

Bamford, Rebecca, and Keith Ansell-Pearson, *Nietzsche's Dawn: Philosophy, Ethics, and the Passion of Knowledge* (Oxford: Wiley-Blackwell, 2021).

Beaulieu, Alain, 'L'Enchantement du corps chez Nietzsche et Husserl', in A. T. Tymieniecka (ed.), *Analecta Husserliana: The Yearbook of Phenomenological Research LXXXIV* (Dordrecht: Kluwer, 2005), pp. 339–55.

Beaulieu, Alain, 'Étude critique: *Le gouvernement de soi et des autres et Le courage de la vérité*', *Symposium* 13(2), 2009: pp. 163–75.

Benoist, Jocelyn, 'Nietzsche est-il phénoménologue?', in Marc Crépon (ed.), *Les Cahiers de l'Herne: Nietzsche* (Paris: Les Éditions de l'Herne, 2000), pp. 307–23.

Bergo, Bettina, and Jill Staufer (eds), *Nietzsche and Levinas: 'After the Death of a Certain God'* (New York: Columbia University Press, 2009).

Berry, Jessica, *Nietzsche and the Ancient Skeptical Tradition* (Oxford: Oxford University Press, 2011).

Berry, Jessica, 'The Pyrrhonian Revival in Montaigne and Nietzsche', *Journal of the History of Ideas* 65(3), 2004: pp. 497-514.

Blondel, Eric, 'Critique et généalogie chez Nietzsche, ou *Grund, Untergrund, Abgrund*', *Revue Philosophique* 2, 1999: pp. 199-210.

Blondel, Eric, *Nietzsche: The Body and Culture: Philosophy as a Philological Genealogy*, trans. Seán Hand (Stanford: Stanford University Press, 1991).

Boehm, Rudolf, 'Husserl and Nietzsche', in Élodie Boublil and Christine Daigle (eds), *Nietzsche and Phenomenology: Power, Life, Subjectivity* (Bloomington: Indiana University Press, 2013), pp. 13-27.

Boublil, Élodie, and Christine Daigle, 'Introduction', in Élodie Boublil and Christine Daigle (eds), *Nietzsche and Phenomenology: Power, Life, Subjectivity* (Bloomington: Indiana University Press, 2013), pp. 1-9.

Boublil, Élodie, and Christine Daigle (eds), *Nietzsche and Phenomenology: Power, Life, Subjectivity* (Bloomington: Indiana University Press, 2013).

Breazeale, Daniel, 'Becoming Who One Is: Notes on Schopenhauer as Educator', *New Nietzsche Studies* 2(3-4), 1998: pp. 1-25.

Brentano, Franz, *Geschichte der Philosophie der Neuzeit* (Hamburg: Meiner, 1987).

Brobjer, Thomas H., 'Nietzsche's Affirmative Morality: An Ethics of Virtue', *Journal of Nietzsche Studies* 26, 2003: pp. 64-78.

Brobjer, Thomas H., *Nietzsche's Philosophical Context: An Intellectual Biography* (Champaign: University of Illinois Press, 2008).

Brown, Kristen, *Nietzsche and Embodiment: Discerning Bodies and Non-Dualism* (Albany: SUNY Press, 2006).

Brown, Richard, 'Nietzsche and Kant on Permanence', *Man and World* 13, 1980: pp. 39-52.

Burnham, Douglas, *The Nietzsche Dictionary* (London: Bloomsbury, 2015).

Cohen, Richard A., 'Levinas, Spinozism, Nietzsche, and the Body', in Jill Stauffer and Bettina Bergo (eds), *Nietzsche* and Levinas: 'After the death of a certain God' (New York: Columbia University Press, 2009), pp. 165–82.

Colera, Christophe, *Individualité et subjectivité chez Nietzsche* (Paris: L'Harmattan, 2004).

Colli, Giorgio, 'Nachwort', in Giorgio Colli and Mazzino Montinari (eds), in Nietzsche, Friedrich, *Menschliches, Allzumenschliches* (Berlin and New York: Walter de Gruyter, 1999), pp. 707–15.

Conant, James, 'Nietzsche's Perfectionism: A Reading of Schopenhauer as Educator', in Richard Schacht (ed.), *Nietzsche's Postmoralism* (Cambridge: Cambridge University Press, 2001), pp. 181–257.

Constâncio, João, 'On Consciousness: Nietzsche's Departure from Schopenhauer', *Nietzsche-Studien* 40, 2011: pp. 1–42.

Constâncio, João, Maria João Mayer Branco, and Bartholomew Ryan, 'Introduction', in João Constâncio, Maria João Mayer Branco, and Bartholomew Ryan (eds), *Nietzsche and the Problem of Subjectivity* (Berlin and New York: Walter de Gruyter, 2015), pp. 1–45.

Cooper, David E., '"The 'New" Nietzsche', *History of European Ideas* 11, 1989: pp. 857–63.

Cordner, Christopher, 'Foucault, Ethical Self-concern and the Other', *Philosophia* 36(4), 2008: pp. 593–609.

Cox, Christoph, *Nietzsche: Naturalism and Interpretation* (Berkeley: University of California Press, 1999).

Crome, Keith (ed.), *JBSP: Journal of the British Society for Phenomenology* 38(1), Special Issue on 'Nietzsche and Phenomenology' (2007).

Daigle, Christine, 'A Nietzschean Beauvoir?: Becoming Who One is As a Being-With-Others', *Simone de Beauvoir Studies* 27, 2010–11: pp. 61–71.

Daigle, Christine, 'Authenticity and Distantiation from Oneself: An Ethico-political Problem', *SubStance* 46(1), 2017: pp. 55–68.

Daigle, Christine, 'Nietzsche: Virtue Ethics ... Virtue Politics?', *The Journal of Nietzsche Studies* 32, 2006: pp. 1–21.

Daigle, Christine, *Le Nihilisme est-il un humanisme?: Étude sur Nietzsche et Sartre* (Sainte-Foy: Presses de l'Université Laval, 2005).
Daigle, Christine, 'Sartre and Nietzsche: Brothers in Arms', in Benedict O'Donohoe and Roy Elveton (eds), *Sartre's Second Century* (Newcastle Upon Tyne: Cambridge Scholars Publishing, 2009), pp. 56-72.
Daigle, Christine, '*The Second Sex* as Appeal: the Ethical Dimension of Ambiguity', *philoSOPHIA: A Journal of Continental Feminism* 4(2), 2014: pp. 197-220.
Daigle, Christine, and Terrance McDonald, 'Introduction', in Christine Daigle and Terrance McDonald (eds), *From Deleuze and Guattari to Posthumanism* (London: Bloomsbury, 2022).
Danto, Arthur C., 'Beginning to be Nietzsche', in Nietzsche, Friedrich, *Human, All Too Human*, trans. Marion Faber with Stephen Lehmann (Lincoln: University of Nebraska Press, 1996), pp. ix-xix.
Daoust, Valérie, 'Foucault et Taylor sur la vérité, la liberté et l'identité subjective: Le vouloir dire-vrai dans la parrhesia', *Symposium* 13(2), 2009: pp. 5-24.
Davey, Nicholas, 'Nietzsche and Hume on Self and Identity', *Journal of the British Society for Phenomenology* 18(1), 1987: pp. 14-29.
De Coorebyter, Vincent, 'Introduction', in Vincent de Coorebyter (ed.), in Sartre, Jean-Paul, *La transcendance de l'Ego et autres texts phénoménologiques* (Paris: Vrin, 2003), pp. 7-76.
Deleuze, Gilles, *Nietzsche and Philosophy*, trans. Hugh Tomlinson (New York: Columbia University Press, 2006).
Descartes, René. *Meditations on First Philosophy. With Selections from the Objections and Replies*, ed. John Cottingham (Cambridge: Cambridge University Press, 2017, 2nd edn).
Descartes, René, *Selected Philosophical Writings*, trans. John Cottingham and Robert Stoothoff (Cambridge: Cambridge University Press, 1988).
D'Iorio, Paolo, and Olivier Ponton (eds), *Nietzsche: Philosophie de l'esprit libre: Études sur la genèse de* Choses humaines,

trop humaines (Paris: Éditions Rue d'Ulm/Presses de L'École Normale Supérieure, 2004).

Diprose, Rosalyn, *Corporeal Generosity: On Giving with Nietzsche, Merleau-Ponty, and Levinas* (Albany: State University of New York Press, 2002).

Doyle, Tsarina, 'Nietzsche's Appropriation of Kant', *Nietzsche-Studien* 33, 2004: pp. 180-204.

Emden, Christian J., *Nietzsche's Naturalism: Philosophy and the Life Sciences in the Nineteenth Century* (Cambridge: Cambridge University Press, 2014).

Ferry, Luc, and Alain Renaut, *Why We Are Not Nietzscheans*, trans. Robert de Loaiza (Cambridge, MA: The MIT Press, 1987).

Figal, Günther, 'Aesthetically Limited Reason: On Nietzsche's "The Birth of Tragedy"', in Simon Sparks (ed.), *Philosophy and Tragedy* (New York: Routledge, 2000), pp. 139-51.

Flynn, Bernard, 'Merleau-Ponty and Nietzsche on the Visible and the Invisible', in Véronique Foti (ed.), *Merleau-Ponty: Difference, Materiality, Painting* (New Jersey: Humanities Press, 1996), pp. 2-15.

Foucault, Michel, 'Afterword: The Subject and Power', in Hubert L. Dreyfus and Paul Rabinow (eds), *Michel Foucault: Beyond Structuralism and Hermeneutics* (Chicago: University of Chicago Press, 1983), pp. 208-26.

Foucault, Michel, *Dits et écrits I* (Paris: Gallimard, 2001), p. 841.

Foucault, Michel, 'Nietzsche, Genealogy, History', in *Language, Counter-Memory, and Practice: Selected Essays and Interviews*, trans. Donald F. Bouchard and Sherry Simon (Oxford: Basil Blackwell, 1977), pp. 139-65.

Franck, Didier, *Nietzsche et l'ombre de Dieu* (Paris: Presses Universitaires de France, 1998).

Franco, Paul, *Nietzsche's Enlightenment: The Free-Spirit Trilogy of the Middle-Period* (Chicago and London: The University of Chicago Press, 2011).

Gardner, Sebastian, 'Nietzsche, the Self, and the Disunity of Philosophical Reason', in Ken Gemes and Simon May (eds),

Nietzsche on Freedom and Autonomy (Oxford: Oxford University Press, 2009), pp. 1-31.

Gemes, Ken, 'Postmodernism's Use and Abuse of Nietzsche', *Philosophy and Phenomenological Research* 62(2), 2001: pp. 337-60.

Gerhardt, Volker, 'The Body, the Self, and the Ego', in Keith Ansell-Pearson (ed.), *A Companion to Nietzsche* (Oxford: Wiley-Blackwell, 2006), pp. 273-96.

Golomb, Jacob, 'Can One Really Become a "Free Spirit Par Excellence" or an Übermensch', *Journal of Nietzsche Studies* 32(2), 2006: pp. 22-40.

Golomb, Jacob, 'Introductory Essay: Nietzsche's "New Psychology"', in Jacob Golomb, Weaver Santaniello, and Ronald Lehrer (eds), *Nietzsche and Depth Psychology* (Albany: SUNY Press, 1999), pp. 1-19.

Golomb, Jacob, 'Nietzsche on Authenticity', *Philosophy Today* 34(3), 1990: pp. 243-58.

Golomb, Jacob, 'Nietzsche's Phenomenology of Power', *Nietzsche-Studien* 15, 1986: pp. 289-305.

Gros, Frédéric, 'Le Souci de soi chez Michel Foucault: A review of The Hermeneutics of the Subject', *Philosophy & Social Criticism* 31(5-6), 2005: pp. 697-708.

Gros, Frédéric, 'Sujet moral et soi éthique chez Foucault', *Archives de philosophie* 65, 2002: pp. 229-37.

Haar, Michel, 'Nietzsche and Van Gogh: Representing the Tragic', *Research in Phenomenology* 24, 1994: pp. 15-24.

Haase, Ulrich, 'Dikè and Iustitia: Between Heidegger and Nietzsche', *Journal of the British Society for Phenomenology* 38(1), Special issue 'Nietzsche and Phenomenology' (2007): pp. 18-36.

Hargis, Jill, '(Dis)embracing the Herd: A Look at Nietzsche's Shifting Views of the People and the Individual', *History of Political Thought, XXXL* 3, 2010: pp. 475-507.

Harris, Daniel I., 'Friendship as Shared Joy in Nietzsche', *Symposium: The Canadian Journal of Continental Philosophy* 19(1), 2015: pp. 199-221.

Hatab, Lawrence J., 'Prospects for a Democratic *Agon*: Why We Can Still Be Nietzscheans', *Journal of Nietzsche Studies* 24, 2002: pp. 132-47.

Heidegger, Martin, *Being and Time: A Translation of Sein und Zeit*, trans. Joan Stambaugh (Albany: State University of New York Press, 1996).
Heidegger, Martin, *Nietzsche: Volumes One and Two*, trans. David Farell Krell (New York: HarperCollins, 1991).
Higgins, Kathleen, 'Nietzsche and Postmodern Subjectivity', in Clayton Koelb (ed.), *Nietzsche as Postmodernist: Essays Pro and Contra* (Albany: SUNY Press, 1990), pp. 189-215.
Hill, R. Kevin., *Nietzsche's Critiques: The Kantian Foundations of His Thought* (Oxford: Clarendon Press, 2003).
Houlgate, Stephen, 'Kant, Nietzsche and the "Thing in Itself"', *Nietzsche-Studien* 22, 1993: pp. 115-57.
Hume, David, *A Treatise of Human Nature* (London: Penguin Books, 1969).
Hunt, Lester H., *Nietzsche and the Origin of Virtue* (London: Routledge, 1991).
Hunt, Lester H., 'Politics and Anti-Politics: Nietzsche's View of the State', *History of Philosophy Quarterly* 2(4), 1985: pp. 453-68.
Husserl, Edmund, *Cartesian Meditations: An Introduction to Phenomenology*, trans. Dorion Cairns (The Hague: Martinus Nijhoof, 1973).
Husserl, Edmund, *Cartesianische Meditationen und Pariser Vorträge*, in Steven Strasser (ed.) (The Hague: Martinus Nijhoff, 1973).
Husserl, Edmund, *The Idea of Phenomenology*, trans. William P. Alston and George Nakhnikian (Dordrecht: Kluwer Academic Publishers, 1990).
Husserl, Edmund, *Ideas Pertaining to a Pure Phenomenology and to a Phenomenological Philosophy, First Book: General Introduction to a Pure Phenomenology*, trans. Frederick Kersten (The Hague: Martinus Nijhoff Publishers, 1983).
Hutter, Horst, and Eli Friedland (eds), *Nietzsche's Therapeutic Teaching* (London: Bloomsbury, 2013).
Ibáñez-Noé, Javier, 'Nietzsche and Kant's Copernican Revolution', *New Nietzsche Studies* 5(1-2), 2002: pp. 132-49.
Jacobsen, Kim André, *Nietzsche and Spinoza: From Ontology to Ethics*, master's thesis in Philosophy, UiT-The Arctic University of Norway, November 2014.

Jensen, Anthony, 'Helmholtz, Lange, and Unconscious Symbols of the Self', in João Constâncio, Maria João Mayer Branco, and Bartholomew Ryan (eds), *Nietzsche and the Problem of Subjectivity* (Berlin and New York: Walter de Gruyter, 2015), pp. 196-218.

Johnson, Dirk K., *Nietzsche's Anti-Darwinism* (Cambridge: Cambridge University Press, 2010).

Kain, Philip J., 'Nietzsche, the Kantian Self, and Eternal Recurrence', *Idealistic Studies* 34(3), 2004: pp. 225-37.

Kant, Immanuel, *Critique of Pure Reason: The Cambridge Edition of the Works of Immanuel Kant*, ed. Paul Guyer and Allen W. Wood (Cambridge: Cambridge University Press, 1998).

Katsafanas, Paul, 'Nietzsche's Theory of Mind: Consciousness and Conceptualization', *European Journal of Philosophy* 13(1), 2005: pp. 1-31.

Kaufmann, Walter, *Nietzsche: Philosopher, Psychologist, Antichrist* (Princeton, NJ: Princeton University Press, 1974).

Kessler, Mathieu, 'La critique des idéaux dans *Choses humaines, trop humaines*', in Paolo D'Iorio and Olivier Ponton (eds), *Nietzsche: Philosophie de l'esprit libre* (Paris: Éditions rue d'Ulm, 2005), pp. 143-51.

Lebrun, Jocelyne, 'Pour une phénoménologie de l'imagination poétique', *Archives de philosophie* 51, 1988: pp. 195-211.

Lupo, Luca, 'Ombres: Notes pour une interprétation', in Paolo D'Iorio and Olivier Ponton (eds), *Nietzsche: Philosophie de l'esprit libre* (Paris: Éditions rue d'Ulm, 2005), pp. 99-112.

Lyotard, Jean-François, *La Phémoménologie* (Paris: Presses Universitaires de France, 2004).

Magnus, Bernd, 'Aristotle and Nietzsche: "Megalopsychia" and "Uebermensch"', in David J. Depew (ed.), *The Greeks and the Good Life* (Fullerton: California State University, 1980), pp. 260-95.

Magnus, Bernd, *Nietzsche's Existential Imperative* (Bloomington: Indiana University Press, 1978).

Magnus, Bernd, 'Perfectibility and Attitude in Nietzsche's Übermensch', *Review of Metaphysics* 36, 1983: pp. 633-59.

Marsden, Jill, 'Nietzsche and the Art of the Aphorism', in Keith Ansell-Pearson (ed.), *A Companion to Nietzsche* (Oxford: Wiley-Blackwell, 2006), pp. 22-37.

Matthews, Eric, *The Philosophy of Merleau-Ponty* (Montreal and Kingston: McGill/Queen's University Press, 2002).
Merleau-Ponty, Maurice, *Phenomenology of Perception*, trans. Colin Smith (London and New York: Routledge, 2005).
Merleau-Ponty, Maurice, *The Visible and the Invisible: Followed by Working Notes*, trans. Alphonso Lingis (Evanston, IL: Northwestern University Press, 1968).
Miller, J. Hillis, 'The Disarticulation of the Self in Nietzsche', *The Monist* 64(2), 1981: pp. 247–61.
Miner, Robert C., 'Nietzsche on Friendship', *Journal of Nietzsche Studies* 40(2), 2010: pp. 47–69.
Miner, Robert C., 'Nietzsche's Fourfold Conception of the Self', *Inquiry* 54(4), 2011: pp. 337–60.
Moore, Gregory, *Nietzsche, Biology, and Metaphor* (Cambridge: Cambridge University Press, 2002).
Moore, Gregory, and Thomas H. Brobjer (eds), *Nietzsche and Science* (Aldershot: Ashgate, 2004).
Moran, Dermot, *Introduction to Phenomenology* (London and New York: Routledge, 2000).
Mullin, Amy, 'Nietzsche's Free Spirit', *Journal of the History of Philosophy* 38(3), 2000: pp. 383–405.
Nabais, Nuno, 'The Individual and Individuality in Nietzsche', in Keith Ansell-Pearson (ed.), *A Companion to Nietzsche* (Oxford: Wiley-Blackwell, 2006), pp. 76–94.
Nietzsche, Friedrich, *Beyond Good and Evil: Prelude to a Philosophy of the Future*, trans. Walter Kaufmann (New York: Vintage, 1989).
Nietzsche, Friedrich, *The Birth of Tragedy* and *The Case of Wagner*, trans. Walter Kaufmann (New York: Vintage, 1967).
Nietzsche, Friedrich (1967), 'Briefe von Nietzsche', *Digital Critical Edition of the Complete Works and Letters*. Based on the critical text by G. Colli and M. Montinari, edited by Paolo D'Iorio (Berlin and New York: Walter de Gruyter, 1967). <http://www.nietzschesource.org/#eKGWB> (last accessed 20 January 2020).
Nietzsche, Friedrich, *Daybreak: Thoughts on the Prejudices of Philosophers*, trans. R. J. Hollingdale, ed. Maudemarie Clark and Brian Leiter (Cambridge: Cambridge University Press, 1997).

Nietzsche, Friedrich, *Ecce Homo: How One Becomes What One Is*, trans. R. J. Hollingdale (London: Penguin Books, 1979).
Nietzsche, Friedrich, *The Gay Science: With a Prelude in Rhymes and an Appendix of Songs*, trans. Walter Kaufmann (New York: Vintage, 1974).
Nietzsche, Friedrich, *On The Genealogy of Morality and Other Writings*, trans. Carol Diethe, ed. Keith Ansell-Pearson (Cambridge: Cambridge University Press, 2017).
Nietzsche, Friedrich, *Human, All Too Human: A Book for Free Spirits*, trans. R. J. Hollingdale (Cambridge: Cambridge University Press, 1996).
Nietzsche, Friedrich (1967), 'Nachgelassene Fragmente', *Digital Critical Edition of the Complete Works and Letters*. Based on the critical text by G. Colli and M. Montinari, ed. Paolo D'Iorio (Berlin and New York: Walter de Gruyter, 1967). <http://www.nietzschesource.org/#eKGWB> (last accessed 20 January 2020).
Nietzsche, Friedrich, 'On Truth and Lies in a Nonmoral Sense (1873)', in Keith Ansell-Pearson and Duncan Large (eds), *The Nietzsche Reader* (Oxford: Blackwell, 2006), pp. 114–23.
Nietzsche, Friedrich, 'Schopenhauer as Educator', in *Unfashionable Observations*, trans. Richard T. Gray (Stanford: Stanford University Press, 1995), pp. 169–255.
Nietzsche, Friedrich, *Selected Letters of Friedrich Nietzsche*, trans. Christopher Middleton (Indianapolis and Cambridge: Hackett Publishing Company, 1996).
Nietzsche, Friedrich, *Thus Spoke Zarathustra: A Book for Everyone and No One*, trans. R. J. Hollingdale (London: Penguin Books, 1969).
Nietzsche, Friedrich, *Twilight of the Idols/The Anti-Christ*, trans. R. J. Hollingdale (London: Penguin Books, 1990).
Nietzsche, Friedrich, *The Will to Power*, trans. Walter Kaufmann and R. J. Hollingdale, ed. Walter Kaufmann (New York: Vintage, 1967).
Nietzsche, Friedrich, *Writings from the Early Notebooks*, trans. Ladislau Löb, ed. Raymond Geuss and Alexander Nehamas (Cambridge: Cambridge University Press, 2009).

Nietzsche, Friedrich, *Writings from the Late Notebooks*, trans. Kate Sturge, ed. Rüdiger Bittner (Cambridge: Cambridge University Press, 2003).
Owen, David, 'Equality, Democracy, and Self-Respect: Reflections on Nietzsche's agonal Perfectionism', *Journal of Nietzsche Studies* 24, 2002: pp. 113-31.
Pieper, Annemarie, 'Die große Vernunft des Leibes: Nietzsches Dekonstruktion des Subjekts', in Barbara Neymeyr and Andreas Urs Sommer (eds), *Nietzsche als Philosoph der Moderne* (Heidelberg: Universitätsverlag Winter, 2012), pp. 59-71.
Poellner, Peter, 'Phenomenology and Science in Nietzsche', in Keith Ansell-Pearson (ed.), *A Companion to Nietzsche* (Oxford: Wiley-Blackwell, 2006), pp. 297-313.
Prange, Martine, *Nietzsche, Wagner, Europe* (Berlin: Walter de Gruyter, 2013).
Reboul, Olivier, *Nietzsche Critique de Kant* (Paris: Presses Universitaires de France, 1974).
Rehberg, Andrea, 'Introduction', in Andrea Rehberg (ed.), *Nietzsche and Phenomenology* (Newcastle upon Tyne: Cambridge Scholars Publishing, 2011), pp. 1-16.
Rehberg, Andrea, 'Nietzsche and Merleau-Ponty: Body, Physiology, Flesh', in Andrea Rehberg (ed.), *Nietzsche and Phenomenology* (Newcastle upon Tyne: Cambridge Scholars Publishing, 2011), pp. 141-61.
Revel, Judith, *Dictionnaire Foucault* (Paris: Ellipses, 2008).
Ricœur, Paul, 'Sur la phénoménologie', *Esprit* 209, 1953: pp. 821-39.
Robert, Jean-Dominique, 'Approche rétrospective de la phénoménologie husserlienne', *Laval théologique et phénoménologique* 2, 1972: pp. 827-62.
Robertson, Simon, 'Normativity for Nietzschean Free Spirits', *Inquiry: An Interdisciplinary Journal of Philosophy* 54(6), 2011: pp. 591-613.
Roos, Richard, 'Nietzsche et Épicure: l'idylle héroique', in Jean-François Balaudé and Patrick Wotling (eds), *Lecture de Nietzsche* (Paris: Librairie Générale Française, 2000), pp. 283-350.

Rosen, Stanley, *The Ancients and the Moderns: Rethinking Modernity* (New Haven, CT and London: Yale University Press, 1989).
Safranski, Rüdiger, *Nietzsche: A Philosophical Biography*, trans. Shelley Frisch (New York and London: W. W. Norton & Company, 2002).
Sallis, John, 'Shining in Perspective: Nietzsche and Beyond', in Andrea Rehberg (ed.), *Nietzsche and Phenomenology* (Newcastle upon Tyne: Cambridge Scholars Publishing, 2011), pp. 19-31.
Sartre, Jean-Paul, *Being and Nothingness*, trans. Hazel Barnes (London and New York: Routledge, 2009).
Sartre, Jean-Paul, *Notebooks for an Ethics*, trans. David Pellauer (Chicago: Chicago University Press, 1992).
Schacht, Richard, 'Introduction', in Nietzsche, Friedrich, *Human, All Too Human: A Book for Free Spirits*, trans. R. J. Hollingdale (Cambridge: Cambridge University Press, 1996), pp. vii-xxiii.
Schmidt, James (ed.), *What Is Enlightenment?: Eighteenth-century Answers and Twentieth-century Questions* (Berkeley: University of California Press, 1996).
Shapiro, Gary, 'Übersehen: Nietzsche and Tragic Vision', *Research in Phenomenology* 25, 1995: pp. 27-44.
Siemens, Herman, and Vasti Roodt, 'Introduction', in Herman Siemens and Vasti Roodt (eds), *Nietzsche, Power and Politics: Rethinking Nietzsche's Legacy for Political Thought* (Berlin: Walter de Gruyter, 2008), pp. 1-10.
Slote, Michael, 'Nietzsche and Virtue Ethics', *International Studies in Philosophy* 30(3), 1998: pp. 23-7.
Small, Robin, *Nietzsche in Context* (Aldershot: Ashgate, 2001).
Sokolowski, Robert, *Introduction to Phenomenology* (Cambridge: Cambridge University Press, 2000).
Spinoza, Baruch, *Complete Works*, trans. Samuel Shirley, ed. Michael L. Morgan (Indianapolis, IN and Cambridge: Hackett Publishing Company, 2002).
Staten, Henry, *Nietzsche's Voice* (New York: Cornell University Press, 1990).
Stiegler, Barbara, *Nietzsche et la biologie* (Paris: Presses Universitaires de France, 2001).

Swanton, Christine, 'Outline of a Nietzschean Virtue Ethics', *International Studies in Philosophy* 30(3), 1998: pp. 29-38.

Swift, Paul, 'Nietzsche on Teleology and the Concept of the Organic', *International Studies in Philosophy* 31(3), 1999: pp. 29-41.

Torjussen, Lars Peter Storm, 'Is Nietzsche a Phenomenologist?: Towards a Nietzschean Phenomenology of the Body', in A. T. Tymieniecka (ed.), *Analecta Husserliana: The Yearbook of Phenomenological Research CIII* (Dordrecht: Kluwer, 2009), pp. 179-89.

Ure, Michael, 'Nietzsche's Free Spirit Trilogy and Stoic Therapy', *Journal of Nietzsche Studies* 38, 2009: pp. 60-84.

van Tongeren, Paul, 'Esprit libre et démocratie', in Paolo D'Iorio and Olivier Ponton (eds), *Nietzsche: Philosophie de l'esprit libre* (Paris: Éditions rue d'Ulm, 2005), pp. 153-66.

van Tongeren, Paul, 'Nietzsche as "Über-Politischer Denker"', in Herman Siemens and Vasti Roodt (eds), *Nietzsche, Power and Politics: Rethinking Nietzsche's Legacy for Political Thought* (Berlin and New York: Walter de Gruyter, 2008), pp. 69-83.

van Tongeren, Paul, Gerd Schank, and Herman Siemens (eds), *Nietzsche-Wörterbuch, Band I* (Berlin and New York: de Gruyter, 2011).

Vartanian, Aram, 'Trembley's Polyp, La Mettrie, and Eighteenth-century French Materialism', *Journal of the History of Ideas* 11(3), 1950: pp. 259-86.

West, Susan, 'When Nietzsche's Texts "disappear under the interpretation": Grasping Nietzsche's Embodied Philosophy', *Philosophy Today*, SPEP Supplement (2009): pp. 98-107.

Widder, Nathan, 'The Relevance of Nietzsche to Democratic Theory: Micropolitics and the Affirmation of Difference', *Contemporary Political Theory* 3, 2004: pp. 188-211.

Wiemand, Isabelle, 'Writing from a First-Person Perspective: Nietzsche's Use of the Cartesian Model', in João Constâncio, Maria João Mayer Branco, and Bartholomew Ryan (eds), *Nietzsche and the Problem of Subjectivity* (Berlin and New York: Walter de Gruyter, 2015), pp. 49-64.

Williams, Linda L., *Nietzsche's Mirror: The World as Will to Power* (Lanham, MD: Rowman & Littlefield, 2001).

Williams, W. D., *Nietzsche and the French: A Study of the Influence of Nietzsche's French Reading on his Thought and Writing* (Oxford: Basil Blackwell, 1952).

Winchester, James J., *Nietzsche's Aesthetic Turn. Reading Nietzsche After Heidegger, Deleuze, Derrida* (Albany: SUNY Press, 1994).

Wollenberg, David, 'Nietzsche, Spinoza, and the Moral Affects', *Journal of the History of Philosophy* 51(4), 2013: pp. 617-49.

Wollenberg, David, 'Power, Affect, Knowledge: Nietzsche on Spinoza', in João Constâncio, Maria João Mayer Branco, and Bartholomew Ryan (eds), *Nietzsche and the Problem of Subjectivity* (Berlin and New York: Walter de Gruyter, 2015), pp. 65-94.

Zeifa, Ammar, 'Nietzsche and the Future of Phenomenology: Der Wille zur Macht and the Criticism of Modern Transcendentalism', in A. T. Tymieniecka (ed.), *Analecta Husserliana: The Yearbook of Phenomenological Research CVIII* (Dordrecht: Kluwer, 2011), pp. 571-609.

Index

a priori, 47
Abbey, Ruth, 12, 24–5, 27
Abel, Günter, 76n, 96
Acampora, Christa Davis, 54–6, 145–6
aesthetics, 5, 6n
   of existence, 114
   of the self, 10, 105
affect (*Affekt*), 9, 64, 67n, 76n, 85–6, 90, 92–3, 106, 177–8
   multiplicity of, 89–90
affirmation, 26, 54, 134, 145, 151n, 162n
   being affirmative, 137, 155
   of oneself, 11
agent/agency, 9, 49, 56–7, 64n, 65, 78, 106, 113n, 154–7, 159, 161, 164
   interpretive agent, 76n
agon, 165, 173, 174n
   agonistic relations, 10–11, 139–41, 173, 176
   agonistic subject, 56n
   democratic agon, 172–3
alienation, 70n, 115, 145, 150–2
   alienating discourses, 12, 125
   alienating moralities, 115
Allison, David B., 51

amor fati, 66n, 137, 149, 162n
Anderson, R. Lanier, 42–3
Ansell-Pearson, Keith, 24n, 50n, 65, 110–14, 137–8, 147–9, 161–2
anthropomorphism, 31–2, 47–8, 59n
aphoristic writing, 8, 32–6
   aphoristic style, 33–6
   as fragmentary, 34–6
   as *Gedanken-Kette*, 33–5
   and perspectivism, 35–6
appearances, 8, 20, 40, 47n, 72
   realm, of, 43–4
aristocracy, 168–9
Aristotle, 160–1
art, 4–6, 12, 15–16, 65n, 106–7, 124–5n
asceticism, 11, 155–6, 162n
authenticity, 10, 104n, 112, 123, 125–35, 144, 163–4

back to things themselves, 4, 8, 19–20, 35, 38, 72, 100n
Bamford, Rebecca, 24n, 50n, 70n, 104–5, 137n
Baron d'Holbach, Paul-Henry Thiry, 108n

Beaulieu, Alain, 3, 77n, 113n
Beauvoir, Simone de, 15–16, 22, 27n
'become what one is' (becoming oneself), 10–11, 131–3, 136, 178
being-in-the-world, 9–12, 19–21, 101–6, 114, 116, 140, 163
being-with-others, 9–12, 104–5, 114, 116, 119n, 127–8, 138–9, 141, 163
Benoist, Jocelyn, 3n
Bergo, Bettina, 23n
Berry, Jessica, 42–3
Bismarck, Otto von, 177n
Blondel, Eric, 34–6, 48–9
body, 5, 29–31, 55, 63–7, 70n, 73–90, 96–9, 101, 131n, 133–4, 148–50, 155–8, 169
  body-subject, 79–8
  conscious body, 9, 77, 97–8
  as grand reason, 9, 75–6, 79, 86, 93–4, 98, 101, 160–1
  lived body, 3, 77
  as mighty commander, 76, 97
  and mind, 6n, 74–5, 150
  and soul, 79–81, 93–4, 154, 158
Boehm, Rudolf, 3n
Boscovich, Roger, 66–7n
Boublil, Élodie, 36n
bracketing, 15, 18, 44, 124n
Breazeale, Daniel, 126–7, 129–30
Brentano, Franz, 17–18, 22
Brobjer, Thomas H., 66–7n
Brown, Kristen, 4–5, 74–5

Brown, Richard S. G., 48
Burnham, Douglas, 73–5, 119n, 177n

care of the self, 9–10, 112–14
categorical imperative, 3, 31, 134, 134–5n
child, 79–81, 152–4
  child spirit, 79–80
Christianity, 29n, 120–1n, 123n, 134–5, 155–6, 160
  Christian beliefs, 51–2
cogito (I think), 9, 18–19, 29n, 78–9, 90–2
  'new cogito,' 19
Cohen, Richard A., 65–6
Colera, Christophe, 94
Colli, Giorgio, 36n
colourist, 8–9, 39–40, 65
  human intellect as, 57–8, 95–6
communication, 84–7, 103
Conant, James, 174n
consciousness, 2–3, 16–20, 34–5, 39–41, 47, 54, 57–8, 61–72, 74–5n, 85n, 87
  as *Bewusstheit,* 69–71
  as *Bewusstsein,* 69–71, 84
  embodied, 7–12, 72, 76–8, 80–1, 101–2, 126, 128, 133–4, 154–8
  as epiphenomenon, 53–4
  inner multiplicity of, 83–4
  intentional, 8–10, 12, 17–20, 59, 70–1, 96–8, 101–2, 163, 178
  multi-layered, 72, 90
  origin of, 49, 83–6, 103
  as tool, 9, 76–8, 87

pre-reflective, 61–2, 68–9,
  78–9, 84–5
 pure, 17–19
 reflective, 78–9
 self-consciousness, 87–8
 self-reflective, 78–9
 topology of, 9, 73–5, 80–1
Constâncio, João, 40–1n, 57n,
  61–2, 103n
constitution, 39–40, 60, 101–2,
  110, 112–13
 co-constitution, 19–20
 of the self, 10, 12, 64–5,
  117–18, 173–4
 of the world, 43n, 46–8
 see also self-constitution
Cooper, David E., 52, 92
Coorebyter, Vincent de, 23
Cordner, Christopher, 110–11
culture, 101, 105–7, 172–3
 cultural progress/evolution,
  107, 120–1n, 124

Danto, Arthur C., 25–7
Daoust, Valérie, 111–12
Dasein (Da-sein), 14–15, 20–1,
  61n, 101–2, 104n
death of God, 58n, 122n, 135
Deleuze, Gilles, 2–3, 36n, 49n,
  50n, 120–1n, 175
democracy, 165, 167, 171–6
 democratic thinking, 11
 Greek democracy, 170–1
 re-evaluated democracy, 175
Derrida, Jacques, 36n, 50n, 53n
Descartes, René, 28–9, 46, 131n
Diderot, Denis, 50n
Diprose, Rosalyn, 4–5, 138–9,
  141

dividuum, 12, 127–8
doer *see* agent/agency
Doyle, Tsarina, 47–8
dream, 155
 logic of the dream, 63–4
drives, 9, 61–6, 68, 75–6,
  88–90, 92–4, 97–9, 106–7,
  116n, 134, 137, 173
 moral, 63
 multiplicity of, 56–7, 90, 93
 physiological, 63
dualism, 67, 79–80, 89, 93–5
 Cartesian, 74–5
 dynamic non-dualism, 5, 75n
 mind/body, 73–5
dynamic becoming, 9–12, 66–7,
  109n, 112–13, 126, 128,
  144, 145–8, 157–8

ego (I), 18–19, 29n, 50–2, 55–6,
  66–70, 72–4, 77–9, 86–7,
  90–3, 97, 130, 137–8,
  148n, 156
 as creation of the body, 78–9
 psychological, 71
 pure, 18, 70–1, 77n
 rejection of, 51–2, 68, 91–2
 transcendental ego, 71, 79
embodiment, 2, 79–80n, 96–7,
  144–7, 153–4, 158
Emden, Christian J., 66–7n
enlightened man, 73–4, 79–81,
  152–3
Enlightenment, the, 25–7, 30–1,
  122
 'children of the
  Enlightenment', 27n, 118
 Enlightenment spirit, 8,
  27, 40

Epicureanism, 161–2
epochè (reduction), 2, 15–17, 19–21, 35n, 37–8, 71, 87, 100
equality, 141, 166–7, 171n, 174–6
essence, 4, 15, 44, 76n, 101, 126, 145, 155, 169, 175
eternal return (eternal recurrence), 66–7n, 149–51, 162n
ethics, 12, 54, 57n, 112–13, 175
  affirmative, 145, 155
  ethical ideal, 10–11, 115–17, 141, 144, 157, 161, 164, 178
  ethical imperative, 140
  see also virtue ethics
eudaimonia, 160–2
existentialism, 18n, 20n
experience, 5n, 19–21, 23, 34–5, 44–5, 49, 52–5, 60–1, 63–5, 68, 71, 75n, 76–8, 83, 92, 94, 100, 104–6, 109, 118, 119n, 123–4, 137, 138n, 163
  inner, 68–9
  lived, 8, 15–17, 34
  'to experience is to invent', 65
experimentation (*Versuch*), 2
  experimenter (*Versucher*), 35n, 118–19, 142
  philosophical, 12–13

fettered spirit, 42n, 116, 122–3, 146–7, 152–3; *see also* free spirit
Fischer, Kuno, 66–7n
flourishing, 10–12, 38, 99n, 133–4, 141, 144–5, 154–5, 157, 160–1, 162n, 164–8, 175
  collective, 11, 178
  ethical, 114–16
  individual, 11, 170–1, 176–8
Foucault, Michel, 2–3, 9–10, 105, 109–14, 175
Franck, Didier, 59n, 76n
Franco, Paul, 12, 24–5, 27, 33n, 35–7
free spirit (*Freigeist*), 6n, 10–12, 30, 109, 114–47, 151–3, 157–8, 161–6, 177n, 178
  free-spirited, 70n, 142, 145, 159–60, 164
  free spiritedness (*Freigeisterei*), 25–6, 105, 116–20, 122, 129, 141
  free thinkers, 27n, 118
  see also fettered spirit
free will, 64n, 66–7, 108n, 118
freedom, 64n, 97n, 107–8, 111–12, 118, 124–5, 143n, 153, 161–2, 174n
friendship, agonistic, 118, 136, 138–44

Gardner, Sebastian, 54–5
Gemes, Ken, 53, 92, 121, 124–6, 132n
genealogy, 34–5, 44, 110
  genealogical thinking, 37
Gerhardt, Volker, 80, 94n
Goethe, Johann Wolfgang von, 6n
Golomb, Jacob, 3n, 35n, 126, 131n, 133, 142n, 159n

grammar, 51, 60, 91, 99n
Greek, 42, 165
  society, 170-1
  virtues, 6n
Gros, Frédéric, 111n, 113-14

Haase, Ulrich, 4
hard determinism, 105, 108n
Hargis, Jill, 109n
Hatab, Lawrence J., 171-3, 174n, 176
health, 26, 102n, 135n, 137, 139, 163
  great, 118-19, 152
  Nietzsche's own, 33
  see also illness
Hegel, Georg Wilhelm Friedrich, 33, 120-1n
Heidegger, Martin, 2, 4, 9, 15-16, 20-2, 60n, 61n, 101, 104n, 130n
helmsmen (*Steuermänner*), 130-1
herd, 3n, 73-4, 76, 87, 108-9, 116n, 119n, 122, 124n, 139, 165, 167, 168n
Higgins, Kathleen, 52-3
Hill, R. Kevin, 40n, 42, 47
historical philosophising, 37-8
Hollingdale, R. J., 147n, 150, 168n
honesty, 129, 132-3
Houlgate, Stephen, 48, 49n
humanism, 2-3, 20n
Hume, David, 91-2
Hunt, Lester H., 168n
Husserl, Edmund, 2-4, 7-8, 14n, 15-23, 29n, 35n, 70-1, 77n, 79, 100n

Ibáñez-Noé, Javier, 46
illness, 179; see also health
imagination, 37, 63-4, 85
immanence, 8, 10
immanent realm, 11, 163
in-itself, 41-2, 45n, 47n, 49n, 83, 92-3, 96
  realm of the, 31-2, 38, 42-5, 57n, 101
intellect, 58-60, 68, 92-3n, 96, 122-3, 125
intentionality, 2, 3n, 8-9, 18, 69-71, 94, 97-8
interpretation, 17n, 38, 48, 50n, 60-5, 68, 83, 89, 91, 94-5, 99, 100n, 136, 158, 175
intersubjectivity, 87, 99, 103n, 141
intersubjective fluidity, 104-5

Jensen, Anthony, 42n
Johnson, Dirk K., 26-7

Kain, Philip J., 90n
Kant, Immanuel, 8, 29-31, 39-43, 46-9, 59n, 75, 86n, 134
Katsafanas, Paul, 85
Kaufmann, Walter, 61n, 98n, 120n, 122n, 130n, 136n, 143n, 160
Kessler, Mathieu, 35n
Kierkegaard, Søren, 16n
knowledge, 6n, 10, 28-31, 39-41, 43, 46, 47n, 51-2, 65n, 67n, 70n, 76n, 78, 82, 86, 93, 100, 102, 107, 109n, 112, 124n, 126-7, 141-3, 149, 154, 163

knowledge (*cont.*)
  acquisition of, 123
  of oneself, 119, 129, 129, 147
  passion for, 66, 120
language, 35n, 47n, 49–50n, 51, 58, 69, 80–1, 87–8, 99n, 101, 109, 145
last man/men, 130, 139n
Lebrun, Jocelyne, 101n
Leibniz, Gottfried Wilhelm, 42n
Lévinas, Emmanuel, 2, 23n, 66n
life, 11, 34, 35n, 56, 60, 61n, 70–1, 81, 88, 94–6, 103, 108n, 114, 132, 146, 148–51, 157–61, 165, 169–70
  affirmation of, 52, 81n, 145, 150, 165
life-world (*Lebenswelt*), 15, 18
Lupo, Luca, 35n
Lyotard, Jean-François, 17, 19

madman, 122–3, 143
Magnus, Bernd, 95n, 151n, 157–8, 160–1
Marsden, Jill, 36
Marx, Karl, 176
Matthews, Eric, 15
meaning of the earth, 10, 148–9, 158
mental states
  conscious, 62, 85
  unconscious, 85
meritocracy, 172
Merleau-Ponty, Maurice, 3n, 5, 14–15, 16n, 18–19, 21–2, 58, 71, 75n, 81, 103n, 138
metamorphosis, 153

metaphysics, 12, 20, 32, 37–8, 45, 54, 99, 124, 124–5n, 137, 151–2
  aesthetical, 42n
  critique of, 8–9, 15–16, 40, 50–1, 72
  Kantian, 42
  metaphysical worldview, 151–3
  metaphysical-religious tradition, 150n, 155–6, 158–9
  rejection of, 26, 30, 45n, 77n
method, 4, 14n, 15, 20–1, 23, 28–9, 31–2, 36n, 37–8, 54–5, 110, 124–5n, 158
methodology, 2, 12
  Nietzsche's own, 32–5, 68
  phenomenological, 8, 16, 32–3, 40, 44
  sceptical, 24
Mettrie, Julien Offray de la, 50n
middle period works, 2, 6, 7n, 12–13, 24–6, 29n, 31, 39, 56, 84n, 113n, 116–17, 126, 128, 144, 159n, 162, 178
Miller, J. Hillis, 68–9, 89
mind, 6n, 20, 47, 63–4, 67–8, 76–7, 95–6, 121, 125, 131n, 134, 150, 172–3
  as a kind of theatre, 91–2
Miner, Robert C., 93, 139–40, 147–8
Montaigne, Michel de, 42
morality, 31, 60, 66n, 105–6, 117, 124, 130–7, 140–1, 146, 153, 169
  alienating, 11–12, 115, 124–5n, 155

Christian, 29n, 123n, 134, 135n
critique of, 16, 26, 30, 38, 56–7, 135
embodied, 157
herd, 116n
as herd instinct, 108–9
master, 116n, 140n
Moran, Dermot, 3n, 16–17, 18n
Mullin, Amy, 120
multiplicity, 34, 35n, 36, 55–6, 63–5, 68, 73–6, 77n, 81, 83–4, 85n, 87n, 88–90, 92–4, 101, 104, 127–8, 134, 148n, 150, 160–1, 172n, 177–8; *see also* subjective multiplicity

Nabais, Nuno, 127
nationalism, 168
natural attitude, 17, 20–1, 71, 80–1, 124n
naturalisation, 135
naturalism, 46n, 54–6, 61n, 66–7n
naturalist interpretation of Nietzsche, 49
scientific, 17
nihilism, 10, 23–4, 35–6, 44n, 89n, 97n, 118, 133–4, 137, 151
noumenal, 41–2

object, 2, 18–20, 23, 38, 47n, 48–9, 58, 69, 71, 81, 83n, 85, 101–3, 139
in-itself, 41
as phenomenon, 41
objectivity, 17, 47n

ontology, 20
other(s), 9–10, 19, 56, 57n, 68, 83n, 87, 99–100, 102–6, 113–18, 119n, 127, 136–41, 145, 172n, 173, 174n, 175, 178
overcoming, 10, 29n, 65–6, 97n, 119–20, 123, 138–40, 145, 157–8, 176
cultural self-overcoming, 120–1n
of metaphysics, 152
Nietzsche's own, 26
of nihilism, 151
of oneself, 11, 126, 153–4
overhuman (*Übermensch*), 10, 140–54, 157–9, 164, 166, 178
Owen, David, 169, 171–5

passion, 66, 67n, 92, 97, 120
perspectivism, 4n, 9, 15–16, 35, 73, 81–2, 118–19, 149
phenomenon (phenomenal), 16–17, 19–21, 35n, 40–5, 47–9, 57n, 58–9, 68–9, 76–7, 84n, 85–6, 98, 173–4
Kantian, 48
phenomenology, 2–10, 22, 100n
definition of, 14–18
existential, 15, 19–21
as science, 20
transcendental, 23
wild, 2, 8, 12, 14, 23, 38, 109n, 113n, 164, 178
wild existential, 23
philology, 1, 18n, 33
philosophers of the future, 142
phronesis/prhonemos, 160

physiology, 54, 102n
Pieper, Annemarie, 47n, 76, 80n, 82n, 153, 154n
pity (*Mitleid*), 136-7
Plato, 35n, 49n, 71n
Platonism, 4n
Poellner, Peter, 3-4
politics, 175-7
  anti-political, 166, 168n, 177
  grand (*große Politik*), 177-8
  political, 8, 10-13, 105, 113-15, 141, 157n, 165-7, 169n, 171n, 172-8
  virtue, 113n, 166-7, 170-1
polyp, 50n, 61-3, 138n
  polyp-being, 102n, 105-6, 108
positivism, 27, 109n
posthumanism, 51n
postmodernism/postmodern, 8-9, 49-53, 57
poststructuralism, 50-4
power, 55, 62-3, 66-7n, 73, 90, 94-9, 101, 104-8, 134, 145, 147-9, 154-8, 159n, 165, 167, 169-70, 177
  and subject, 9-10, 109-14, 116
practical wisdom, 160, 163
Prange, Martine, 6n
preparatory human being, 144
progress, 107, 109, 120-1, 124, 128, 168
  toward oneself, 26, 30, 144

question of meaning, 22n

rationalism, 27-9
  rationalistic tradition, 3
  rejection of, 30, 75n

reality, 19, 34-5, 43-4, 48, 55, 63, 66-7, 82-3n, 92, 96-9, 150-1, 156
phenomenal, 45
reason, 28-9, 31, 40-3, 47, 80, 120, 123, 132
  aesthetic, 79-80n, 153
  as embodied, 21n
  'eyes of reason', 21
  grand reason (great intelligence), 9, 73-7, 79, 86, 94, 97-8, 101, 134, 156-8, 160-1
  life of, 160-1
  little reason (little intelligence), 73-8, 86-7, 92-3n, 96, 158
  poetic, 58n
  rejection of, 30
reception of Nietzsche's philosophy, 1, 24
Rehberg, Andrea, 3n, 16n, 86
religion, 12, 16, 30, 38, 108-9, 123-4, 124-5n, 137, 156, 160, 168n
Revel, Judith, 114
Ricœur, Paul, 15, 100n
Robert, Jean-Dominique, 16n
Robertson, Simon, 128n, 129-30
romanticism, 12
Roodt, Vasti, 165-6
Rosen, Stanley, 58n, 77n, 80n

sacred Yes, 79-80n, 153
Safranski, Rüdiger, 32-3
Sallis, John, 4n
Salomé, Lou, 25, 117

INDEX

'sapere aude!', 30-1
Sartre, Jean-Paul, 15, 16n, 18-19, 20n, 21-3, 37n, 71, 78-9, 83n, 97n, 111n
scepticism, 10, 28-9, 124
  Pyrrhonian, 42
Schacht, Richard, 33
Schmidt, James, 31
Schopenhauer, Arthur, 2, 4n, 40, 41n, 42, 49n, 108
science, 15, 18n, 29n, 37, 54n, 55, 83, 89, 106
self, 5, 8-12, 20, 49-57, 65-8, 72-5, 77-80, 82-3n, 87-91, 98-9, 107-8, 109n, 111-14, 124-7, 139-41, 145, 159, 175
  deepest, 26, 93, 148n
  higher, 126, 140, 148n
  as mighty commander, 73-4, 81n, 97
  self-constitution, 10, 12, 65, 118, 173-4, 178
  self-knowledge, 65n, 126-7, 131-3, 138, 156, 163
  self-mastery, 116, 128, 133, 138, 146
  self-overcoming, 119-20
  self-scrutiny, 10, 63
  self-transformation, 53
  selfhood, 8, 40, 127, 129-30
  they-self, 104n
  true, 126, 148n
  unity of (*Einheit*), 126
sensualism, 6n
shepherd, 76, 150-1
Siemens, Herman, 165-6
socialism, 167-8
Sokolowski, Robert, 18, 104n

solitude, 35n, 104, 112, 119-20, 140n
soul, 50n, 73-4, 79-81, 88, 104, 106-7, 132n, 139, 152-5, 158, 160, 163
  Christian soul atomism, 89
  as subjective multiplicity, 9, 89, 92-4, 177-8
sovereign individual, 172-3
spider's net, 82-3n
Spinoza, Baruch, 42n, 50n, 51n, 61n, 64n, 65-7, 95n, 157n
Staten, Henry, 104-5
Stendahl (Marie-Henri Beyle), 142
Stiegler, Barbara, 47, 86n
stoic/Stoicism, 159n, 161-4
structuralism, 3n, 9-10, 105
subject, 10, 41, 47-9, 55, 58-9, 69, 80-1, 85-7, 90-1, 95, 99, 100n, 102, 103n, 104-6, 109-14, 128, 130, 137-9, 150, 178
  agonised, 10, 146
  agonistic, 145-6
  corporeal, 94
  critique of, 46, 51
  death of, 50n
  as fiction, 52
  as multiple, 56, 135
  of power, 110-11, 116, 128n
  rationalist, 53
subjectivation, 110-13
subjectivity, 17, 19, 23n, 46-8, 57n, 58, 68, 100, 104-5, 111-12, 141
  corporeal, 94
  embodied, 2, 23-4, 116, 135n

203

subjectivity (*cont.*)
  subjective multiplicity
    (*Subjekts-Vielheit*), 9, 34,
    55-6, 73, 87n, 89-90,
    93-4, 101, 132n, 134,
    145-6, 160-1, 172n, 177-8
suspicion, 28-9, 118

things, 19, 35, 38, 40, 46, 51,
    57-60, 65, 70, 82-3n, 83,
    100-1, 102n, 122, 128,
    136-8, 142-3, 148-9, 152
  closest, 12, 39, 45, 118, 125,
    135, 162-3
  small, 11, 82, 151, 163
  in themselves, 3-4, 48-9, 60,
    136
Tongeren, Paul van, 174n
Torjussen, Lars Peter Storm,
    14n, 81n, 88
transcendence, 77n
  transcendent reality, 19
  transcendent realm, 31-2, 42,
    148
  transcendental being, 70-1
Trembley, Abraham, 50n
true being (*Eigentliche Selbst*),
    3n, 130-1
truth, 8, 10, 16-18, 24, 28-31,
    35-41, 44, 45n, 47, 50n,
    52, 59, 63, 86, 88, 99n,
    118-24, 126-7, 140, 143-4,
    152, 163, 177
  critique of, 51
  incorporation of, 11, 149,
    154, 156, 164
  and method, 31-2
  problem of, 31-2, 100
  quest for, 30

Übermenschlichkeit, 11-12,
    79-80n, 128, 151n
Ure, Michael, 159-62

value, 3n, 24n, 38, 44-5,
    58-9, 64n, 79-8n, 108-9,
    116, 118, 126, 132, 136,
    146-9, 153-7, 165,
    168-9, 176
  re-evaluation of, 144, 156-7,
    175, 177
  transvaluation of, 133-4
Vartanian, Aram, 50n
virtue, 6, 37-8, 60, 101, 125-9,
    132-3, 135, 139, 148-9,
    155, 163, 166-7, 170-6
  ancient virtue ethics, 11,
    159-61, 164
  virtue ethics, 11, 113n, 133n,
    134, 146, 159-62, 164,
    166, 170
Voltaire (François-Marie
    Arouet), 26-8, 29n, 30n,
    40, 168

Wagner, Richard, 2, 6n
wanderer, 45n, 125
West, Susan, 93-4
Widder, Nathan, 175
Wiemand, Isabelle, 46n
will to power, 9, 62, 66-7n, 73,
    94-9, 109n, 114, 145-9,
    154-7, 169
  as cosmological force, 95
  world as, 98
Williams, Linda L., 62, 99n
Williams, W. D., 29n
Winchester, James, 50n
Wollenberg, David, 67n

world, 2, 5n, 8–12, 17, 28, 30, 37–43, 47–9, 51, 57–67, 70–3, 75n, 76–81, 88, 92, 94–105, 114–18, 122, 124n, 125, 128, 131–5, 145, 150, 153–8, 163
  apparent, 44–5, 142, 152
  external, 62, 68
  illusory, 44
  inner, 64, 68–9, 81–2n, 85, 89n, 119
  phenomenal, 41–5, 59
  pre-given, 18–19, 101
  real, 44–5, 48, 82–3, 151–2

Zarathustra, 77–9, 95, 119n, 139n, 146–52
Zeifa, Anmar, 4n

EU representative:
Easy Access System Europe
Mustamäe tee 50, 10621 Tallinn, Estonia
Gpsr.requests@easproject.com

www.ingramcontent.com/pod-product-compliance
Lightning Source LLC
Chambersburg PA
CBHW050551160426
43199CB00015B/2623